PHANTOM
FLEET

ALSO BY ALEXANDER ROSE

Kings in the North:
The House of Percy in British History

Washington's Spies:
The Story of America's First Spy Ring

American Rifle:
A Biography

Men of War:
The American Soldier in Combat at Bunker Hill,
Gettysburg, and Iwo Jima

Empires of the Sky:
Zeppelins, Airplanes, and Two Men's
Epic Duel to Rule the World

The Lion and the Fox:
Two Rival Spies and the Secret Plot
to Build a Confederate Navy

PHANTOM FLEET

THE HUNT FOR NAZI SUBMARINE U-505 AND WORLD WAR II'S MOST DARING HEIST

ALEXANDER ROSE

LITTLE, BROWN AND COMPANY

New York Boston London

Little, Brown and Company
Hachette Book Group
1290 Avenue of the Americas, New York, NY 10104
littlebrown.com

First Edition: May 2025

Little, Brown and Company is a division of Hachette Book Group, Inc. The Little, Brown name and logo are trademarks of Hachette Book Group, Inc.

The publisher is not responsible for websites (or their content) that are not owned by the publisher.

The Hachette Speakers Bureau provides a wide range of authors for speaking events. To find out more, go to hachettespeakersbureau.com or email hachettespeakers@hbgusa.com.

Little, Brown and Company books may be purchased in bulk for business, educational, or promotional use. For information, please contact your local bookseller or the Hachette Book Group Special Markets Department at special.markets@hbgusa.com.

Print book interior design by Jeff Stiefel

ISBN 9780316564472
LCCN 2024948939

Printing 1, 2025

LSC-C

Printed in the United States of America

For Rebecca and Edmund,
again and as always

They that go down to the sea in ships,

that do business in great waters;

These see the works of the Lord,

and his wonders in the deep.

For he commandeth,

and raiseth the stormy wind,

which lifteth up the waves thereof.

They reel to and fro,

and stagger like a drunken man,

and are at their wits' end.

Then are they glad because they be quiet;

so he bringeth them unto their desired haven.

———

—Psalm 107:23–25, 107:27, 107:30

CONTENTS

PHANTOM
FLEET

"WONDERS IN THE DEEP"

(Psalm 107:24)

A t 11:09 a.m. on June 4, 1944, when the destroyer escort USS *Chatelain* heard the distinctive sound of a sonar hit on her elusive prey, the German submarine *U-505*, three men's lives changed—two for the better and one for the worse.

For Captain Daniel Gallery aboard USS *Guadalcanal*, the aircraft carrier leading the task group of which *Chatelain* was a part, that sharp, metallic *ping* had resounded like the tolling of a Gothic cathedral bell. Earlier that morning—a Sunday, notably—Gallery had faithfully attended Mass on the flight deck, and now *Chatelain*'s revelation that the submarine he'd sought for months had been delivered unto him answered his prayers.

He had always known this day would come. For Gallery, his destiny had been inscribed, as he put it, in the "Book of Fate." His long, winding path to this moment had been providentially ordained by the Lord, and he had treaded it dutifully. By endeavoring to fulfill His ends, just reward was now his.

For Commander Kenneth Knowles in Washington, D.C., on the other hand, Fate, Providence, Destiny—whatever you wanted to call it—had nothing to do with the matter. There, he headed the most secret room in the United States, known only as F-21—the submarine-tracking unit of the Navy's mysterious Tenth Fleet, which was tasked with a single mission: Hunt and kill Nazi U-boats.

There, Knowles acted as a storyteller in the sense that he told stories about submarines. He could imagine, just like a novelist or screenwriter, what they would do, how they would do it, and *why* they did it because he understood them as real *characters*, not as mere mechanical objects moving to and fro. As a master of narrative, he had *known*, or at least suspected, that *U-505* would be where he said she would be, and he had guided Gallery to this rendezvous. His colleague may have believed that he was unrolling a sacred scroll, but Knowles was in fact writing it as he went.

And finally, for *Oberleutnant zur See* (Senior Lieutenant) Harald Lange, luckless commander of *U-505*, his number had finally come up when he ran straight into Gallery and was hurled headlong into a personal hell. From Lange's perspective, his fall was due to none but the haphazard of chance, the play of dice, the joker in the deck. At one key moment, for instance, had he turned *this* way rather than that, *U-505* would never have intersected with Gallery.

But such were the vagaries of war. And Lange, like every U-boat captain, spun the wheel of fortune every time he ventured onto the high seas. He had been lucky so far, but *U-505* was notorious for being the unluckiest boat within the German submarine fleet. Now, it seemed, the odds had caught up with him.

As different as they were, all three men served in phantom fleets—Lange in one that could not be found, and the Americans in one that did not exist. Common, too, was that by whichever route they had taken to their destination—via Providence, Imagination, or Fortune—it had been a long Odyssean voyage for the three of them.

But one way or another, it would end here, very soon.

It had *begun,* however, nearly two and a half years earlier, in the grim aftermath of Operation *Drumbeat*—the German attack on America.

ACT 1

"THEIR WITS' END"

(Psalm 107:27)

ONE

THE EMERALD CITY

I

As *U-123*, dark and venomous and shielded from sight by the waves breaking against her low silhouette, killed time until the big-game night hunt, the best Fritz Rafalski could make out was that Mr. Way was arguing with Mrs. Way and that matronly Molly Goldberg, bless her sweet, interfering heart, was trying to calm the stormy waters of marital strife.

The blond, goateed Rafalski, twenty-seven years old, had never heard a Jew on the radio, or at least not since he'd been a teenager in 1933, when the Nazis took charge of the airwaves, but here there was a show devoted to the everyday doings of the Goldberg clan and their zany neighbors in a tenement building at 1030 East Tremont Avenue in the Bronx, wherever that was.

The radioman's confusion over the distantly German-sounding Yiddishisms and the incomprehensible New Yorkese in that day's episode of the hugely popular soap opera/comedy, *The Goldbergs*, was only the first, but by no means the last, clue that *U-123* had arrived in the New World.

Relegated to his cupboard-sized wireless room, Rafalski had grown accustomed to hearing only the staccato bark of coded orders from headquarters. When the U-boat's antenna had begun picking up signals from New York City, he listened in, curious to learn more about this strange and barbaric culture.

Trying to ignore the crackling static through his headphones, he shuffled past WOR's 710 frequency and stopped at WABC's on 880, where a cheerful fellow named John Reed King was hosting *Missus Goes A-Shopping*.

The contestants, all female, appeared to be playing a game in which they guessed the weight of a mighty joint of ham. Amidst their unimaginable abundance, they seemed so carefree. Did these *Hausfrauen* not realize there was a war on their doorstep?

Back in Europe, Stalin's legions had recently shoved the *Wehrmacht* more than 100 miles back from Moscow. Gone, at least for the time being, was the prospect of exploiting Soviet territory as Germany's granary, farm, and abattoir. Food shortages were beginning to bite on the home front. Women's magazines now advertised recipes for dandelion tea and acorn coffee; bread, meat, and butter rations had been halved, and lines stretched around corners whenever rumors of a potato delivery circulated.

At least Rafalski, subsisting on a submariner's tedious diet of diesel-infused water, soggy bread, greenish eggs, and dubious sausage, wouldn't have to dwell much longer on the thought of the Yankees feasting so lavishly and enjoying their silly radio shows. Soon after the sun had set that chilly evening of January 14, 1942, Rafalski picked up what *Kapitänleutnant* Reinhard Hardegen had been eagerly awaiting the last seventeen hours.

On the 6:30 news, there was a brief bulletin belatedly acknowledging that a tanker had sunk, possibly hit by a torpedo, south of Montauk on the eastern edge of Long Island. At last, Hardegen's latest kill had been confirmed.

Not long after—around 8 p.m. on that near-moonless night—*U-123* gunned her engines. There was no time to rest on their laurels. The slaughter was about to begin.

II

New York presented a blinding festival of light to the dark-doused eyes of a submarine skipper.

During the weeks when Hardegen and his crew had been waiting out there, deep in the Atlantic, the nights had blackly enveloped them. As their experience of fighting the British had shown since 1939, darkness cloaked submariners from prowling destroyers and questing bombers, and the men on *U-123* had done everything they could to stay hidden. When at sea, watchmen were banned from smoking on the conning-tower bridge, and carelessly letting a glimmer of light emerge from the chink of an opened hatch incurred a harsh penance.

But here, now, anyone standing topside could see bubbles of luminescence along the Long Island and New Jersey coastlines, each representing a carefree city or high-living town. Twinkling ribbons marked the paths of automobiles along highways; the crewmen could even make out the flickering neon signs by the roadside.

Bobbing lightships, like the one off Fire Island whose 18,000-candlepower lamps could be seen thirty miles out to sea, helpfully radiated their warnings of dangerous shoals while buoys flashed a rhythmic *dash-dot-dash-dash* guide to the nearest shipping lane. The passing cavalcade of steamers, freighters, tugs, and tankers was lit up like a funfair.

Directly north of *U-123*, Hardegen could even see a real one—a funfair, that is. Checking the cheap tourist map of New York given to him by U-Boat Command, the best available at short notice, Hardegen confirmed that it was Coney Island. One highlight—a more than 300-foot-high tower—was the famous Parachute Drop ride, next to which stood the huge Wonder Wheel, built twenty years earlier.

Despite their filamented garishness, these sights paled beside the main attraction: an incandescent glow suffusing the night sky. Emanating from the millions of lights illuminating Times Square and Manhattan's thicket of skyscrapers, it was a view similar to the one that had astonished Dorothy a few years earlier when she first laid distant eyes on the Wizard's Emerald City.

Against this aureole one could spot the silhouettes of ships gliding unwittingly past the hunter as they entered or cleared New York harbor. Hardegen, who'd visited the city in 1933 during a training cruise and had marveled at the metropolis from atop the Empire State Building's observatory, surveyed the scene from *U-123*'s bridge. "I cannot describe the feeling with words," he wrote soon after, "but it was unbelievably beautiful and great."

Hardegen's rapture was not occasioned solely by the view or his fond memories. No, it was the *moment* that signified, for "we were the first to be here, and for the first time in this war a German soldier looked out upon the coast of the U.S.A."

Yet there was no U.S. Navy to be seen. It was as if the Americans were suffering from some kind of cognitive failure to grapple with the horror of the fact that a ship had gone missing in their home waters. Perhaps they had decided to ignore the problem in the hope that it would go away.

It wouldn't. A few hours later, at 1:40 a.m., Hardegen found his next prey. It had not been difficult. The *Coimbra*, a full-bellied tanker carrying some 80,000 barrels of lubricating oil, had been steaming along with her navigation lights nonchalantly ablaze.

Hardegen maneuvered *U-123* into position, gently turning to set himself up perfectly for the kill as his crew assiduously calculated the target's course, speed, and track angle. Finally, just over an hour after the first sighting, with *Coimbra* silhouetted 800 yards away against the hazy lights of New York, Hardegen ordered Tube One to be flooded.

III

For fifty-eight seconds after Hardegen fired, *Coimbra* continued steaming along placidly while the eel, as the Germans called their torpedoes, slithered through the water. Then the projectile violently collided with its target just aft of the bridge.

The explosion—a column of yellow and red flame hundreds of feet high—lit the night sky "as bright as day," Hardegen noted in the ship's war diary. Chunks of superheated metal soon plummeted into the sea, hissing as they landed. Dark, oozing pools of fiery oil illuminated the horizon.

It had been a near-perfect hit, but Hardegen was nevertheless worried that the inferno was burning so fiercely its flames could be seen from New York, which meant the cavalry must surely be on its way. Just as bad—though ironic testament to the excellence of the German shipyard that had built her in 1937—was the fact that *Coimbra* had not sunk. Worse was that, by the glow of the fire, he could see men running to a mounted 4-inch gun on the tanker's listing deck—and if he could see them, they could see him.

Hardegen unleashed a second eel, which would prove to be the coup de grâce, at 2:59 a.m., eighteen minutes after his initial shot. This one struck the ship beneath the funnel. Another explosion and her back was broken. Settling on the seafloor by the stern in 170 feet of cold water, *Coimbra* marked her own grave with her bow protruding from the water at a 30-degree angle. As he left, Hardegen thought she'd make a "pretty buoy for the Yankees."

Of her forty-six crew, twenty-five went down with the wreck, and another eleven would die of exposure. There would be just ten survivors.

An Allied tanker sinks, 1942.

IV

But it never happened—at least according to the local newspapers.

In that morning's early edition of the *Brooklyn Eagle,* for instance, a small article cryptically mentioned the loss of "an Allied vessel of un-revealed nationality and tonnage" off Long Island. By the time the evening edition appeared, however, the story had been scrubbed. Instead, a correction noted that the "Sinking of 2nd Tanker Proves to Be a Myth," and quoted a Navy Department spokesman in Washington denying that anything out of the ordinary had occurred.

Not until Saturday, January 17—after a couple of gruff Long Island police chiefs had unhelpfully contradicted the Official Government Version by asserting that survivors and wreckage had in fact been spotted—did *Coimbra*'s name first appear. Even then, the *Eagle* buried the revelation in a tiny story at the bottom of page 7. It was easy to miss—deliberately so.

Radio stations and other newspapers (among them the *New York Times*) followed a similar policy. They did not suppress the fact that at least one U-boat was operating off the East Coast, yet they did not exactly promote it, either.

Life thus went on as normal—exactly as Washington had intended when officials had discreetly urged reporters to play down the news for fear of provoking panic. Front pages were devoted instead to the death of "Hollywood's Laughingest Actress," screwball comedian Carole Lombard, in a plane crash outside Las Vegas.

Traders at the New York Stock Exchange accordingly registered no signs of the alarm that would have greeted the news that the Germans were sinking ships off the Hamptons. On Friday, for instance, stocks had dipped a little in sluggish trading only because brokers were closing positions so they could depart early for leisurely weekends of golf at the country club.

In one downtown Manhattan office several blocks from Wall Street, though, nobody had gone home all week.

V

At 10 p.m. on Monday, January 12, five days earlier, Lieutenant Richard Braue's face-gleamingly polished black shoes clacked on the tiled floor as he hurried down the corridor to the office of Vice Admiral Adolphus Andrews, commander of the Eastern Sea Frontier (ESF), a zone extending 200 miles out and stretching from Canada to Florida.

In his hand, the communications officer carried a small metal case; in his holster, a service .45. You could never be too careful, even here in the ESF's headquarters on the 14th floor of the Federal Office Building, a confident monolith of standard United States Government architecture presiding stolidly at 90 Church Street in Manhattan, across from what is today the World Trade Center and 9/11 Memorial.

Braue had orders to shoot anyone who attempted to steal the case, though it contained but a single slip of paper. He knew nothing more about the terse message it bore than that it had originated from some-place in Britain informally called "The Citadel."

Even Andrews was in the dark as to the paper's mysterious prove-nance. But when Braue handed over the case, the old man treated its con-tents with the kind of reverence the Greeks once reserved for the sacred pronouncements of their oracles.

VI

The British had been interested in *U-123* since Christmas Day, when one of their listening stations had picked up a radio signal from Captain Har-degen to U-Boat Command relating his position.

Just after the New Year, another message was similarly intercepted, this one indicating that *U-123* was heading toward Newfoundland. By January 4, alarmingly, five more submarines seemed to be following her there.

Five days after that, U-Boat Command referred to this coalescence of submarines as *"Gruppe Paukenschlag."* This was the first time the cover name *Paukenschlag*—translated as *Drumbeat* or *Roll of Drums*—had been used, and it implied a major operation was in the offing.

Yet *Drumbeat's* objective remained unclear until January 12, when it was confirmed by eavesdropping on German radio traffic that the group was bearing on New York. The first attacks on the East Coast were scheduled to begin the next day.

The Americans had to be warned, urgently. London sent the message—the one borne by Lieutenant Braue—shortly afterward.

Within minutes of its reaching Vice Admiral Andrews, a pride of senior Navy officers gathered in the ESF's conference room. Four hours later, at 2 a.m., Andrews ended the meeting.

He had been through two wars (the Spanish-American and the Great), but here he was, aged sixty-three and just a year away from mandatory retirement, facing the ignominy of losing his final one.

Yet there was no avoiding what had to be done. He ordered an alert. After Braue flashed a signal to all civilian ships at sea—SUBMARINE MENACE ON NORTH ATLANTIC COAST—Andrews directed local air and naval units to prepare themselves for an imminent onslaught.

In the event, the rest of that day, the 13th, was unexpectedly quiet, as was the 14th. Perhaps the Brits' entrail-reading prescience had failed them. Maybe there were no submarines after all.

But Andrews's hopes were dashed on the Wednesday evening of January 14, when a report arrived that a Panamanian tanker, the *Norness*, had sunk. Until the survivors could be rescued, though, it remained to be confirmed whether she had been the victim of a torpedo or of a storm. But in his heart Andrews already knew that the first beat of the drum had been struck by *U-123*.

After reading the torn-off teletype reporting the loss, he glumly murmured to Braue, "Well, they are here."

VII

Glum he was right to be. Just a couple of weeks earlier, after all, Andrews had warned his superiors that "should enemy submarines operate off this coast, this command has no forces available to take adequate action against them." Now, he was expected to take them on anyway.

Admittedly, Andrews was something of a laughingstock in high Navy circles. In the mid-1920s he had captained *Sequoia*, the presidential yacht—not exactly an onerous posting—he loved to attend society parties, and yes, his nickname was "Dolly." Those facts alone might not have been damning, but in port and speech Andrews resembled some antiquated Gilbert & Sullivan comic-relief admiral and he was known among his peers as a "terrible old fusspocket."

Too often forgotten, though, was that Andrews was a highly capable commander who possessed more combat experience than most. Perhaps owing to his imminent retirement, too, he was one of the few gold-braided officers brave enough to have pointed out the emperor's lack of clothes.

It was true that the United States *was* virtually naked, its might and majesty covered by nothing but the quivering fig leaf of 21 small ships and 103 old naval aircraft.

Of the vessels under Andrews's command, four were 200-foot Eagle Boats, built in 1919 and described by the Navy as "almost completely useless" and "materially unreliable." His four small, wooden "submarine chasers" were likewise hopelessly ancient—so much so that they could chase a modern submarine about as well as a jogger pursuing a sprinter. Joining them were two larger gunboats that had been in service since 1905, almost as long as had Andrews himself. And finally, there was a quartet of luxury yachts that had been sold to the Navy by their well-heeled owners to aid the war effort. Although each was now armed with a pair of machine guns, they were unlikely to strike fear into the heart of any U-boat captain.

The best ships, in fact, belonged to the Coast Guard. They included seven modest cutters, six of which had been commissioned in 1927 to catch Prohibition rumrunners. Each had since been fitted with a 3-inch cannon and ten depth charges. The remaining one, *Dione,* was bigger and had entered service in 1934, but she carried the same small gun as her sisters.

U-boats weren't unarmed smugglers who'd dump crates of hooch overboard at the first sign of trouble, of course, and if it came to a knockdown fight a Nazi submarine would win on points. Not only was Hardegen's *U-123* some 251 feet in length—more than half again that of the 165-foot *Dione*—but she was armed with a 4.1-inch deck gun, thoroughly outclassing the Coast Guard's puny armament.

As Andrews laconically remarked of his tatterdemalion collection, "The limited capabilities of these vessels are apparent."

Their limited *number* was apparent, too. Andrews may have had on paper twenty-one vessels, but few were fit for operations. Nearly half, for instance, were being repaired or were unsuitable for wintry conditions. Others were stationed far south of New York. As of January 12, if one counted only the vessels immediately available for combat, Andrews was the grand admiral of an armada of three ships.

Naval aviation was in an almost equally parlous state. Most of his airplanes were in maintenance or waiting for pilots, meaning that Andrews could summon only thirty-eight in-service aircraft from local naval air stations. They were a mix of dated biplanes such as Grumman Ducks, usually employed for air-sea rescue, and newer scout floatplanes such as Vought Kingfishers.

Each was armed with two elderly depth charges. These bombs were capable of buckling a submarine hull, but in order to be effective they had to be dropped within an absurdly small radius of the target—thought to be around fourteen feet to be sure of a kill. The chances of a U-boat skipper idling helpfully within that bull's-eye while waiting for one to fall next to him were around zero.

In better news, Andrews was able to request the assistance of the Army Air Forces, which had a modest contingent of bombers, but no aid was guaranteed. At the time, the contentious relationship between the Army and Navy resembled less a team of rivals than a rivalry of teams, so much so that they occupied separate wings at 90 Church Street and met in the no-man's-land of a room designated for the purpose situated midway between them.

In any case, it wasn't clear how helpful the Army could be even with the best will in the world. Nearly all its veteran pilots had been urgently reassigned to the Pacific after Pearl Harbor a month earlier, and the green crews that remained hadn't the foggiest notion how to hit a small, moving target at sea using bombs designed to flatten cities.

Shortly afterward, the predictable disaster-waiting-to-happen happened when a quartet of Army pilots spotted the sinister outline of a U-boat and eagerly swooped for the kill.

All their bombs went wide, and a good thing, too, because the targeted "U-boat" turned out to be USS *Trippe*, an American destroyer that was 100 feet longer than (and traveling twice as fast as) any known German submarine. Completely untrained in basic sea recognition—to such a degree that to them the wake of a shark's fin was indistinguishable from that left by a periscope—the pilots had avoided a friendly-fire tragedy owing only to their spectacular inability to hit anything.

Andrews knew there was little he could do to stop the coming rampage along the East Coast. "Whatever possible grounds there may be for optimism," he depressingly concluded, lay in a single forlorn hope: that his skeleton force might "limit losses to bearable proportions" among civilian and merchant ships until the Germans decided to go home.

Two

THE GOLDEN TIME

I

Vice Admiral Adolphus Andrews was being perfectly reasonable in hoping that the U-boats off the East Coast would not be there long. In the summer of 1918, five U-boats had similarly made a nuisance of themselves along the seaboard, but only for a couple of months.

Several lightly armed submarine chasers—the ones still in service, actually—and converted yachts had been sufficient to drive them off. As the Navy had languidly concluded at the time, "There was no stampede on the Atlantic coast; no excitement; [and] everything went on in the usual calm way."

This general sense of equanimity helps explain why the Navy had devoted little time to anti-submarine training or to strengthening defensive forces before Pearl Harbor. *Even if they do come, they won't be here long.*

In fact, no one really knew what the U-boats were doing there in the first place. Some thought they had been sent to ambush Prime Minister Winston Churchill as he returned from his American visit with President Franklin Roosevelt. If so, they must have been bitterly disappointed;

Churchill was flying, not sailing, back to Britain. Perhaps, in their pique, the German captains had decided to sink some ships? Others suggested that they were just passing through on their way south to disrupt the Inter-American Conference in Rio de Janeiro. Whatever the objective was, the submarines would hit-and-run and surely go home.

For an unconscionably long time, then, no one bothered to order coastal towns to dim, let alone extinguish, their streetlights, theaters, and boardwalks. And for every good citizen—the *New York Times* turned off its famous 14,800-bulb sign in Times Square—there were scofflaws aplenty, like Roosevelt Stadium in New Jersey, where night baseball games served as a convenient lighthouse to U-boats fifty miles out to sea. Worse yet, many ships still persisted in sailing with their lights on.

None of this mattered, of course, because the U.S. Navy was handing Hitler's U-boats a whipping they would never forget. "The recent visitors to our territorial waters will never enjoy the return portion of their voyage," gloated a senior Navy official to newspapers in late January. No fewer than fourteen had been sunk so far, he said. By April 1, that total had risen to twenty-eight. At the time, some ninety-one German submarines were operating in the entire Atlantic Ocean, meaning the Navy had destroyed nearly a third of the fleet in damn short order.

An impressive accomplishment, except that the actual figure was zero, at least until April 14, when the destroyer *Roper* killed *U-85* off North Carolina's Cape Hatteras, a feat attributable more to the German skipper's cockiness than to anything else. After that the Americans got a little more proficient, but even so, during the entire first half of 1942 U.S. forces would sink a mere six U-boats off their own coast.

That senior Navy official may have been exaggerating, but he was not, to his knowledge, lying. He genuinely believed that submarines *were* being sunk—because that was what captains and pilots were reporting when they returned to their bases. In late January, for instance, the pilot Donald Mason earned himself a Distinguished Flying Cross when, as his report stated, he "dove to low altitude, and dropped two depth bombs which straddled the periscope" of a submarine, which soon disappeared. After sending the sibilant message SIGHTED SUB, SANK SAME, he found himself famous.

But Mason hadn't sunk anything. So lamentable was the quality of American anti-submarine warfare and intelligence that he, like many others, mistook standard operating procedure for a kill. *Every* U-boat commander *always* dived as soon as he spotted an airplane. It was simply a part of the getaway plan—and get away, Mason's target had.

II

Greeks, Persians, and Romans had once marveled at the bones of unimaginably vast monsters—we know them as dinosaurs—they found in the deserts and swamps of their empires. The same might be said of the befuddled U.S. Navy as it sought to come to grips with the U-boats. What *were* these things?

The vessels were mystifying. Their behavior was unknown. So too were their purpose and capabilities. All anyone knew was that they were still here—and becoming ever more lethal.

On a single day—January 19, four days after his attack on *Coimbra*—Captain Hardegen torpedoed *City of Atlanta* and then *Ciltvaira*, on her way from New York to Savannah, while his comrade Richard Zapp in *U-66* hit the *Lady Hawkins,* a Canadian liner carrying 212 passengers and 109 crew. Of those aboard, only 71 survived.

When the waters around New York grew too hot, Hardegen turned south to Cape Hatteras. The busy sea-lanes there soon became known as "Torpedo Junction" when four other U-boats in *Drumbeat's* first wave joined him. It got so crowded that two U-boats crashed into each other and had to hobble home for repairs.

By January 24, both Hardegen and Zapp had run out of torpedoes, but the killing did not stop. A second wave of U-boats had since arrived to carry on the work. And then in mid-February, a *third* wave began to wreak havoc in the Caribbean and off Florida.

Among the U-boat crews, this was known as *die goldene Zeit*—the Golden Time.

III

The dire statistics told as dreadful a story as the sight of beaches covered in washed-up corpses and the black plumes of smoke from burning ships just a few miles offshore. In January and February, a mere five U-boats sank twenty-seven ships without suffering a single casualty. After sneaking into the Caribbean, a handful of submarines destroyed thirty-three more, again without being unduly annoyed by the Navy. Then in March alone, another twenty-seven ships disappeared along the East Coast.

Putting those figures into perspective, from 1939 to 1941, the British and their allies had lost an average of 2.1 million tons of shipping per year to all causes, including accidents and storms. In March 1942 alone, by comparison, more than a million tons were lost due solely to submarines, the vast majority of it in American waters. Over the entirety of that year, U-boats would destroy 6.1 million tons of cargo and oil, a level of destruction out of all proportion to the number of submarines deployed off the East Coast and in the Caribbean, which never totaled more than a baker's dozen.

Even Adolf Hitler, who hadn't held out high hopes for the campaign, told the Japanese ambassador to Berlin at the end of March that he was "surprised at the success we have met with along the American coast lately. The United States kept up the tall talk and left her coasts unguarded. Now I daresay *she* is quite surprised."

It looked as if the Führer's opportunistic declaration of war on the United States on December 11—four days after the Japanese attack on Pearl Harbor—had paid off brilliantly. The Americans, he thought, were in no shape to withstand the hammer blows of a seaborne *Blitzkrieg*.

Hitler had always quickly seized any chance to benefit from his opponents' disarray and panic. The Americans would soon collapse, he expected. They had to, because the United States was known to be a sleeping giant: weak and dopey when first awoken, but capable of extraordinary strength when roused to anger. Hitler could recall as well as anybody that in 1916 the German commander General Erich Ludendorff had casually remarked, "I don't give a damn about America," only to be confronted by a fresh, million-man army arriving in Europe a year later.

Although the prewar American military was puny—in 1939, the Army numbered some 270,000 men, making it the world's seventeenth largest, just a shade smaller than mighty Romania's—Hitler understood, if he did not deeply appreciate, that the U.S. would soon place its matchless productive capacity on a war footing. Within German High Command, the year 1943 was determined to be the key inflection point: After that, ramping U.S. superiority in numbers would remorselessly begin to tell against the Axis powers.

But not if Operation *Drumbeat* succeeded. Hitler's gamble was that the Americans' will to wage war against *Germany*, as opposed to the hated Japanese, was for the time being soft and malleable. If the United States was confronted by dispiriting losses at the outset, the dragon of isolationism, so recently slayed by Roosevelt, might well resurrect itself—and enter the arena in Berlin's favor.

There was never a doubt in Hitler's mind that the Yankees would cut and run. He admired their pluck and their flint, their system of national parks, and their sound views on eugenics, but ultimately they were ruled by a corrupt, plutocratic democracy almost as rancid as Soviet

Bolshevism. "The Americans put business above all else," Hitler wrote of their most contemptible weakness. Confronted by a hard strike on these financial interests, the Americans would fold and let their British allies hang rather than sacrifice their effete luxuries.

But it had to be done *now*, not later, when they would compete with Germany for mastery of the globe.

IV

It seemed a practical plan, for in December 1941, if analyzed from a certain perspective, Germany was at the height of its power and looked like a surefire winner. Among other things, the territories under Hitler's direct and indirect control had a combined population of 290 million people—about 100 million more than that of the United States and Britain combined—and the Reich's GDP was greater than either. Compared to the five measly Army divisions the Americans could send into the field, Germany had already deployed 180.

But when viewed in the round, the picture was decidedly less rosy. In June 1941, only six months earlier, the Soviet Union had been an ally, the United States was at peace, and a beleaguered Britain had been the only obstacle to the Nazi domination of Europe. After Hitler's declaration of war on December 11, by contrast, Germany had descended into an existential struggle against not just an obstinate British Empire, but a bellicose America and an insatiably vengeful USSR.

Worse even than the deteriorating strategic situation, the declaration had come as such a surprise that no one at Hitler's headquarters had even begun drafting a plan of attack against the United States, and alarmingly numerous German admirals could not locate Pearl Harbor on a map.

The *Drumbeat* campaign to knock out the Americans had thus been a hastily concocted one. At the last minute, however, the Führer—always his own worst enemy—got it into his head that the British were about to invade Norway. He therefore ordered eleven U-boats originally assigned to the attacking fleet to stay behind to guard his possession.

Which was why the first wave had comprised just six submarines—a lucky escape for the Americans, had they but known it.

V

Even if Hitler's blunderous reallocation had dulled the shock power of *Drumbeat,* the operation succeeded not only in fraying the lifeline of supplies heading to Europe from the United States, but in exacerbating tensions between Britain and America. In mid-March, when Prime Minister Winston Churchill expressed his alarm to President Franklin Roosevelt at the never-ending losses in American waters, the president testily pointed a finger back at him for not bombing the U-boat bases on the Continent to eliminate the trouble at its source. The British already knew, however, that would be futile: The concrete pens were impregnable.

Squabbles aside, Churchill was correct to cite "the immense sinkings of tankers" as especially worrisome in his letter to Roosevelt. In January, for instance, 70 percent of the ships sunk were tankers; in March, 57 percent. That was no coincidence.

The Germans were not, it was becoming clear, hitting ships randomly. Instead they had focused on choking off the flow of oil to the Allied war machine. The Americans, German naval analysts argued, owned few domestic pipelines and lacked sufficient railway or road capacity to transport the black gold overland to their factories and shipyards. They were thus dangerously dependent on their tanker routes, with 95 percent of Texas and Oklahoma oil bound for the East Coast traveling by sea.

Because it would take at least a year to build a pipeline from Texas to New York, they estimated, the analysts confirmed German High Command's assessment: American manufacturing would be throttled until 1943, at the very earliest, if the U-boats continued their bloody task.

More enticing still was the possibility of shutting down New York. That city's port was the busiest in the world, as well as the biggest: Its 1,800 docks, piers, and wharves could accommodate some 600 ships at a time.

In short, New York was the heart, lungs, and sinews of the American war effort relating to Europe, and everything in, on, under, over, and near it ran on oil. To cripple operations, all the Germans had to do was target the huge, lumbering tankers arriving from the Gulf of Mexico or heading north toward Halifax in Canada, where the transatlantic convoys originated.

It would not take much to disrupt this tanker traffic. There were only some 260 U.S.–flagged vessels transporting Texas crude. In the six weeks from mid-January to March 1 alone, a few U-boats had destroyed forty-five tankers and damaged thirteen—a little more than one-fifth of the fleet. What would happen if *half* of it was lost over the coming months?

Quite aside from devastating the country's economy, stanching the flow of American oil would cause British resistance to collapse; their bombers and fighters simply could not take off. What's more, any planned invasion of North Africa would have to be canceled because there would be no fuel in the depots, and Stalin's tanks would clank to a halt when they ran dry.

Freighter losses presented a similarly frightening outlook. An average cargo vessel carried as much matériel as four 75-wagon trains. For every two modest, 6,000-ton freighters and small, 3,000-ton tanker that were sunk, what ended up on the bottom of the sea was the equivalent of 42 tanks, 8 6-inch howitzers, 88 25-pound guns, 40 light guns,

24 armored cars, 50 Bren carriers, 5,210 tons of ammunition, 600 rifles, 428 tons of tank parts, 2,000 tons of stores, and 1,000 tanks of gasoline.

Put another way, in the first couple of months of 1942 alone, a handful of submarines had inflicted the same amount of loss as would have, statistically speaking, *96,000* bombing sorties. And the U-boat war was just getting started.

But so too was a new broom at Navy headquarters.

Three

SHEEPDOGS AND WOLVES

I

In March 1942, the first sign of change at this nadir of American fortunes came in the tall, bleak form of Admiral Ernest King, the newly appointed Commander in Chief, U.S. Fleet, and Chief of Naval Operations.

Throughout his long career, most of King's subordinates had despised him, and not even his few admirers had loved him, a notorious bully and bellower. Contemptuous toward those who did not meet his elevated expectations, King loudly cursed hapless captains and youthful lieutenants alike in language that shocked even old sea dogs. On land, a drunk in all but name, he could turn charming and debonair at cocktail parties, all the better to proposition his colleagues' wives as his hands wandered beneath the table.

He did, however, maintain a small retinue of loyalists. The upside to serving under King, if you survived the gauntlet, was that he would grant his officers leeway to a degree unheard-of among American admirals. Like Napoleon, whose marshals were batoned on the basis of their enterprise, King prized initiative above any other value; a superior's responsibility, he believed, was to tell a subordinate what needed to be done but not how to do it. Juniors needed to learn to think for themselves and to act independently when they judged it necessary. "Stop nursing them," was one of his maxims.

Nevertheless, there was no excusing King's philandering, not in the starched-white Navy, and Roosevelt disliked his heavy boozing and wild poker games. For that reason, he'd

Admiral King, as approachable as ever.

been passed over for promotion until *Drumbeat* came along within weeks of his mandatory retirement, an event that everyone save King had been looking forward to.

No one could have guessed that the admiral, who had gloomily expected he'd soon be spending his dotage duck-hunting—a sport at which he was a grim enthusiast, if not a crack shot—would be summoned to leave his proverbial plow and return to war.

Roosevelt's appointment of King to the Navy's top spot had about it the sound of a barrel being scraped, and King knew it. But he also knew that when the going gets tough, they call in the bastards.

King may have lacked the easy congeniality of an Eisenhower, but he possessed the unrelenting aggression of a Patton. King was an attacking admiral—one who, like the legendary Lord Nelson, demanded that his ships engage the enemy more closely. Playing defense did not come naturally, or sit well, with a commander like King. Battle was his mettle.

Granted this unexpected opportunity, King immediately cleaned himself up. The furious chain-smoking endured, but out went the Scotch and in came a modest glass of sherry. The poker parties and the weekend affairs stopped, replaced by late-night meetings and all-day order-giving.

As Commander in Chief, U.S. Fleet—CINCUS—King's very first act was to change this unfortunate acronym to COMINCH, or plain Commander in Chief. His second, and more consequential, was to fix America's embarrassing response to the U-boat onslaught.

II

Admiral Karl Dönitz, King's opponent across the water, is known to have cracked a single joke in his life. It was when he suspected the presence of a spy in his headquarters and everyone but him and his chief of staff had been thoroughly questioned by investigators. When no spy was found, Dönitz said to the man, "Now it can be only me or you."

No one, alas, said it was a funny joke. It's even possible that Dönitz wasn't attempting to lighten the mood but was instead being entirely serious: At that stage, the spy really could be only one of them. Aside from there being no spy at all, that was, after all, the only logical conclusion.

Seriousness, manifested in a zeal for remorseless, self-critical improvement, had been Dönitz's default mode since his motherless childhood, when his authoritarian father had pushed and shoved and driven him ahead at all costs. Although his subsequent rise through the German Navy wasn't explosive, it was steady: Dönitz was always competent, always punctual, always prepared.

Following four years of sterling service during the Great War, Dönitz's one great, unforgivable failure came in its closing weeks, when as commander of the submarine *UB-68* he was forced to surrender his vessel to the British after damage rendered her unable to dive. To his mortification, he survived—albeit humiliatingly dressed only in a shirt, his underwear, and a sock—while his engineer heroically sacrificed himself to stay below to scuttle the U-boat.

Dönitz appears to have suffered some kind of mental breakdown in captivity as he turned over that day's events repeatedly in his mind. He blamed himself: for the shame of failure, for betraying the Kaiser, for personally losing the war for Germany. His interrogator wrote that Dönitz "was very moody and almost violent at times and it was very hard to make him talk at all."

Despite his self-flagellation and possibly suicidal intent, the loss of *UB-68* was not Dönitz's fault at all. He eventually pulled himself out of his funk by resolving *never* to break again.

In the 1930s, as chief of the Führer's growing submarine force, Dönitz had become a true believer. An out-and-out anti-Semite, Dönitz was already temperamentally inclined to be mesmerized by Hitler's power and the blood-cult of his omnipotent will. The seaman's ramrod, compact form—until the end of his days he could still fit into his midshipman's uniform—and rigidly controlled, taciturn exterior concealed a roiling core of molten fanaticism, the only giveaway being the dark, piercing eyes of the silent zealot.

Absolute faith in the Führer, absolute hatred of the enemy's creed, absolute commitment to the U-boat weapon, absolute determination never to yield: These were Dönitz's guiding stars. But his Polaris was *control.* During the war ahead, he would govern his U-boat fleet as tightly as he did his own body and mind, orchestrating the wolf packs' sweeping movements from his headquarters as much as his brain regulated his own limbs.

Unlike the case of King, however, his men were fond of "Uncle Karl," who saw in their comradeship the spirit of the German *Volk* in microcosm. And a good thing, too, for they would end up dying for him in their tens of thousands.

III

Handed unfettered command over the Navy, the force of nature that was Admiral Ernest King quickly made itself felt.

In early April 1942, he demanded a near-total blackout along the East Coast and ordered ships never to sail independently. These two steps alone brought an immediate drop-off in sinkings, with monthly losses in the Eastern Sea Frontier plummeting from twenty-three to five.

At first, Admiral Dönitz could not understand what was happening. The U-boats' sudden lack of success could be ascribed to the new precautionary measures—that was only to be expected—but more mysterious was how the Americans were still able to fight. An astonishing 112 tankers now lay rusting at the bottom of the sea. Surely their machines must be sputtering for lack of oil by now?

By mid-May, it had become distressingly clear not only that the oil-starved American economy *hadn't* juddered to a halt, but also that it wasn't even oil-starved in the first place. If anything, the Yankees were almost swimming in the stuff: Since *Drumbeat* began, thousands of miles of pipeline from Texas to the East Coast had been rush-built and the railroad system overhauled. In January, trains had hauled 100,000 barrels a day eastward, but by June that figure had rocketed to 726,000.

These overland oil deliveries nearly completely replaced the losses caused by Dönitz's U-boats. Just before *Drumbeat*, seaborne tanker shipments to the East Coast had amounted to 1.3 million barrels a day, but by June they had plummeted to 226,000. That collapse would otherwise have sparked a major political and economic crisis, but in fact all that happened was that lead-footed drivers were asked to go a little easier on the gas. Only modest rationing was needed because the remaining sea shipments, added to what the new pipelines and tank cars were bringing, totaled nearly 1.2 million barrels. In terms of oil supply, it was almost as if *Drumbeat* had never happened.

Dönitz conceded that *Drumbeat* had run its course; no longer showing results, the operation would have to be scrapped. But the relentless
mariner wasn't giving up. In August, with sinkings having fallen precipi-
tously, Dönitz decided to transfer not only the *Drumbeat* submarines but
also forty-eight newly built U-boats to the North Atlantic.

The war was about to enter its next, deadlier phase.

IV

Two thousand years before, the Romans had secured their shipments
of olive oil and spices from Sicily and North Africa by aggregating merchant vessels in port and assigning warships to watch over them as they
sailed.

Then, in the sixteenth century, Philip II of Spain's grand galleons,
groaning and creaking under the weight of their cargoes of New World
gold, had similarly warded off Elizabeth I's sea dogs by herding together
on their Atlantic voyage.

And a hundred and fifty years earlier, the British had protected their
own trade from Napoleon's raiders by escorting it through the English
Channel, the North Sea, and the Mediterranean.

Convoying worked, in other words, against corsairs, pirates, privateers, and insolent Frenchmen alike. Early in World War II, nevertheless, some British merchant vessels had sailed alone in the hope of
evading the enemy through either guile or speed, but that hope had been
dashed: Loss rates among these independents had been at least five times
higher—occasionally one hundred times higher—than among convoyed
ships.

The reason was that when ships sailed independently they presented
multiple opportunities to attack. If a U-boat missed one, another target would soon come along, and then another. The compact mass of a

convoy, on the other hand, gave U-boats a single shot. If they flubbed it, it might be weeks before the next one arrived.

On this general principle, Admiral King and the British agreed: Convoying was crucial for continuing the uninterrupted supply of fuel and matériel to Europe. But there the concordance ended.

The major point of dispute concerned not whether merchant ships should be convoyed but the role of the *warships* escorting the convoys. To the British, the presence of several of these wardens tended to deter submarines seeking easy kills, in the same way that a flock guarded by a sheepdog or two often went unravaged by a wolf. "We U-boat men knew well enough that a big convoy," as the ace Kapitänleutnant Peter Cremer of *U-333* put it, "escorted by even only a few destroyers and corvettes, could not be attacked even by a whole pack of U-boats without loss to ourselves."

The British attitude was that an attack that either did not happen or failed to succeed was a victory, making it almost irrelevant whether *any* U-boat was sunk so long as the merchant vessels arrived safe and sound. Their yardstick of success lay in the amount of tonnage ferried to Britain to prepare for the coming invasion of continental Europe, to beef up resources for the Mediterranean and African campaigns, and to load up the arms convoys heading north to the Soviets.

For the British, preserving these supply lines was their highest priority. Their country was serving as a combination of warehouse and refinery while producing very little of the raw materials necessary for modern war. Some 95 percent of all petroleum products, 90 percent of copper ore, 90 percent of bauxite, and 100 percent of rubber, for example, had to be imported simply in order to keep fighting. "The people of Britain can tighten their belts," advised one Admiralty expert, "but our armies cannot be let down by failure to provide equipment, guns, and tanks. This means ships and more ships, and safe escort for them."

The arrival of the Americans was adding to that already heavy burden. Until then, no one had realized just how much *stuff* was needed to maintain a single soldier—an American one, at least. Each GI sent abroad was accompanied by five tons' worth of equipment and supplies, and every month he required another ton shipped over. Japanese soldiers of the time may have survived on a bowl of rice a day, but on the Anzio beachhead in 1944 the Americans would amass *18,000* vehicles *just for transport.*

Given these logistical requirements, it was understandable that the British would prefer keeping their own vessels afloat to sinking the enemy's. King, however, saw this strategy of avoidance as a passive half measure. It *managed* the U-boat problem by getting more ships through than Dönitz could sink, whereas King wanted to *solve* it by sinking more submarines than Dönitz could build.

To his mind, wars could not be won by sidestepping combat. As King put it in a memorandum to Roosevelt, it was instinctual to be initially defensive in the face of danger, but ultimately "no fighter ever won his fight by covering up—by merely fending off the other fellow's blows. The winner hits and keeps on hitting even though he has to take some stiff blows in order to be able to keep on hitting."

Until he built up his strength, he'd put his guard up—but then King intended to hit back hard.

V

Well, that was all right for *him*, retorted the British. King could afford to wait, enjoying as he did the luxury of oceanic moats around his fortress, an invulnerable continent connected by land to the riches of South America and Canada. They, on the other hand, were located on a small island twenty miles away from an aggressive enemy who had recently tried to invade it. So, yes, managing their supply lines to avoid suffocation was a rather important consideration.

King understood that his ally's focus on trade protection rather than on decisive battles was the sensible, even necessary, approach in the short term—but he knew that it would eventually become a self-defeating one because the U-boat struggle was not static. It was *dynamic* in that Dönitz would build hundreds more submarines, with each successive generation more technologically advanced than the last. Aside from the boats' better torpedoes, faster speeds, and enhanced performance, every day their crews spent unmolested at sea gained them invaluable tactical experience. The lessons they learned, logged and annotated by their captains, would be passed on to subsequent cadres of German submariners.

One could already see that both machines and men had improved in short order. Just two years earlier, the life expectancy of a U-boat had been three months; now it was thirteen. Blooded U-boat crews were these days sinking an average of nineteen enemy ships before their own vessel was sunk. In 1940, that "exchange rate" had been eleven for one.

In time, unless the Allies stopped trying simply to manage the U-boat threat, the challenge of keeping the U-boats at bay would become *unman*ageable. Eventually these ravenous wolves would overwhelm the sheepdogs and ravage every flock. To preempt such a disaster, King believed, the wolves must be brutally culled before they got anywhere near a convoy.

The only way to do that was for destroyers and airplanes to sally out and hunt them down in their lairs.

There was just one small problem with King's strategy: Searching for a submarine was like trying to find one particular haystraw in a field of haystacks.

VI

In a sense, submarines are more like airplanes than ships. The latter exist in a two-dimensional environment and are therefore relatively easy to detect on the flat surface. Submarines, however, operate in three dimensions, only aquatic rather than aeronautic. Planes can change their heading, altitude, and airspeed just as much as submarines can vary their bearing, depth, and knots.

A related complication was that, even if the hunters managed to locate a submarine lingering on the surface—a difficult enough proposition, given the vast areas involved—the U-boat's ability to maneuver in three dimensions gave its opponents only a limited time (about thirty seconds) to wound or kill one that crash-dived upon being spotted. Once it was underwater and maneuvering evasively, only guesswork and good fortune enabled a depth-charge hit.

To be sure, the Germans were manacled, too. Take a Type IX U-boat, of which *U-123*—the submarine that under Kapitänleutnant Reinhard Hardegen helped kick off Operation *Drumbeat*—was a typical example. While surfaced, her diesel engines could propel her at more than eighteen knots (twenty-one miles per hour). When submerged and running on battery-powered electric motors, by contrast, her maximum speed dropped to seven knots (about eight mph). If Hardegen throttled down his diesels to an economy speed of ten knots (twelve mph), his official surfaced range was 14,000 miles without refueling; if he did the same with the electrics and dropped to four knots (five mph), his cruising range plummeted to a mere 74 miles.

Even so, a Type IX could enjoy sixteen hours' continuous running time underwater—more than enough to shake off its frustrated pursuers. With 74 miles as the radius of the U-boat's operating circle from initial point of contact, and given its maximum operating depth of around 750 feet, we can form a cylinder of sorts, with the circular, 148-mile-diameter "top" being the ocean surface and the "body" extending 750 feet down. The volume of water within this cylinder amounts to 2,444 cubic miles, or 360 trillion cubic feet.

That's a lot of *theoretical* space to lose oneself in. To put it into perspective, a Type IX U-boat was 250 feet long. That slight metal sliver might be anywhere, pointed in any direction, moving at any speed or depth. During those sixteen hours underwater, the submarine could have changed bearing countless times, dived deeper or risen to periscope depth, sped up or slowed down.

Under real-world conditions, of course, no captain would stay submerged for so long, he would avoid diving to anywhere near maximum operating depth, and the U-boat would surface at night to recharge its batteries and vent its stinking air. That act of self-revelation hardly mattered, though, since the craft was as good as invisible way out there in the blue.

Except to one man currently aboard an American Export Airlines flying boat en route to Washington.

ACT 2

"THE STORMY WIND"

(Psalm 107:25)

FOUR

THE SEASON ON THE LINE

I

The transatlantic flight that August 4, 1942, was comfortable: The Sikorsky VS-44's forty-inch-wide seats converted into beds, the white-jacketed steward mixed a fine Old-Fashioned, and, most relievedly, the Luftwaffe was not causing trouble. Since tourism had been killed by the outbreak of war, American Export Airlines had contracted its small fleet to the Navy, meaning that most of the sixteen passengers on the half-full plane were traveling on government business of one sort or another.

Divided almost equally between Americans and Britons—the grand alliance at work—most of those on board were blandly described as "officials," but many were actually intelligence officers of one sort or another. One of the travelers that day was, for instance, Archibald MacLeish, the well-known poet and current Librarian of Congress, who was then working in the Research & Analysis Branch of the newly formed OSS, forerunner of the CIA.

The man listed as Passenger No. 2, however, was not a spy, though he had recently become deeply immersed in a secret world. Indeed, the

43

arcane knowledge he carried in his head was more valuable than anyone else on board could imagine.

His name was Lieutenant Commander Kenneth Alward Knowles, he was thirty-eight years old, and he was the only American bestowed with the priestly power to foretell the whereabouts of German submarines in the wild.

Kenneth Knowles, captured in a very rare photograph.

II

The induction of Knowles into such seeming necromancy had begun four months prior, in mid-April, when Commander Rodger Winn had limped into the office of Admiral Ernest King's deputy chief of staff, Rear Admiral Richard Edwards. Winn declined to sit, preferring to stand and lean on the back of the chair for support.

He wore a naval uniform, but one bearing the distinctive gold "Wavy Navy" rings on the sleeves indicating that he was Royal Naval Volunteer Reserve. A civilian with no sea experience, then, granted only a temporary officer's commission. And how he'd got one of those, Admiral Edwards couldn't begin to hazard.

The first thing that struck people when they met Winn was his broad shoulders and powerful forearms—a typical wrestler's build. The second was his polio-twisted spine, his cane, and his relatively spindly legs. And the third was his indomitable use of the first set of attributes to overcome the challenges of the second.

It had been a slog for Winn to see Edwards. Sent to Washington without any guidance, he'd started with the bottom rung of officers at the

Navy Department Building (known as "Main Navy") and wheedled his way up the ranks. Even when, after four days of meetings with various functionaries, Winn was finally ushered into Edwards's office, he found that it still was not smooth sailing. Quite the opposite, in fact.

Winn considered King's deputy overbearing, unreceptive, and "frankly hostile." Edwards had reason to be unwelcoming, though, given that Winn came across as crazy by claiming that he could *forecast a U-boat's movements*:

Rodger Winn, around the time of his Washington visit.

where it was, where it was going, when it would get there, and what it would do once it did. And not for just one enemy submarine—*for all of them.*

Edwards, who looked like a cross between a bloodhound and a bulldog, thought Winn was treating him like his poodle. It was a truth universally acknowledged within the U.S. Navy that finding a submarine was a matter, as Edwards pointed out, of "sheer chance and the law of averages." A golfer had better odds of successively hitting several holes in one.

So it was impossible, Edwards insisted, to do what Winn said he could do. He knew baloney when he heard it. Submarines' behavior was unpredictable, and the dismal mathematics of volume and area multiplied by time gave them every advantage.

False, Winn shot back. For some time, his "Room 41" had been tracking dozens of U-boats at a time and diverting convoys, as was the British preference, around their predicted interception points with U-boat packs onto safer routes.

It took Winn three meetings, an insolent remark referring to "your bloody incompetence" regarding American performance during *Drumbeat,* and a very boozy lunch to induce Edwards to concede that Winn's method *might* work.

Really, it was the lunch that did it. Winn had said something off-handedly that finally piqued Edwards's interest. Until then, Winn had been emphasizing how tracking allowed him to reroute convoys *past* submarines. Over the third martini, however, Winn mentioned that, since he already knew where the U-boats were, he could probably guide destroyers and aircraft *to* them.

It was at that point that Edwards stopped drinking and started thinking. If Old Man King wanted a more aggressive approach to killing U-boats, mused the admiral, this would be the way to go about it. Of course, the question remained: *Could* this odd little wizard really perform such dark magic? But when Winn described how the trick worked, he certainly sounded convincing.

The admiral had no idea just how convincing Winn could sound. At first, the gold braid at the Admiralty had been similarly skeptical that Winn could peer into the future, but he had won them over by being right most of the time. There was no chance to give an impromptu exhibition of his talents here in Washington, so Winn instead deployed his fearsome powers of persuasion. In his previous life, the Cambridge-educated Winn (with additional stints at Yale *and* Harvard) had been a first-class barrister in London, accustomed to arguing his clients' cases dexterously before unyielding judges and skeptical juries.

Gruff American admirals were not immune to similar rhetorical sleight of hand, it seems. Winn knew he'd won his case, at least in the lower courts, when Edwards said, "I'm quite clear that this must be done, now."

Edwards still had to gain the approval of his boss, Chief of Staff Vice Admiral Russell Willson, who would decide whether to take the appeal to *his* boss, Admiral King. Willson knew that Winn's January tip had alerted Admiral Andrews that Dönitz was about to launch *Drumbeat,* which was strong enough grounds to arrange a hearing with Chief Justice Ernest King to present his closing argument.

A week later, Winn found himself in the belly of the beast, Main Navy 3048—King's imposing and austere office.

King had a terrible reputation in London for being obnoxiously anti-British. So as Winn waited to see the admiral, he was, naturally, trepidatious as to what awful fate awaited him.

It turned out not to be so bad. In reality, King was less anti-British than single-mindedly pro–U.S. Navy—as his numberless Army enemies could attest. He became exasperating and stubborn only when outsiders made a play to control his forces in the name of "joint command." Since Winn wasn't here to do that, King was curt but not rude.

The meeting went as follows: Winn was ushered in, King heard him out, nodded his approval at setting up an American version of Room 41, and Winn was ushered out.

American was King's watchword. This new Tracking Room that Winn had sold him on was not to be a combined Anglo-American venture, nor were British officers to be attached to it. An all-American naval officer was to be in charge, and a good candidate was soon found: Kenneth Knowles.

III

As a junior officer in the late 1920s and 1930s serving aboard the battleship USS *Pennsylvania* and the destroyer USS *Paul Jones,* Knowles had become known to several of the big shots now in COMINCH headquarters; even King, whom he'd once seen coming home late from a party "considerably under the weather and carrying his shoes in his hand," was dimly aware of Knowles's existence.

His diligence, smarts, and application had impressed the brass as much as they had his fellow midshipmen at the Naval Academy. Back then, they had said he was destined to make two-starred flag rank.

But the stars had not aligned for Knowles after this promising start. In 1937, soon after getting married to Velma Sealy, the daughter of a well-to-do Texas surgeon, he was ordered onshore for hearing and serious eyesight problems. The ears could be fixed, but his newly diagnosed nearsightedness was an insuperable obstacle in the Navy, where the ability to see distant objects clearly when traveling at thirty-five knots—especially when you were a gunnery specialist like Knowles—was critical. Soon afterward, he was discharged as a lieutenant into the Naval Reserve.

Friends in high places ensured him a soft landing and arranged for him to take over as editor of *Our Navy* magazine, headquartered in the pleasant surroundings of the neo-Romanesque skyscraper at One Hanson Place in Brooklyn. His neighbors included the Catholic newspaper *The Tablet* and the Bureau of Internal Revenue, together ensuring that human affairs were properly rendered between God and Caesar.

Our Navy was an easy-reading lifestyle outlet for patriotic sailors and their families, and while it may not have been the *Naval War College Review* or some other highfalutin rag, as he enjoyed the expansive views of the bustling Brooklyn Navy Yard from his tenth-floor office Knowles was grateful for employment of any kind in a tough job market.

Still, as the Navy geared up for war in early 1941, Knowles itched to command a destroyer. He put in to be reactivated but was instead assigned to the University of Texas's Naval ROTC to teach navigation. And there the landlocked Knowles might have stayed for the rest of the war had he not been called with a most enigmatic offer of a berth at Main Navy.

Only when he appeared in Washington did Knowles learn that he would head the Submarine Tracking Room—whatever that was—and that he should fly to London pronto to learn the ropes from Winn—whoever *he* was.

The ensuing Atlantic flight was probably Knowles's first time in an airplane, but more worrying was what awaited him there, a stranger in a strange land.

IV

Fifteen years earlier, Kenneth Knowles had been the Naval Academy's star marksman. As 1926's captain-elect of the rifle team, he was the crack shot who helped lead Annapolis to its most successful year ever, yielding first place only to the sharpshooters of the Quantico Marines, bitter rivals of ancient vintage.

At the time, to be good with a rifle garnered a man broad plaudits. More than a sport, marksmanship demonstrated *character*. To be able to hit a bull's-eye consistently from 600, 900 yards or more required coolness, nerve, focus, and obsessive dedication to the pursuit of perfect accuracy.

Expertise in the science of ballistics alone did not, however, an elite marksman make. Understanding the *art* of shooting was more important. Wind, elevation, humidity, trajectory, spiraling, altitude, recoil, stance, heart rate, respiration: These factors influenced the track of the bullet as it hurtled from muzzle to target, and all had to be controlled for, compensated against, and contended with. Even when ideally adjusted, though, bullets still inexplicably missed the target, which meant that a shooter also had to have a feel, an instinct, a nose for unpredictability and to possess the kind of wisdom to make an on-the-fly correction that came only with experience.

For Knowles, rifle-shooting's orderliness substituted for the instability of his earlier life. His father, who'd pursued a variety of occupations ranging from stylish boulevardier to gentleman farmer to silver-mine owner, oscillated between states of affluence and destitution with metronomic regularity, while his exasperated mother had alternated between gentle kindliness and terrifying rages. The fortunes of the Knowles family could be discerned from their address, which shifted from upscale manor to modest rental to one-room shack depending upon the success of pater's latest financial wheeze.

A divorce left young Kenneth and his older brother, Frank, in the care of their father, while their sisters stayed with their mother in Wisconsin. A stepmother, one Lotta Faust, entered the scene and imposed an austere form of Christian Science on the lads. Frank loathed her strictness, but Kenneth later granted that she'd instilled in him the virtues of self-discipline, a determined work ethic, and sound organization.

Escaping from the embrace (or clutches) of "Aunt Lotta," Knowles briefly attended Cornell University and joined the Army ROTC there. But he hated all the parade-ground drill so he jumped to the Marines, somehow laboring under the misapprehension that the Corps would require no marching. Soured by the experience of being required to don a replica Confederate uniform and embark on Pickett's Charge at Gettysburg during an official Civil War reenactment (he was assigned to be killed), Knowles took the entrance exam for the Naval Academy in 1923.

He did very well there academically, his marks falling generally on the upper reaches of "Credit" and the lower end of "Distinction," with Mathematics, Gunnery, Seamanship, and Navigation being his best subjects and Modern Languages his weakest. Still, his steady accumulation of points over four years at the Academy earned Knowles the honor of graduating 16th in a class of 579.

Knowles was genial but not gregarious, a serious though not humorless man. In the class yearbook, an Academy pal described him as a "quiet and unassuming" fellow who had few friends but no enemies. Tall, lean, intense, controlled, Knowles stood out from most of the dashing blades in his class with their prep-school nicknames ("Oogy"), joie de vivre ("Good looks, a good dancer, an officer and a gentleman—if not a scholar"), and Bertie Wooster antics. While one of his classmates used to bring "a different member of the deadlier sex" to each hop—swooning afterward, "She isn't much to look at, but Lawd how I love her," and solemnly swearing to get engaged after every first date—Knowles was always "too busy to pay much attention to the fair sex."

V

In an encouraging sign of Anglo-American amity, the U.S. and Royal Navies shared a wartime habit of throwing up brutally ugly buildings along the more elegant boulevards of Washington and London. In the American capital, Main Navy dominated Constitution Avenue and ruined every view of the Lincoln Memorial, while its British counterpart, The Citadel—dubbed "Lenin's Tomb" by its unfortunate inhabitants—disfigured the majesty of The Mall and Horse Guards Parade.

The Citadel had been hastily constructed in 1940–41, when British fears of invasion had been rampant, and it was intended to serve as a Last Stand bunker for the government before the oncoming Nazi hordes. Rendered both siege resistant and bombproof by its windowless, concrete walls, maze of tunnels, twenty-foot-thick roof, and machine-gun emplacements, the fortress also served as a greenhouse for ceaseless viral infections and colds. The Citadel's sole concession to beauty was a luxuriant rooftop garden, but that was there only as camouflage from Heinkel bombers.

Located deep within The Citadel was the Operational Intelligence Centre (OIC), sometimes known as Section 8, whose Room 41, presided over by Commander Rodger Winn, was the holy of holies. This was the Tracking Room—the place where the movements of Dönitz's submarines were plotted.

In June, when Knowles arrived in London and entered Winn's little realm, he found a very different atmosphere from that of the U.S. Navy. The diffident man from Wisconsin felt somewhat out of place, a kind of Twainian "Innocent Abroad" among Winn's fifteen-strong collection of Very Curious People.

There, an Englishy, old-school-tie ethos prevailed, one binding together, say, Winn and his deputy, Patrick Beesly, both of Oundle School and Trinity College, Cambridge—medieval institutions several centuries older than America—and their penchant for trading Latin witticisms. Its other denizens had similar backgrounds: a litany of Oxfords and Cambridges, with perhaps a University of London scattered in for the sake of diversity.

Knowles, taught in local schools of dubious quality, could not have helped feeling a little country mouse amid the casual sophistication. For instance, Beesly, a decade younger than Winn, had been partly educated in Bonn, Vienna, and Brussels, and his mother was a cousin of the late prime minister Neville Chamberlain (himself the scion of a powerful political dynasty).

It was, above all, a humanities shop: Winn had taken a First Class university degree, specializing in Classics and Law, while Beesly had read History. Other Room 41 personnel included barristers and solicitors, an art collector, a literary critic, a professor of geography, and an archaeologist.

Spods—a derisive Cambridge term for dull mathematicians and pasty chemists who had never felt a woman's touch—were in short supply. A charitable exception was made for accountants, whose heads for precision, organization, and detail Winn considered optimal for spotting errors and omissions, but otherwise *never* were scientists to be put in charge of anything important. In his world, they were only to be on tap, not on top.

Yet neither was Room 41 a true-blue Navy outfit, despite being part of the Admiralty. Like his chief, Beesly, for instance, was in the Wavy (not Royal) version. For the room in which his writ ran, Winn had purposefully sought out those who lacked any experience of the actual sea. He needed people who could see many sides to a problem and juggle alternative interpretations of the same material. Professional officers, Winn felt, tended to override contrary evidence with their own nautical experience and so remained wedded to preconceived ideas.

One illustrious admiral, for instance, had flatly told Winn that it was impossible for a pack of U-boats to patrol in line abreast fifteen miles apart for hours at a time. Winn showed that was in fact *exactly* what the Germans were doing, and they had inflicted serious losses on Allied convoys as a result. The same went for a frankly unbelievable claim by Winn that U-boats routinely lurked for days on the seabed until searchers gave up; that, too, was soon proven correct.

It had taken someone who knew nothing about navigation, was ignorant of common practice, and had never participated in a battle to break free of the straitjacket of conventional wisdom by getting inside a German submarine commander's head to predict what he could, and probably would, do.

The freewheeling environment of Room 41 was unsettling at first to an orthodox Navy man like Knowles, accustomed to a strict hierarchy where a clipped "Aye, Aye" followed every command. In Room 41, by contrast, everyone called each other by their first name and there was no saluting. It was even permissible (indeed, encouraged) to contradict and challenge colleagues—including Winn himself.

Knowles, perhaps to his own surprise, took to the place quickly. Winn's eagerness to teach him the secrets of U-boat tracking spurred him to put in long days learning the rituals and incantations of this high priest of the temple. Fascinated by Winn, Knowles found his mentor "utterly brilliant"; as his acolyte, he hoped "that some of that brilliance would brush off on me."

For his part, Winn initially hadn't expected much of Knowles. His view of U.S. Navy officers, gleaned from his brief Washington trip, was none too flattering: They were stiff-necked, closed-minded, and bull-headed. King's faults, Winn believed, had clearly poisoned the officers below him. As he wrote in a report, during their meeting King had presented "a facade, without much behind him." Yes, he was "well informed" and "inspire[d] fear in his subordinates," but "I got no impression of a really first-rate mind. He was insanely vain and a megalomaniac."

The problem with American sailors, Winn believed, was that, like King, they "knew how to make a decision" and issue commands but not how to arrive at *judgments* after weighing conflicting or missing evidence, positing a range of outcomes, evaluating alternate possibilities, balancing probabilities, drawing on deep experience, and detecting biases and omissions—which is what submarine-hunting, like history, law, and classics, was all about. One had to possess the imagination to see the world from the enemy's perspective; the wisdom to sense when something was just slightly off, as a marksman would.

Having prejudged Knowles as yet one more arrogant King clone, Winn was overjoyed to be proved wrong. It turned out that Knowles was just two weeks younger than he was, laughed at his jokes, and was a smart, capable understudy—one who would prove to be a prized comrade in the fight ahead.

VI

To hunt and kill a submarine, Knowles learned, you needed the Three Ts: By far the most important of these was *Tracking*, with *Technology* and *Tactics* being secondary and not his concern. Ultimately, if you don't know where the target is, or likely will be, then all the advanced technology and expert tactics in the world won't do an ounce of good.

In that sense, tracking a U-boat is like hunting a whale. In *Moby-Dick*, Herman Melville described the preternatural ability of a few sea dogs such as Captain Ahab to plot a quarry's movements and estimate its destination.

Quenchlessly obsessed with finding the elusive White Whale, Ahab would consult a "large wrinkled roll of yellowish sea charts" and mark out places where the monster had been spotted, as well as courses it might subsequently have taken. Each night he threaded a maze of sea currents and wind eddies on the parchment, erasing some possibilities and adding new ones.

"It might seem an absurdly hopeless task thus to seek out one solitary creature in the unhooped oceans of this planet," Melville commented, "but not so did it seem to Ahab." The captain "knew the sets of all tides and currents," accounted for the drifting of the whale's food, understood its temperament, and recalled "the regular, ascertained seasons for hunting him in particular latitudes."

From there, Ahab would arrive at "reasonable surmises, almost approaching to certainties, concerning the timeliest day to be upon this or that ground in search of his prey."

Now, among the Nantucket captains who lacked it, this rare talent of finding an invisible enemy was ascribed by some to sorcery or fate, and by others to mere good fortune.

But Ahab was no Merlin or Pythia; nor did he have Lady Luck to thank. Instead, he had accumulated *wisdom* by means of deep knowledge, long experience, careful observation, profound empathy, and a creative imagination. He had seen that whales favored particular feeding grounds, traveled along known corridors, behaved in foreseeable ways.

The old mariners had coined a term for this phenomenon: the "Season on the Line."

If Ahab knew the Season, or time, a whale would be following the Line, or bearing, to its probable destination, then the "great fish" was dangerously vulnerable to interception and attack.

The same went for submarines. Tracking—an updated version of the

Season on the Line—was based on the insight that the seemingly mysterious actions of a foe, be it beast or boat, were often in fact *predictable* and not (as Admiral Edwards had said during his meeting with Winn) the result of "sheer chance and the law of averages."

And thus began the apprenticeship of Kenneth Knowles.

FIVE

THE LAVATORY MAN

I

Dan Gallery was having a bad war. It was the morning of August 20, 1942, and even if he'd had any notion who Kenneth Knowles was, Gallery still wouldn't have cared that he'd left London more than two weeks earlier on some American Export Airlines flight. He had more important things on his mind.

About two and a half months earlier, Gallery's naval-aviation comrades had been flying Wildcat fighters and Dauntless dive-bombers and earning immortality at the Battle of Midway, and today they were launching from mighty aircraft carriers plowing their foamy furrows through the turquoise Pacific. Gallery could imagine the sun glinting off the propeller blades as the promise of R&R in gorgeous Pearl Harbor beckoned.

Yet here *he* was, condemned forever, like some modern Count of Monte Cristo, to what he had dubbed "Camp Kwitcherbelliakín" in Iceland, where the weather was nowhere near as inviting and where the natives, while at least not hostile, were very much indifferent to the Americans, like cats tolerating their tiresome human benefactors.

The nearest he'd come to living the Pacific dream was when some of the boys had enterprisingly erected a couple of steel pipes and covered them in rough burlap bags to simulate a palm tree's bark. Then they'd liberated a few curved reinforcing rods for concrete runways to serve as stems, stuck on some worn-out softballs as coconuts, and added flattened five-gallon kerosene cans for the leaves, finishing them off with a coat of green camouflage paint. Even his old classmate from naval flight school, Admiral King, briefly stopping by after a conference in London, had been impressed with these incongruous additions to the local flora.

Not impressed enough, alas, to hand him a better posting there and then. Instead, Gallery was bumped from commander to captain as compensation for having to make do with being in charge of a squadron of vintage PBY Catalina patrol-bombers expected to fight their way through the worst flying weather in the world. On the bad days, they contended with gusty Arctic winds and freezing rain, a cloud ceiling of 300 feet and 500-yard visibility. There were no good days.

II

When Gallery had arrived in Iceland nearly nine months earlier, on December 30, 1941, he had found nothing but a few dilapidated huts eagerly abandoned by their previous owners, the British, who had moved into newer quarters. The food was terrible, there was no plumbing, and salvaged junk was masquerading as working equipment.

In the early spring, however, a supply ship had come in carrying one complete air base and a detachment of Seabees to put it all together like naval Lego. Because the work kept you warm, everyone pitched in to build the runway. Even the unit's dentist and chaplain had volunteered to help dynamite rocks.

Soon enough, just as the modern conveniences of Roman civilization had once followed her legions into barbarian lands, American luxury would ease the men's burdens. Phonographs, electric lights, hot water, radios, lampshades, rugs, writing desks, ovens, kettles, gym equipment, steak and eggs, even automatic dishwashers, turned Quonset huts into homes. Wallpaper was a jerry-rigged affair, consisting of posters of come-hither pinup girls. These days, whenever they visited, the eyes of Gallery's British colleagues widened in envy at the sheer opulence on display (and perhaps also at whatever Rita Hayworth was displaying).

Gallery's relationship with his Anglo peers down the road was at first frosty, but had soon thawed. The Brits had been worried that as a Catholic of Irish pedigree he'd be reluctant to work with them, but he assured them that "I am eternally grateful to your ancestors for persecuting my ancestors, so that I was born in the U.S.A."

Then there was the time that he noticed that his opposites signed their official letters with a cascade of impressive suffixes—KCB, DSO, CBE, and the like—and so he started doing the same, adding DDLM after his name. As intended, it piqued their curiosity and one well-bred air commodore finally ventured to ask what it stood for. Gallery replied that it was one of America's highest decorations, awarded only to the few and the proud: Dan, Dan, The Lavatory Man.

Daniel Gallery, DDLM.

Humor, like Gallery's christening his air base Camp Kwitcherbelliakín, with its Icelandic ring in a land where the mountains were called things like Snæfellsjökull and the lakes

Frostastaðavatn, was the only thing that broke the monotony. His squadron's thankless task was to depart from near Reykjavík, fly for five hours south, rendezvous with a convoy, escort it for a couple of hours, then turn home for the tedious trip back.

Worse yet was the lack of action. On several occasions, one of the Catalinas had spotted a U-boat heading toward the convoy, but each time, adhering to the American preference for enthusiasm over competence, the chance to hit it had been wasted. Gallery attributed the misses to a combination of buck fever and clumsy fumbles, and went so far as to close the officers' club until there was a kill.

III

As one of the very few American aviators who had ever "sunk" a submarine, Gallery had the standing to administer such an unpopular move—withholding his pilots' sacred right to a stiff drink—in a bid to focus them on the task at hand. Admittedly, Gallery's success had been in 1935 during a naval exercise, the submarine had been an "enemy" American one cruising unwarily on the surface, and he had been credited with the kill merely by buzzing the sub's conning tower. But that was still more than virtually anyone else had achieved.

He'd exulted in his victory at the time, little suspecting that the reason he'd be exiled to Iceland seven years later was because someone at Main Navy had decided that such an expert sub-hunter would be wasted on attacking Japanese battleships in the Pacific.

Gallery had always stuck out among the stiffer-necked elite of the Navy. He was small, wiry, and jug-eared, and had a nice line in Dang It to Heck!–style comedy. For him, the Navy was a place where stuck-up admirals were always disarmed by cheeky retorts from seen-it-all sea salts, where everything was FUBAR and the shit rolled downhill, where nothing went according to the plans drawn up by Washington pencil-necks but where there's a will there's a way and the U.S. Navy would inevitably muddle through thanks to good old American know-how—as exemplified by Dan Gallery, Lavatory Man.

Wherever this romantic idealism and corny humor came from, it wasn't from his father, a mirthless Chicago lawyer, who in photos comes across as a caricature of a Stern Victorian Patriarch. In his letters to Gallery, no hint of levity was ever apparent, he weirdly referred to his son in the third person, and he was ever ready to admonish his progeny for disappointing him in some minor way. If the Irish—and it was difficult to be more Irish than Dan Gallery, three of four of whose grandparents had come over during the Potato Famine—are supposed to have the gift of blarney, well, Gallery senior hadn't kissed that Stone.

The Old Man had been a terrifying figure in the younger Gallery's life. He brooked no dissent, enjoyed never sparing the rod, and reigned over his household like a tyrant of yore. His iron rule extended to dictating his four sons' careers. His father, Gallery recalled, had been set on a naval career as a young man but had lost an eye, and thus his chance to captain a ship. To execute his ambitions, he decreed, they would enter the Naval Academy—and indeed all but one (who became a naval chaplain) did so.

As it happened, Dan enjoyed his time at the Academy—he was sworn into service as a midshipman in 1917—becoming a champion wrestler and a solid B+ student (much to the ire of his father, who exhorted his professors to punish him). It was there, too, that his taste for the unorthodox came to the fore.

His father had always blocked any way but his way, so Gallery had long ago learned that bypassing obstacles required one to do the unexpected and the unconventional: If the front door was locked, then wriggle through a side window.

Gallery applied this lesson to the wrestling mat, where he invented a hold adapted to his lanky frame. "It was a scissors on the near arm and a far-side half-Nelson," he later recalled, and "it was such an unusual hold that when you first applied it your opponent's reaction seemed to be *What the hell is this crazy guy doing now?*" For the rest of his life, people would always seem to be saying something similar about Dan Gallery.

It was a good enough move that Gallery was promoted to the U.S. Olympic wrestling team and traveled to Belgium to compete in 1920. The crazy-hold strategy, alas, did not work wonders against the best in the world and Gallery was knocked out early in the featherweight category.

That disappointment aside, it was in Antwerp that Gallery's life changed when he paid 50 francs for a 15-minute jaunt in a biplane. At the time, few people had ever flown as airplanes were commonly regarded as wood-and-fabric death traps held together by screws, glue, and luck.

This was a just conclusion, for airplanes of that era *were* wood-and-fabric death traps held together by screws, glue, and luck. There were no regulations or pilot licenses in early-1920s America, so literally any-one, even a child, could fly without taking a single lesson; hard-drinking wartime aces-turned-barnstormers awed onlookers with death-defying stunts that often turned out not to be as death-defying as they'd antici-pated; and in a mere eight years, the new U.S. Air Mail lost no fewer than 200 planes and 31 pilots in crashes and collisions.

That was tediously irrelevant, of course, to those red-blooded junior officers who hankered to join the most glamorous outfit in the Navy: the aviators. Gallery was no exception. He wanted more than anything to fly planes.

After returning from Antwerp, Gallery was assigned in December 1924 to USS *Idaho*, a Pacific battleship. Normally this would have counted as a plum posting, but Gallery chafed at the job. All they ever did was train, he recalled, for "the coming great naval battle" against Japan that would take the form of two columns of battleships slugging away at each other with their guns. The air weapon, however, held out the prospect of a different future—a high-tech one of bombers and fighters, scouts and torpedo planes, searching out the enemy fleet and delivering a precise knockout blow from afar.

Finally, he got his opportunity. At the end of 1926, he was approved for flight school in Pensacola. Gallery's timing was impeccable. Thanks to the introduction of safety regulations, aviation was booming: Aeronautical schools were opening and dozens of passenger airlines had launched. Towering above all would be Charles Lindbergh's solo flight across the Atlantic in 1927, a feat that instantly made him the world's most famous man. Together these developments heralded a technological shift from traditional, putt-putt, Edwardian-looking biplanes to the streamlined, curvedly Art Deco monoplanes of the 1930s.

And Dan Gallery was right in the thick of it. Over eight months, he learned to fly every sort of airplane in one of the toughest courses around. The failure rate was high—by halfway through, more than half the class had dropped out—as was the fatality rate: Within a year of graduating, six of his class of twenty had been killed.

Gallery had his own share of close calls. Once when he was practicing slow rolls, his seat belt unlatched and he almost fell out of the plane. He ended up in a vertical dive at 7,000 feet, holding on by his toe. He could have bailed out but he wanted to save the plane, so Gallery crawled back into the cockpit and managed to pull up in time.

The incident highlighted Gallery's characteristic approach to danger. He was rarely shy about assuming extreme risk, but at the same time he was never insouciant about it. Despite his jocularity, there was nothing careless or carefree in his makeup. Unlike the barnstormers, he planned ahead and rarely improvised. *Not* flying by the seat of their pants was how bold pilots became old pilots.

In January 1941, Gallery was sent to England to liaise with the Royal Air Force as an assistant naval attaché. Part of his job was to gather technical information on fighter defense and radar, just in case Britain fell and the U.S. needed to fight alone. He even had the opportunity to fly a gorgeous Spitfire and a first-rate Hurricane.

Being an attaché was a stepping stone to a bigger job, and come October of that year Gallery was appointed prospective commanding officer of a huge new seaplane base being built in Scotland at Loch Ryan. Once it was operational, he would be in charge of several patrol squadrons, even a wing, and assigned to take over anti-submarine duty in the North Atlantic.

Perhaps the most important thing Gallery did at this time was to take a tour of *U-570*, a Type VII submarine that had been captured by the British after surrendering on August 27, 1941. Her crew had managed to destroy virtually all their secret documents, but the Brits made lemonade by towing their prize back to Barrow-in-Furness in the north of England in early October. When she arrived, newsreel cameras and reporters were on hand to immortalize the moment. As an interested party, and because Loch Ryan was only a few hours away, Gallery inspected the submarine after things quieted down.

He wasn't overly impressed by what the Limeys had done. In common with many other American officers before *Drumbeat* wised them up, Gallery was too arrogant to give the British the credit they deserved for developing practical anti-submarine techniques. They "do a tremendous amount of flying, drop lots of bombs and depth charges, but they don't get any kills," he dismissively told a friend in November. "All they do is worry the submarines."

Gallery didn't understand that "worrying" the U-boats, and thus keeping them away from convoys, was exactly what the British intended to do. To his mind—and in this he echoed Admiral King—aggression was the name of the game. But he would soon discover that even worrying submarines was much harder than it looked.

On December 6, a day before Pearl Harbor, while he prepared to take command of his spanking-new Scottish air base, he received the surprise order to ship out to Reykjavík. "I'm still hanging over the ropes from the blow," he lamented to his diary a few days later.

Iceland was Siberia. Just after he arrived, a message from Main Navy told him that a hundred troublemakers had been given a choice: a stern court-martial or being posted to Reykjavík. Not all of them had chosen Iceland.

Gallery complained that the brass was trying to turn his base into a "penal colony," and thankfully the bosses backed down. To gin up everyone's spirits, Gallery created the Order of the F.B.I.—the Forgotten Bastards of Iceland—which he solemnly bestowed on every man who made it past a hundred days and kept his sanity.

Still, there was no disguising the fact that for more than eight months after he arrived in Iceland, Captain Gallery's detachment hardly worried a U-boat, let alone sank one.

And then, on the evening of August 20, 1942, he reopened the officers' club and the lads "damn near blew the roof off the joint."

Dan Gallery was going to have a good war after all.

IV

Because Gallery had been putting the crews through their paces to cool their buck fever, Lieutenant Robert Hopgood was at the top of his game when at dawn that August 20 he spotted *U-464* lolling on the surface 160 miles south of Iceland.

U-464 was a Type XIV "U-tanker," whose job was to replenish the attack submarines with fuel, rations, and torpedoes at sea. This was her first time out, and it showed. Kapitänleutnant Otto Harms had carelessly lingered too long on the surface, and as Hopgood swooped the boat was slow to sound the alarm.

A Catalina on patrol.

Hopgood's Catalina descended from the low and dirty clouds amid roaring gusts and he released a stick of six depth charges, set to explode underwater at the recommended twenty-five feet and expertly spaced forty-five feet apart.

One of the 325-pound charges got stuck in the Catalina's rack, but the other five badly wounded the U-boat before she could submerge. One bomb exploded to starboard, one to port, and the other three landed on the deck. When the latter were gingerly thrown overboard by the crew, they exploded as they sank, inadvertently damaging the pressure hull.

Worth mentioning here is that U-boats had two hulls. The outer was a thin and non-watertight shell of sorts, its job being to provide the sleek hydrodynamic shape that submarines needed to slide through the water. Separated by a gap from this outer hull was the inner "pressure hull" of three-quarter-inch steel, safely encasing the submarine proper with its living quarters, control room, and engines.

Badly damaging the outer hull was one thing, the pressure quite another, as the men aboard *U-464* understood very well. The first was survivable, the second was likely not. So when Hopgood disappeared into cloud cover rather than dropping more depth charges, the shaken submariners were elated to have seen him off with their deck guns. In fact, as they would soon discover, Hopgood had ascended only to radio for assistance.

In the meantime, listing perilously, the crippled *U-464* could not be saved. Captain Harms spotted an Icelandic fishing trawler nearby, sidled up to it, and commandeered the craft. All but two of his crew were rescued before he scuttled *U-464*. A short time later, a pair of British destroyers, detached from convoy protection after Hopgood's urgent signal, forced the trawler's surrender.

The destruction of *U-464* broke Gallery's eight-month-long curse; it would be the first of six kills for his Forgotten Bastards of Iceland.

As for Hopgood, he would be awarded the Navy Cross for his actions. More importantly, on his way back he radioed Gallery with the message SUNK SUB, OPEN CLUB—gladly done. Gallery also donated a $20 bounty to the young lieutenant, but for Hopgood that night the drinks were free.

V

Most important of all, however, was the drunken conversation that took place among the pilots that night.

As the fire crackled and liquor loosened tongues, the men's imaginations ran riot. When Gallery brought up the fact that *U-464* had been sitting vulnerably on the surface after Hopgood's attack, thereby giving the skipper time to scuttle his boat, some bright spark suggested that maybe it would be possible to use a Catalina to board and capture a sub before it sunk.

Great idea! So they gamed it out. Taxi the airplane close to the submarine, Gallery fantasized out loud, "put one wing over the deck, throw grappling hooks over him and get hold of him. Meantime, we'd have our machine guns peppering away at the conning tower to keep people down below. And we'd get a couple of people over into the sub, and run up to the conning tower and heave a hand grenade down there to let them know we really mean business. Then we'd throw a chain down so that they can't close the conning tower hatch and submerge. And then we'd get possession of the thing."

Every man there had dancing in his head the same image of the captured *U-570*, shown off by the Brits in newsreels and written up in the papers the year before. Those involved had become celebrities, their exploits acting as catnip to any passing female with an eye for a man in uniform. So why couldn't, and why shouldn't, Americans heist their own submarine, with medals for every buccaneer and immortal glory for the great Dan Gallery, the John Paul Jones of World War II?

It was all going to be easy. Of course it was. Because when bars stay open so late, Gallery mused, "small difficulties are solved immediately and big ones are soon whittled down to small ones." Anyway, by then it was "one o'clock in the morning and we all decided to go to bed and sleep it off."

Yet while the audacious scheme was put down to nothing but bourbon bravado by most of the boys the next morning, the kernel of an idea had been sown in Gallery's mind.

He decided there and then that one day he would take a U-boat alive.

VI

In the harshly hangovered light of day, *unorthodox* was a major understatement to describe such an off-the-books (and perhaps off-his-meds) operation. What Gallery wanted to do was a sublime combination of smart and nutty, brilliant and stupid, a product of watching too many swashbuckling Hollywood movies like *Captain Blood* involving ker-chiefed pirates clutching knives between their teeth and swinging from the yardarm, cutlasses afrenzy.

Quite aside from how an eight-man Catalina crew was supposed to overcome the fifty sailors aboard a U-boat that would be firing its guns at the cumbrous plane slowing to land on churning water, the plan was a relic of a more glorious age. The last time the U.S. Navy had boarded a hostile craft at sea had been during the War of 1812, which made Gallery's derring-do seem as antiquated as Nelson's ordering his fleet to "Cross the T" at Trafalgar.

Well, in his wrestling days they'd said his signature move was too "unorthodox" to work, yet he'd ended up in the Olympics. Of course they'd also wondered, *What the hell is this crazy guy doing now?*, which would be a pretty good question if Gallery ever actually tried to hijack a submarine.

Still, all it would take for Gallery to dare attempt the marvelous, or perhaps the mad, was to be in the right place at the right time, and to be armed with the right tool.

Six

THE HERBIVORE

I

On August 25, 1942—three weeks after Knowles had flown home and five days after Gallery triumphantly reopened the officers' bar—Kapitänleutnant Axel-Olaf Loewe returned to port in *U-505*.

He had just completed an eighty-day combat patrol, his boat's second. At Lorient in France, where the Second Flotilla was based, Captain Loewe and his men received the customary welcome, with the usual grandees congregated alongside to garland Germany's gallant heroes. Although his surname translated to *lion*, Loewe cut something less than a dashing figure. It was normal for returning crews to look sallow—a lack of sun tended to do that to you—but their commander looked disturbingly haggard, even haunted.

Built in Hamburg, *U-505* had been commissioned into service almost exactly a year earlier (August 26, 1941), and had embarked on the standard training and shakedown cruises in the Baltic until mid-November. The crew were put through their paces, for no captain went to sea without running his men through numerous exercises. Machinists, for example,

A U-boat comes home.

were expected to know where each pipe led, every gauge's purpose, and the color code for the high- and low-pressure lines that ran the length of the boat. Above all, they had to be able to recognize every valve by feel so they could be operated in the dark—which could make the difference between life and death if they were attacked.

Nothing distinguished *U-505* from her sisters joining Admiral Karl Dönitz's U-Boat Command as the submarine war heated up. Larger and slightly faster, but with significantly greater range and equipped with more torpedoes and launch tubes than the more common Type VIIs (the workhorses of the fleet), she was a Type IX of the new "C" variant, earmarked for longer patrols farther away from home base.

No, what made *U-505* exceptional among the other fifty-three new Type IXCs was not the submarine herself, but rather her captain.

Loewe was something of a relic in the U-boat division. This was his first submarine command and he was thirty-three—not quite the oldest captain in a service where his peers' average age was twenty-six, but

Axel-Olaf Loewe, first captain of U-505.

old enough to have served, unlike them, in the pre-Nazi Navy, then still rooted in the conservative traditions of the Wilhelmine Germany of 1914.

That Navy, at least until the end of the Weimar era, was a place where officers had been forbidden to wear middle-class raincoats or to carry a businessman's briefcase to avoid offending baronial sensibilities, or worse, to look like some ghastly, glamorous Luftwaffe showboater. Neither were they permitted to affect a monocle—that was the kind of thing social-climbing Army officers did—and an admiral had to approve their choice of wife. All of this helps to explain the aphorism of the time that Hitler had gone to war with a Prussian army, a Nazi air force, and the Kaiser's navy.

Glib, of course, but in Loewe's case apposite. He'd entered the *Reichsmarine*'s highly selective "Crew" (or Class) of 1928—fewer than 2 percent of applicants made the final cut—and had graduated second out of thirty-nine in 1932, a year before Hitler came to power. The young man had brains, but even more than that, he had blood: At U-Boat Command, Loewe was counted as an aristocrat of sorts. Two uncles had commanded U-boats during the Great War, and his cousin was the legendary submarine ace Fritz-Julius Lemp, who'd sunk seventeen ships and damaged two others, including a British battleship.

In short, Loewe was a promising officer—one who also had much to live up to. But that didn't explain his ghostly pallor when he pulled into the U-boat pen in Lorient that summer.

II

On February 11, 1942, with Operation *Drumbeat* in full stride, *U-505* had left the Bay of Biscay, where Dönitz had built five bases after the fall of France: From north to south, these were Brest, Lorient, St. Nazaire, La Rochelle, and Bordeaux. Their being perched on the edge of the Atlantic allowed his U-boats to spend an extra ten days at sea; no longer did they have to slog from the Baltic Sea to reach their patrol lines.

U-505's destination, however, wasn't the East Coast or even the North Atlantic. She was one of the rare birds heading south for the winter: the balmy climes of West Africa, where Freetown in Sierra Leone was a port of call for ships heading around the Cape of Good Hope to and from the Persian Gulf, Asia, and South America.

Despite its status as one of Britain's most important colonial bases as well as a waypoint for American shipping, Freetown was a quiet posting. The last time U-boats had disturbed it was in May and June of 1941, when seven German submarines had sunk seventy-two Allied ships. Since then, aside from the occasional interloper, not much had happened.

That was about to change. With the American entry into the war, Admiral Dönitz wanted to force the Allies to divert escorts from the Atlantic convoys to protecting West Africa. For her first mission, then, *U-505* was to serve as a decoy—a lure to draw the enemy away from the more important action up north.

Hers was not expected to be a dangerous assignment. Freetown was low on the Admiralty's list of priorities, and few stationed there were eager to go hunt submarines. The recently arrived Bob Whinney, a British anti-submarine expert, was appalled to find "the unhappiest collection" of fellows he'd ever meet. Living conditions were so abysmal that the men could hardly summon the energy to do much more than drink duty-free gin and swat mosquitoes.

Cold comfort, perhaps, was that the Germans had to contend with the sea, whose climate was as unbearable as the land's. The men of *U-505* had been accustomed to frigid Baltic and Atlantic winters, where mountainous waves boiled and foamed under the lash of gales and frozen spray lacerated your face. But once they crossed the Equator, they found themselves in the height of summer, which came with its own challenges.

On the surface of this watery desert, the boat felt "like a furnace in the daytime," recalled one crewman. "Off watch, we went up on the bridge to get a little relief from the stifling heat down below." The temperature was made worse by the humidity, which caused streaks of condensation to run down the inner walls. That, at least, the men could handle. Cold or hot, north or south, nearly everything inside a U-boat was always wet to one degree or another. If it was not dripping, it was slippery; if it was not damp, it was clammy; and if it was not soggy, it was slimy.

By now, at least, the newbies had grown accustomed to riding the boat. In *U-505*'s case, that was almost everyone on board. Of her complement of fifty, only Loewe, two petty officers, and a lone seaman had any experience of active duty underwater.

You could always tell a green submariner from a veteran simply by how he passed through the ship. In rough weather, the former tried to walk as naturally as he did on land and ended up cracking his head on hatches, falling down ladders, or tripping over valves; the old hands, however, swung, swayed, rocked, and rolled with the boat as it moved through the water and the water moved it.

With his crew working so well together, Loewe was soon able to make a minor nuisance of himself. Since there were so few U-boats in the area, Freetown had lazily allowed too many ships to sail independently. A British steamer, *Benmohr*, became an easy target on March 5, and the Norwegian tanker *Sydhav* the following day. After that, there were slim pickings as the alerted British switched to convoy tactics, holding ships back in port until they had a full complement and the escorts to dispatch alongside it.

For the next twenty-nine days, as Loewe fruitlessly prowled back and forth, the crew began to show signs of strain. "Looking at the same faces day in and day out, listening to the same stories, grown old after the first few weeks, and now the dismal luck on the hunt had frayed nerves here and there," recalled one sailor. "It showed in little ways—sharpened remarks and glum faces, lined with fatigue that resulted from stifling, sleepless days and nights."

Adding to the pressure, there was no getting away from people in the cramped confines of *U-505*. In the bow torpedo room, for instance, where crewmen shared their quarters with five torpedoes—each about twenty feet long and costing the equivalent of a medium-sized house—they longed for combat because every eel fired meant more space. The top bunks were particularly tight: Wolfgang Schiller's had a pipe running above it, so he could sleep only on his back; others had just sixteen inches of headroom between pillow and ceiling.

The only privacy to be had anywhere on the boat was in either of the two toilets, but nobody spent much time in there. First, constipation was rampant. Captain Loewe eventually solved the problem by placing a can of prunes in the control room; every man who passed through had to eat a couple and spit out the pits as proof.

Second, the heads were so small that one's knees lodged against the wall, and they were made smaller still by the food stored in them. U-boats used every conceivable nook and cranny to stash the fourteen tons of provisions that were diligently packed for each patrol. Sausages and hams hung like washing from pipes in the control room; loaves of bread were kept in hammocks strung between bunks; potatoes, vegetables, and eggs—2,000 of them—were wedged in wherever they could fit.

Which meant, third, that because after two weeks those eggs began to rot, the first fortnight was always an orgy of their consumption. On *U-230*, for example, Kapitänleutnant Herbert Werner and his crew often found themselves eating virtually nothing but eggs for days. Eventually, inevitably, lethally, the diet manifested itself in an indescribable, mephitic fug of fifty men's farts that only enhanced the nauseating potpourri inside an enclosed U-boat, with its almost viscous stench of sweat, diesel oil, mildew, semen, and Kolibri, every sailor's favorite—and necessarily potent—cologne.

And fourth, in a tribute to overthought German engineering, the flushing mechanism was so complex that crewmen needed to be given lessons in how to use it, after which a certificate was issued attesting their competence. This was no joke degree: The unsuccessful flush of a high-pressure "thunder box" at depth could lead to disaster. A terrifying instance of a bowel evacuation gone wrong occurred on the first patrol of the ill-fated *U-1206,* which suffered a reverse flow of seawater that not only flooded the boat but seeped into her batteries, producing wafting clouds of chlorine gas. After she surfaced, an aircraft attacked and the unfortunately named Kapitänleutnant Schlitt—author of the defecatory mishap—had to scuttle the craft, leaving three men dead and the rest captured.

But the worst part of U-boat life was that when it wasn't dangerous it was *boring.* Like many captains, Loewe ran a mostly dry ship, with a few bottles of Cognac reserved for "medicinal purposes" and 150 bottles of beer locked away in a pressure-tight crate otherwise reserved for the dinghy's motor. These were opened only on special occasions, and strictly by order of the commander. Following regulations, smoking was banned inside the boat for fear of exploding the storage batteries, but Loewe set up a sign-up system so that two men at a time could go topside for a quick smoke, if only during the day.

For those confined below, there was always a card game or a chessboard to be found, along with other diversions. *U-505,* like her sisters, carried a collection of around eighty records and a hundred books. Her library was maintained by one of the radiomen, and in it one could find several works by such popular 19th-century novelists as Theodor

Fontane. For the men's edification, Loewe insisted on keeping a copy of Goethe's *Faust* on hand, but no one seems to have read the highbrow stuff. According to Heinrich Klippisch, a crewman, he and his friends passed the time with pulpy cops-and-robbers thrillers and cowboys-and-Indians adventures.

Music was almost entirely popular songs, tangos, foxtrots, and the like, with a sprinkling of military marches and hummable classical pieces. Sometimes, just sometimes, a few illicit American jazz records were smuggled aboard. Listening to such "Negro music" at home might risk a spell in a concentration camp, but the rules were different at sea.

In this respect, *U-505* was again unexceptional, for the great majority of U-boats were not overtly politicized: The Gestapo placed no informants aboard; no SS officers were present; and members of the Nazi Party were rare among the crew. Indeed, only the more fanatical submarine captains like Wolfgang Lüth of *U-181* insisted on haranguing glazed-eyed crewmen with improving lessons from the Führer's life. (The abstemious Lüth was also responsible for banning pinup posters, primly noting, "If you are hungry, you wouldn't paint bread on the wall.")

Still, the U-boat service was as thoroughly suffused with Nazism as everything else in Germany. Because the average age of the crewmen was twenty-one, only the older officers had ever voted in a free election, and virtually every sailor had been programmed by a compulsory stint in the Hitler Youth.

The U-boats, then, did not need to be politicized—they essentially policed themselves. With or without informers lurking in the ranks, critics and defeatists would have soon been discovered and punished, for Dönitz had decreed that "complainers" and "deprecators" be court-martialed and shot. Even if it did not conform to the stereotype of die-hard SS–style fanaticism, the U-boat corps would nevertheless remain unswervingly loyal to Party, state, and ideology over the course of sixty-eight months of nonstop combat. Revealingly, among the 1,156 commissioned German U-boats of World War II, there is not a single recorded case of mutiny—not even under the harshest conditions or during the hardest times.

Notwithstanding the camaraderie that bound together the men, as the days and weeks passed the ceaseless tedium numbed minds and depressed spirits. At first, the symptoms were mild. For instance, radio-man Gottfried Fischer once got so bored, he confided to his diary, that he longed for a radio to break—or perhaps to break a radio—just so he could repair it.

The next stage was a descent into the sickness they called *Blechkoller*. The slenderest difference of opinion, the merest jostle, or the minutest error would cause sufferers to explode into screaming rages while throw-ing punches. The typical remedy was for everybody to shout, "Shut up!," which usually sufficed to bring the aggressor back to his senses.

Combat, however, was the most effective cure for this disease. Although the boat's war diary recorded a few instances of *Blechkoller* on *U-505*, no further outbreaks were reported after April 2–3, when Loewe's luck finally turned and he hit an incautious American cargo vessel, the *West Irmo*, followed by a Dutch merchantman on April 4. After that excitement, he didn't spot so much as a fishing boat for the next fortnight.

Captain Loewe would have preferred a more explosive send-off to cap his mission, but such were the fortunes of war. On May 7, *U-505* had returned to Lorient, with her captain and crew eager for their next outing.

III

It had been an unremarkable patrol—"well and thoughtfully carried out," commented Dönitz, who pored over every captain's report—and, now blooded, Loewe could look forward to receiving a more active assignment. He wanted to impress. His own view was that *U-505*'s record so far was "nothing better than normal," and he was "definitely not satisfied" with his own performance off Freetown.

On June 7, 1942, Loewe again departed Lorient and headed to the Caribbean, there to prey on American tanker traffic. No longer was *U-505* a decoy; henceforth she'd be the hunter.

Promisingly, on June 28 Loewe destroyed the American freighter *Sea Thrush*, heading from Philadelphia to Capetown via Trinidad with military supplies. The next day, Loewe sank the *Thomas McKean* en route to the Persian Gulf with a cargo of planes, tanks, and munitions for Russia. This was by far Loewe's biggest score to date in terms of military utility, indicating that he was getting better at target selection as well as more confident.

Until then, for instance, Loewe had relied exclusively on firing torpedoes at a safe distance, most of which missed. But this time he had released just two at closer range, with one hitting the target. Afterward he'd surfaced, boldly closed the gap, and shot up the *Thomas McKean* with seventy-two incendiary rounds of his deck gun.

And then, silence. The next occasion when *U-505* would crop up would be nearly a month later, when she reappeared in Lorient on August 25.

IV

Loewe's return marked his final patrol. He had sunk his last ship, but it hadn't been the *Thomas McKean*.

On July 22 at 1:35 in the afternoon, *U-505* had been sunbathing off a speck of a Caribbean atoll called the Courtown Cays, about 420 nautical miles northwest of Colombia, when a three-masted schooner hove into sight. Flying a Colombian flag and named *Roamar*, it was a slip of a thing, nothing but a rich man's pleasure craft out for a jaunt from Barranquilla.

There was even a luxury car lashed to the deck for touring one of the nearby idylls.

Around 130 feet long, or half the size of *U-505*, but at 150 tons just 10 percent of the submarine's displacement, the *Roamar* had been purchased only the year before by three friends—Eladio Rodriguez, Pablo Arango, and a Señor Martinez—who'd christened the boat after their surnames: RO, A, MAR.

Loewe issued a "challenge"—some warning shots—but *Roamar* did not stop; instead she seemed to embark on a series of evasive zigzags.

It was a horrible case of wrong-time-wrong-place, and *Roamar* had seen too much: a vulnerable German U-boat at a moment when Loewe's nerves were already on edge. Only the day before, he had reported a worryingly "strong patrol by land-based aircraft" to U-Boat Command, and *U-505* had been forced to crash-dive several times at night over the past few weeks when American planes, in a frightening new tactic, had lit up the seascape with giant flares.

Every time a U-boat was forced to crash-dive, it wore out the ship, and the men, a little more. There would be a shout of *Alarm!*, instantly followed by the bridge watchmen tumbling down the ladder as bells ear-splittingly shrieked the length of the ship, hatches were slammed shut, machinists weighed down valve handles with their bodies to flood ballast tanks faster while others frantically spun handwheels, and each man grabbed hold of something solid to prevent slipping on the deck plates. As all this was going on, the engineers had to undertake the tricky task of maintaining forward movement while switching off the diesels and clutching in the electric motors.

A well-ordered Type IX could crash-dive in just thirty-five seconds—about five seconds longer than it took a smaller Type VII—but owing to the many recent interruptions, Loewe had been unable to fully recharge *U-505*'s batteries or replenish her air supply. If the enemy caught him now in the open, it would be over for *U-505*.

For that reason, Loewe feared that the *Roamar* would report his position. There was nothing else for it: He ordered his deck gunners to sink the ship. Twenty-two rounds later, she vanished forever.

None of her thirteen crew and passengers survived the encounter. Aloysius Hasselberg, a *U-505* crewman, recalled half a century later that he saw three to six people emerge from the stern cabin and desperately run forward to clamber belowdecks through a hatch, only to be killed by a direct hit on the bow. "It wasn't nice," was all he would say about it.

V

What exactly happened throughout the engagement remains unknown, but what is certain is that Loewe's actions were completely out of character.

Until that day, despite the risks of being spotted by eagle-eyed aircraft, he had always aided survivors after an attack, providing them with rations, medicine, cigarettes, liquor, and compasses. In every case, the only known fatalities occurred during the initial torpedo hits, generally when crewmen were trapped belowdecks, such as on the *West Irmo,* when ten of her sixty-five African longshoremen had died. Quite often, in fact, no one was killed. Loewe, for instance, had granted the time it took to disembark *Sea Thrush*'s forty-one sailors, fourteen U.S. Army personnel, and eleven Naval Armed Guards into lifeboats before he sank her.

Everyone has heard, then and now, horror stories of U-boats mercilessly machine-gunning hapless sailors in the water or peppering lifeboats with bullets, but such cases of outright murder were in fact extremely rare—despite Dönitz's casually brutal assessment that killing as many merchant seamen as possible to deter others from volunteering was key to increasing the pressure on the Allies' trade routes.

The admiral, however, had never gone as far as his Führer, who on

January 3, 1942, had boasted to the Japanese ambassador, Baron Hiroshi Oshima, that he'd ordered his U-boats "to surface after torpedoing and shoot up the lifeboats."

Some of that was the usual Hitler bluster, for no such instruction is known to have been given—or if it was, even Dönitz did not enforce it. The admiral instead quietly permitted captains to use their discretion whether to provide aid, the critical imperative being that they never risk their boat to do so.

During the *Roamar* incident, though, *U-505* was never in any immediate danger. Yet Loewe had murdered a group of harmless day-trippers and made sure to leave behind no trace of their ship by firing no fewer than twenty-two rounds from a 105mm deck gun.

Loewe's bizarre behavior had a simple explanation: He was attempting a cover-up to convince the Colombian authorities that *Roamar* had succumbed to some tragic accident at sea. The Colombians were already angrily aware that U-boats were skulking in their waters, and several other neutral South American countries, not least Brazil and Argentina, were complaining to Berlin that their ships were being sunk.

Just one month earlier and in similar circumstances, a thirty-five-ton Colombian schooner named *Resolute* had been hit by *U-172*'s deck gun, and most aboard had been killed. Losing a *second* ship to a U-boat might be enough to tip Colombia into declaring war against Germany (as Brazil would do that August). The last thing Berlin wanted right now was to lose Germany's sole source of platinum, essential for aircraft instruments, while also seeing the Americans get invited to use Colombia as a base for their anti-submarine air patrols.

That terrible day, Loewe chose, on the spot, not to repeat *U-172*'s mistake of leaving behind living witnesses. But he had committed a crime, and he knew it.

VI

When *U-505* arrived in Lorient a little more than a month later on August 25, there was the usual celebration and congratulations, but to one crewman "the cheers and hurrahs seemed a little hollow." As well they might. Loewe had sunk only two ships—the *Roamar* did not count—but worse, *U-505* had broken off operations prematurely.

Returning home early from a patrol, at least without severe battle damage and empty torpedo tubes, was an extreme rarity in U-Boat Command. Yet *U-505* had come in with most of her eels and nothing troubling her more than a malfunctioning compass.

Dönitz picked captains for their spirit of unceasing aggression, their belief in the primacy of the will to overcome long odds, their ability to improvise in the face of material inferiority, and their routine acceptance of colossal risk. Anything less than that was dangerous evidence of faltering commitment to the cause of National Socialism. Naturally, there were questions to be asked about *U-505*'s performance.

To the men, it seemed as if Loewe had lost his killing instinct shortly after 1:35 p.m. on July 22, when he'd been startled by the *Roamar*. The first signs of his mysterious malady appeared within a day or two, when a crewman, Hans Goebeler, noticed that Loewe, "usually a paragon of steely calm, began to show signs of nervous distress." Soon afterward, he retired to his bunk, drew the curtain, and refused to talk.

The crew believed that their captain was "literally worrying himself sick" over *Roamar*, and his second-in-command, First Watch Officer Herbert Nollau, assumed his responsibilities. On July 28, with Loewe getting worse not better, Nollau alerted Dönitz that *U-505* had sunk a "Colombian sailing ship."

He didn't have to explain the details; U-Boat Command instantly understood the diplomatic implications of the message, though they were still unaware of the psychological crisis aboard *U-505*. Then on

July 31, the submarine sent a request "to return due to the state of health of the Kommandant"—a subtle signal that there was trouble on *U-505*.

Whatever else Dönitz was, he was doggedly loyal to his crews, and in Loewe's case there would be no black mark on his record upon his return. Having suffered a mental breakdown himself during the Great War, Dönitz was more sympathetic than might be expected to captains who had succumbed, so long as they had performed to their utmost. In his subsequent remarks appended to *U-505*'s war diary, then, Dönitz mildly praised Loewe for using his "few attack opportunities" to good advantage and attributed the premature end of his patrol solely to "illness."

Still, Loewe had erred by destroying the *Roamar*, then made a bad situation worse by killing the passengers and crew. As Dönitz stingingly concluded, "The sinking of the Colombian sailing vessel would have been better left undone."

So far, there had been no reaction from Bogotá, so at least Loewe appeared to have covered his tracks. In case anyone investigated further, he had also taken the precaution of entering in the log that the *Roamar* had not stopped even after he'd fired "several warning shots." This was an important qualification. According to the London Naval Treaty of 1936, Germany had agreed to guarantee civilian ships immunity from submarine attack *except* in cases of "persistent refusal to stop." *Roamar*, in other words, was being carefully painted as a legitimate target when she manifestly was not.

Nevertheless, it was clear that Loewe could not again put to sea—not because of what he had done but of what he could not do.

The U-boat war was entering a new phase and Loewe was not cut out for it. Guilty of destroying innocents, Loewe had been irretrievably rattled by the sight of punctured corpses and scarlet clouds in the clear blue water. As an older veteran of the Weimar-era Reichsmarine, with family roots stretching back to the old Imperial Navy, he had revealed himself to Dönitz as a herbivore in a world of carnivores.

VII

The days of easy hunting on the high seas were drawing to a close, Dönitz had realized. In June, his U-boats had sunk a monthly wartime high of 124 ships along the North Atlantic convoy routes, and from there the numbers trended down. By December 1942, an unimpressive forty-six ships would be sunk, despite the launching of more U-boats than ever. More alarming in that context was the number of submarines being lost. In June, there had been just three; in September, ten; in October, sixteen.

From this, Dönitz rightly concluded that convoy protection and Allied anti-submarine techniques were improving. The Americans had survived the German attack on their oil supply and they had pulled through *Drumbeat,* making it almost a certainty that in the coming year, just as predicted, they would be escalating their production capabilities.

The meaning was as clear as the solution: 1943 would witness a final battle of annihilation between U-Boat Command and its enemies, and for that fight Dönitz needed a new style of captain. Loewe's inability to continue his mission because of a few dead Colombians was an early warning sign that men of his ilk would be unsuited to the harsh new exigencies of the coming struggle. The hearts of the older generation were too tender for the fight; he required men forged in the fire of National Socialism with souls, like his, pierced by iron.

U-505's new commander, the admiral resolved, must be very different from her last.

SEVEN

THE HUMAN FACTOR

I

On the first day of his apprenticeship in Room 41 in London, the American Lieutenant Commander Kenneth Knowles learned that Rodger Winn's typically wry term for the "Season on the Line"—the art of submarine tracking—was the "Working Fiction." It was a story he weaved, a tale "to be taken as fact and acted upon," about a given U-boat and her behavior when all he often had were some clues, a hunch, an estimate, and maybe a best guess.

Winn, in other words, wrote novels and composed scripts in his head to make narrative sense of an otherwise confusing and overwhelming welter of isolated snippets, weird incongruencies, conflicting signals, and factoids of varying dubiety. When successful, the technique allowed him to construct a storyline that coherently explained a U-boat's seemingly arbitrary or contradictory actions for his audience.

In the colorful world that Commander Winn mentally built within his office in The Citadel, every captain had a character arc; every crew its quirks; every U-boat a backstory. The life of a submarine, from the moment she launched in the Baltic for training until her final mission on the high seas, was divided into acts, paused by cliff-hangers, and punctuated by reveals.

Most important of all was that there was no iron logic to Winn's storytelling, no AND/NOT/OR. Those were computer-style syllogisms, and in the U-boat war there were too many alternatives, too many possibilities, to bind Winn to such constrictive rules for his plots.

It was *never*, for instance, the case that a submarine was definitely in Place 1 *or* Place 2; it could be in fact anywhere within an almost infinite range of places, for nearly all options were equally possible. What allowed Winn to plump for one place over another was his understanding of that nebulous trickster, the human factor, where MAYBE/UNCERTAIN/PERHAPS reigned.

Penetrating the mind of the enemy—Dönitz—was key to the Working Fiction, for only then were you enabled to see the global situation through *his* eyes rather than your own. As Winn instructed Knowles, he needed to replicate Dönitz's own chart as closely as he could. He had to see what Dönitz saw in his map room to understand what he would think—and from that scry what he would do.

II

In Paris, Dönitz was doing the same thing. The admiral was unique in serving throughout the war as a one-man C-Suite: All at once he was the CEO, Chief Operations Officer, Chief Information Officer, Chief Human Resources Officer, Chief Technology Officer, and Chief Product Officer. Karl Dönitz *was* U-Boat Command. So when Winn and Knowles read the hundreds of messages sent from his Paris headquarters in an apartment block on the Avenue du Maréchal Maunoury, they were essentially eavesdropping on Dönitz's private conversations with his submarine captains.

Inside Dönitz's map room, there was a "U-Boat Disposition Chart" that displayed Allied convoys marked in red based on sightings radioed in by his submarines, colored blue. He and his tiny, six-man staff then asked themselves, as Dönitz put it: "In the enemy's place, how would we react to these dispositions?" Would he alter the convoys' courses or allow them to drive straight ahead "on the assumption that we had already redisposed our forces in anticipation of the evasive action we expected of him"?

This form of strategizing in, as Dönitz called it, "the first and second degree" was a high-stakes version of *I know that you know that I know that you know,* but the admiral lacked Winn's breadth of imagination and storytelling genius. Unlike Winn, he didn't understand the enemy as being *people* capable of autonomous action and thought—the human factor, in other words. To Dönitz, they were only pieces to be moved by him in a giant board game in which he played both sides. The year before, the captured German ace Otto Kretschmer of *U-99* had put his finger on the difference when he conceded to the British that the latter owed their success to seeing the U-boat service as a "living entity" with its own habits, tics, and characteristics, whereas "to us, on the other hand, the enemy was no more than an anonymous mass."

Which was why Winn's mirror of his opponent's pieces was much larger and finer than Dönitz's ever was. Room 41 was dominated by a giant table, eight feet by eight, covered by a massive chart of the North Atlantic. Day and night, a concentrated light, similar to those hanging over pool tables, radiated downward, leaving puddles of gloom in the corners of the room but brilliantly illuminating the oceanic battlefield.

On it, every Allied warship and every convoy was represented by a pin with a colored tab stuck to it. Elastic cords and thread marked their courses, and every incident—a sighting, a sinking, a signal—was marked on the map in pencil with the date and time. Each incident was a clue that might ultimately lead to a U-boat.

Once a submarine had been *definitively* detected, it received a bigram (*AB* or the like) for identification and was represented by a pin: red for a hard fix, white for a sighting, and blue for an intercepted radio transmission. There were different levels of certainty associated with each color: For a sighting, for instance, *how* had the U-boat been spotted? By a trained observer in an airplane, or by a merchant seaman who thought he'd glimpsed a periscope? At what range had it been detected, and in what weather conditions?

For Winn, nothing was or ever could be 100 percent certain. He dealt in probabilities, possibilities, and likelihoods. He never forgot that each piece of information on his map was not necessarily accurate, varied in its timeliness, and existed on a sliding scale of trustworthiness. Above all, even if judged accurate, timely, and trustworthy, it still could be interpreted in multiple ways, like some maritime Delphic oracle. There was no, in other words, absolute truth that one could induce from the available data, just a medley of contending scenarios, some more probable—at least for the time being—than others.

To say that what Winn had created propelled the Royal Navy into the future while leaving the U.S. Navy in the Stone Age would be an insult to the Stone Age, whose inhabitants at least knew how to use stones to great effect. During his visit to see Admiral King and his deputy, Rear Admiral Edwards, Winn himself had seen the sorry state of American submarine tracking when he was ushered around the Office of Naval Intelligence's grandly named "U-Boat Intelligence Room." Winn's depressing impression: The Americans knew nothing. They had but a few charts recording the positions of sunk ships, some photographs, and a number of files containing estimates of German construction timetables. "None of the 3 officers," he reported, "revealed any grasp of the strategic or tactical function of U-boat intelligence."

Knowles, much to Winn's relief, quickly grasped the real nature of the great game. Colleagues spoke of Winn's undefinable "flair" for the work, by which they meant his ineffable gift for intuition—a kind of second sight, third eye, and sixth sense rolled into one. It was not, however, a superpower but a talent—one that could be taught to, or learned by, those with the right aptitude. Knowles himself said he watched Winn for ten or more hours a day during his time in Room 41 and picked up the knack of tracking U-boats by the power of "osmosis."

At which point, Winn showed him what was really hiding behind the Wizard's curtain.

III

Information from a multitude of sources, Knowles learned, flowed into Room 41 by telegram, teleprinter, telex, and telephone. Every scrap of data pertaining to U-boats—no matter how apparently insignificant or tangential or just plain wrong—was sent there for Winn to see, assess, and add to the Working Fiction.

By the time Knowles arrived in mid-1942, things had come a long way since the outbreak of war in 1939, when the best available intelligence on U-boats, relatively speaking, had come from a black-market dealer in silk stockings with a chatty friend in the German Naval Post Office. These days, the British had access to a few spies working for the Germans in one capacity or another. One was a laundress who kept her French Resistance contact informed about upcoming U-boat departures by noting when a boat's bed linen was picked up.

But overall, spies were not of much use. Prisoners of war proved far more valuable. They were treated well, according to the theory that it was much more efficient to extract information from men if they loved you rather than hated you. For that reason, no torture was ever used in these interviews. One experienced American interrogator, Angus MacLean Thuermer, later said the most shocking incident of abuse he'd ever seen was when a Royal Marine colleague poked a prisoner in the chest with the eraser end of a pencil.

Instead of pulling-out-fingernails routines, which only produce junk intelligence, captured officers were seduced into revealing secrets when their friendly interrogators, using colloquialisms picked up as journalists or students in Germany before the war, gossiped about how the much-disliked Admiral So-and-So was scared of mines. Other times they were taken to expensive restaurants to loosen their tongues with a decent vintage or smooth Scotch.

To persuade U-boat crewmen that there was no point in holding back information, interrogators specialized in seeming to know more than they did. One trustworthy technique involved using Houses of Prostitution cards. In an effort to reduce the incidence of venereal disease erupting during war patrols, sailors were given cards during their visits to French brothels that catalogued their favored nymph, date, and location. Then if a crewman came down with something unpleasant at sea, headquarters would be radioed with the details on his card so the girl could immediately be taken off duty.

When the men's uniforms were confiscated after their capture, their pockets were rifled for these helpful cards, which they had invariably forgotten to destroy in the confusion. From them the interrogator could glean enough information to make nudge-nudge-wink-wink conversation about whether good old Marie was still working at *Le Chat Noir*. From there, they would demonstrate that they already knew everything about U-boats the POW could possibly tell them, but had one or two questions—just to clarify a few things, of course.

At that point, it all tumbled out. The details supplied by prisoners on technical specifications, weapons capabilities, training methods, construction bottlenecks, morale, and advanced countermeasures allowed their interrogators to compile a giant dossier on U-boats—once so mysterious, but now an open book.

Of particular interest to Winn was a chronology of a U-boat's patrols. He pressed interrogators to ask what to them seemed like trivial questions about course corrections, speed, length of voyages, and rendezvous points for gathering wolf packs. The primary purpose of these data was to allow him to detect underlying patterns and upcoming shifts in Dönitz's fleet deployments.

Just as useful were the psychological insights into the captains and senior officers that emerged from the interrogations. That, say, Kapitän-leutnant Hans Speidel of *U-643* was, according to his men, "a complete swine" who wore a Golden Hitler Youth Badge, slept all day, and was "hated and feared by all on board" was immensely useful to Winn. From such gossip he could hypothesize how other submarines captained by similar individuals would act under the same circumstances that had netted *U-643*.

In the absence of a captured crew, Winn relied on photo reconnaissance by aircraft overflying the U-boat pens and the Bay of Biscay. These pictures were minutely examined by experts for telltale hints of departures and arrivals, thus allowing Winn to improve his understanding of German habits. Routine, it would prove, was lethal to U-boats as it allowed one to predict their movements.

More important, perhaps, was his analysis of the emblems painted on their conning towers. To frustrate easy vessel identification, Dönitz had forbidden the use of numbers. But he turned a blind eye to emblems, because the benefit to crew morale outweighed—or so he thought—the risks of tracking. Every commander had his own, from the "Three Little Fishes" of *U-333* to the "Snorting Bull" of *U-47*. (Loewe's *U-505* insignia was a lion rampant brandishing an axe.) By matching hints extracted from other sources, Winn could eventually put a number to a boat and a name to its captain, and once he had those he could begin constructing their stories.

Occasionally, Winn's job was made easier when a group of captains adopted a shared emblem. Among commanders who had attended the German equivalent of the Naval Academy in 1936—the year of the Berlin Olympics—the famous five-rings symbol was universally popular. From that single clue, experts could cross-reference against a class list to extrapolate the commander's age, experience, and skill level.

Media monitoring was another rich source of information. German propaganda broadcasts and newspapers were picked over for mentions of a heroic captain being garlanded or medaled. From a simple report of his homecoming *fête*, a careful ear and eye could glean the length and track of a cruise, confirm the number of ships sunk, and identify an up-and-coming commander eligible for promotion.

The results were impressive. After the war, for instance, one U-boat captain was shown his file and "there, neatly registered in minute detail, was everything ever published in the German daily press and periodicals about me and my boat." He was even more surprised to discover that the dossier included a list of "the most important dates in my life, my career, my weakness for sport, down to my favorite drink, rum."

Winn's specialty was to parse any public announcement by Dönitz for clues to imminent changes in strategy. On July 27, 1942, near the end of Knowles's London assignment, Dönitz—concerned that the German press was getting too rosy-spectacled about the damage inflicted on the Americans during Operation *Drumbeat*—gave a speech intended to tamp down these exaggerated hopes by pointing out "that even more difficult times certainly lie ahead of us." Monitors twigged that Dönitz was indirectly referring to potentially higher U-boat losses, signaling a shift away from U.S. East Coast operations and back to the North Atlantic, where the going would be harder.

IV

All these techniques were important to gain information, but the *most* important, as Winn told Knowles, was radio, the chink in the U-boats' armor. To coordinate movements and attacks, and to report home and receive orders, U-boats *had* to communicate via radio—which meant that those transmissions could be overheard or traced by one means or another.

The Germans took precautions, of course. Admiral Dönitz admonished submarine captains who were overly talkative; a boat's radio was to be used only briefly, and even then solely for important matters. But the critical precaution was to encrypt every transmission in the Enigma, the toughest code of them all—especially the exclusive naval version.

It's a popular conception that "Enigma" was a single code. It wasn't. While the basic idea remained the same, there were actually dozens of Enigma versions, some more advanced than others. Moreover, some were broad, such as *Red* (a general-purpose key for secret traffic), but others were specific, like *Scorpion,* which was used for ground-air cooperation in Africa.

Because Dönitz (rightly) distrusted the quality of Luftwaffe and Army security discipline, the Atlantic U-boats used their own system, called *Triton,* as of October 5, 1941. At the time, the standard Enigma machine was the M3—it had three rotors for encryption and decryption—and when used at the highest security settings it was theoretically capable of 160 trillion combinations.

Nevertheless, through the clever use of "cribs," the British codebreakers at Bletchley Park were able to penetrate *Triton.* A crib was a hack into the M3's apparently randomized keys, which changed daily, by exploiting a vulnerability repeatedly caused by operator error, such as all too predictably signing off with *Merry Xmas* during December.

That source of free information ended on February 1, 1942, when

Dönitz introduced an upgraded Enigma machine—the M4—to his fleet. It was a masterpiece. Using four rotors as opposed to the M3's three, the device exponentially multiplied the number of possible combinations. To give an example of the magnitude of the challenge now facing Bletchley Park, the M3's rotors had around 17,500 possible starting positions; the M4's, 450,000. When used properly with *Triton,* German signals were rendered, literally overnight, unreadable.

At a stroke, Bletchley Park had been blinded—and would remain so for more than another ten months, until mid-December of 1942, when it finally managed to again crack open the Enigma.

For Winn the loss was annoying but survivable, since he could still exploit Enigma even in its raw, undecrypted form. As he taught Knowles, the *signal itself was a signal* because U-boats still needed to transmit and receive via radio—even if you couldn't understand what they were saying.

For this reason, the British had developed a technique called High-Frequency Direction-Finding—snappily known as Huff Duff, or HF/DF. It relied on women reservists assigned to remote radio-monitoring posts, whose task was to listen for German transmissions on a range of frequencies. Headphones clamped over their ears, a cigarette burning at their fingertips, they listened for hours through an audio fog of static pierced by overlapping, jumbled radio signals from who knows where just for the chance to pick out the curt, distinctive sound of U-boat Morse.

As they rapidly scribbled down the code transmission, a supervisor contacted the nearest direction-finding station in a chain of *Wuthering Heights*–style outposts, situated atop bleak coastal cliffs to which no roads led, where the huts were rudimentary, the food abominable, and the heating nonexistent.

The station quickly tuned its rotating antenna to the same frequency to find the general direction the U-boat signal was coming from. After this was called through by the operator to at least two other stations, they together tried to certify the result before the U-boat signed off, often within twenty-five seconds, sometimes less.

If the operators managed to get a fix, as it was called, the information was telephoned to The Citadel, where experts in the Plotting Section—over in a corner of Room 41—used strings and colored drawing pins to triangulate the submarine's position on a large map. Winn then performed his magical interpretation of the findings to add detail to the Working Fiction.

At least, that was how Huff Duff worked in theory.

In practice, because the radio bearings hardly ever intersected, like an X marking the spot, a given U-boat's position was rarely precise. Instead, it was usually reckoned to be somewhere within an area shaped like a cocked hat—otherwise known as the "Triangle of Error," because as often as not the submarine was actually outside it.

The size of this hat varied widely. Very occasionally, the fix was astoundingly accurate—on one marvelous day a British bomber sank two U-boats in the Baltic Sea half an hour after being directed to within three miles of their estimated position—but a good fix was defined as being between forty and fifty miles of the target's actual position. The typical estimate, however, was off by an average of one hundred miles—a figure equating to 10,000 square miles, or about the size of Maryland or Vermont.

At that stage, analyzing the radio traffic helped pinpoint locations and nail down intentions. More often than not, the Atlantic airwaves crackled with signals. Who chattered to whom, when messages were sent and at which priority level, what call signs were used, which frequencies were favored—all these provided clues to German activity.

Deviations from the norm, though, could be just as revelatory. If a certain radio circuit, routinely quiet, suddenly began buzzing, it often meant an operation was afoot. And when a busy circuit died, so too had its operator.

Of particular interest were individual radiomen's idiosyncrasies—their "fist" on the telegraph key—as well as the unique "voice" of each U-boat radio set. These could be catalogued to cough up hints as to deployment areas and maintenance schedules.

From all this, and without having the faintest idea of its encrypted contents, Winn could often extrapolate from a message the identifying number of a submarine, its fuel and torpedo situation, its position and likely objective, and much more. On one occasion, for example, he knew from just the relatively extended *length* of a single message that the transmitting U-boat was homeward bound and reporting mechanical problems—making her vulnerable to airplane attack.

V

Hamlet's observation—that "there are more things in heaven and earth, Horatio, / Than are dreamt of in your philosophy"—probably best describes the way Knowles's head was spinning at the esoteric knowledge into which he had been inducted. He had never dreamed that one could, by constructing a story from such disparate elements as radio chatter, a prisoner's remark, a news bulletin, even the flaming datum of a torpedoed ship, reveal the secrets of the U-boats, tear off their veil, peer at their hidden workings, *understand* them.

Until Knowles's time in London, the Americans had superstitiously believed that U-boats were an amorphous menace that struck randomly and vanished into the night, like some medieval fairy-tale monster. But this wasn't the case at all, Knowles now knew. They were part of a system with weaknesses and strengths, and they were governed by the human factor. They could be tamed. Which meant they could be beaten.

Once back in Washington, Knowles got right to work.

VI

Within the hulking edifice of Main Navy, unadorned offices stretched interminably down government-gray corridors floored in regulation-brown linoleum. Since Pearl Harbor, the arrival of several thousand staffers had resulted in a permanent state of organized pandemonium in the building's endless catacombs. Whistling messengers on tricycles cheekily weaved in between flag officers on their way to strategic conferences, while ensigns' wives brought the kids into the dispensary and sweating workmen pushed dollies bearing filing cabinets and furniture from one room to another. Occasionally, the lost lamb of a visitor could be witnessed forlornly wandering hall and stairwell in desperate search of the cafeteria.

The only place where a brisk, seagoing air prevailed and an urgent silence presided was along the front corridor of the third deck, overlooking the main entrance: Admiral Ernest King's COMINCH headquarters.

Located down the hall from King's office, the room Knowles had been assigned was nothing out of the ordinary—deliberately so. Adhering to the ancient principle that the more boring the name of a committee or department the more influential it was, his section had been slotted into the bureaucratic table of organization as "F-21." Following suit, Knowles was promoted to commander, the most junior of senior ranks, the bump giving him enough power to get things done but not so much as to garner any attention.

F-21's plain exterior concealed its more striking interior. There were the usual federal-issue desks and chairs, of course, with Knowles's at the back of the room, but dominating the place was a huge map of the Pacific to his right on the wall, a similar-sized world map to his left, and two giant ones of the South Atlantic and North Atlantic covering the entire wall facing him. This layout had been Knowles's idea, because if there was one thing he could not do, it was to clone Winn's Room 41.

There, like some high-seas buccaneer, Winn's writ ran uncontested and he recognized no master. Despite holding only an essentially honorary rank, Winn got away with virtually banning even the highest brass from visiting. He believed they basked in what he called "VSOV"—Very Senior Officer Veneration—which gave them the right, or so they believed, to ask impertinent and ignorant questions of their subordinates.

That freewheeling attitude did not, to put it mildly, fly in COMINCH, where King expected *his* F-21 to replicate a crisp ship of the line. So whereas Winn had enjoyed theatrically holding court over the huge map table in the the center of Room 41, Knowles eschewed the horizontal for the vertical. Wall maps prevented anyone from monopolizing the discussion—necessary because, unlike Winn, Knowles lacked the sway to ban mere admirals from dropping by, and he was scheduled to hold daily fifteen-minute briefings at 9 a.m. for half a dozen high-level visitors at a time, all of whom expected a ringside seat and due VSOV.

Outside of these conferences, Knowles used a scrambled telephone line to talk to Winn several times a day to exchange views and trade scraps of intelligence. While his counterpart, with his prodigious memory, could speak off the cuff about any submarine on the map, Knowles, lacking the same, relied on an increasingly comprehensive database of 5-by-8 index cards (known as "sub cards") listing a given U-boat's hull number, number of patrols, captain's name and background, favored hunting grounds, associated wolf packs, and various other tidbits such as sightings and radio fixes.

"We had a nice working relationship," Knowles fondly recalled decades later, but he would eventually begin to chafe at Winn's still treating him as an acolyte rather than as a colleague, let alone as his peer. Already, hairline cracks were starting to appear on the smooth surface of their relationship. During each call, said Knowles, Winn would deploy his "brilliant wit" to "try to push me around a bit, and I would come back at him."

In F-21, there was no lone genius tinkering away in his workshop: Knowles was assisted by a staff that eventually grew to twelve lieutenants, two lieutenant commanders, and five enlisted yeomen. Like Winn, Knowles insisted on permanent staff because, as he put it, "familiarity with enemy thought processes as applied to his operations and the characteristics of individual U-boat commanders can only be developed with long practice."

Knowles had selected each one for a specific set of skills. His deputy, for instance, was Lieutenant John Parsons, a blue-blooded New Yorker who'd set up his own deliberately unbusy law practice to give him more time to indulge his three abiding interests: hunting, fishing, and writing about hunting and fishing. A seemingly incongruous choice for a submarine-tracking outfit, perhaps, but Knowles had talent-spotted the lieutenant's masterly command of *detail*.

Parsons's expertise in Greek and Latin made him attentive to the smallest subtleties. So careful was he about getting the facts right that he would devote a decade to writing an unfinished, unpublished, and possibly unreadable monograph entitled *The Aroostook Dispute and the Bounding of Maine,* which minutely examined the history of the border between that state and Canada in the 1840s.

In short, Parsons was the ideal candidate to oversee the crucial cataloguing, indexing, processing, and charting that enabled F-21 to function efficiently, thereby freeing Knowles to focus on the big picture.

Like Parsons, the other officers were civilians called up or volunteering for the naval reserve, and just one of the five yeomen was a Navy professional. Equally striking was that half the officers and 80 percent of the enlisted were Women Accepted for Volunteer Emergency Service, or WAVES, surely one of the cleverest acronyms of the war.

Allowing females into the hallowed precincts of Main Navy was a form of socio-military experiment intended to release men for active duty. Every WAVE—most aged twenty to twenty-four and carefully selected for their Hepburnian levelheadedness, refusal to crack gum, and choice of sensible shoes—had taken a crash course in Navy lingo, organization, and traditions before taking up her post.

For obvious reasons, rules on fraternizing with other naval personnel were exceedingly strict: WAVES were enjoined to behave in such a ladylike way that their manners would escape comment "in a small town." On the plus side, though, they wore uniforms designed by the Franco-American couturier Mainbocher, who'd made many a Hollywood starlet's frock (to say nothing of Wallis Simpson's dress for her wedding to the abdicated King Edward VIII). More appealing still was that they received pay equal to that of their male equivalents—a benefit then unheard-of.

But most importantly, a large proportion of WAVES were directed into highly sensitive intelligence positions. In F-21 they maintained the log of sightings, contacts, and attacks on U-boats, as well as recording torpedoings and sinkings of Allied ships. They were also in charge of accurately plotting data on the map boards and posting Huff Duff fixes. Two WAVES ran the Statistics and Records unit; another assisted on the General Combat Intelligence desk.

In other departments at Main Navy, WAVES were regularly asked by officers junior to them to make the coffee—a blunt *No* generally ended the patronizing attitude—but that was never the case at F-21, where Knowles was regarded by his WAVES "in awe, almost as a god," and his coffee was always topped up.

VII

On August 25, the day when Captain Axel-Olaf Loewe brought *U-505* back to Lorient, Rodger Winn had been as usual laboring in the depths of The Citadel—dank even at the glorious height of a warm English summer.

He read the intercepts recording the customary proud announcement of *U-505*'s safe return on German radio and dutifully noted her arrival, but otherwise he took no especial interest in her.

Winn then telephoned Knowles with the update, who added it to his rather bare *U-505* sub card. Neither man thought any more about the matter. During her patrol, this Loewe character had bagged the unimpressive total of two ships, marking him as below-grade, perhaps at best run-of-the-mill, but nowhere near a superstar. As for *U-505*, she was just another U-boat.

Not for much longer, she wouldn't be.

EIGHT

THE CARNIVORE

I

On September 15, 1942, a few weeks after returning to Lorient and being (very) briefly noticed by Knowles and Winn, U-505 was again ready for action and the crew was excited to greet their new captain. To cheers, Loewe, promoted and reassigned to Dönitz's operations staff, appeared alongside the flotilla commander to hand over his boat formally.

In Lorient's bars and brothels, the cover story was circulating that Loewe had been suffering from appendicitis during the patrol. But everyone knew that wasn't the truth. A bout of appendicitis didn't get you assigned to shore duty—a move otherwise assumed to be, as U-505 crewman Hans Goebeler put it, a "catastrophic" end to a combat career.

The crew had adored Loewe, but there was no avoiding the fact that U-505 had underperformed on his watch. By reputation alone, however, his successor promised to vault U-505 into the premier league.

Oberleutnant Peter Zschech was one of Dönitz's favorites. He was on the cusp of celebrating his twenty-fourth birthday, making him young even among his peers, and he always seemed to have something

Peter Zschech, in his yearbook photo.

to prove. Handsome and cultured, Zschech was, according to a crewman, "a perfect example of the new breed of U-boat commander that the Propaganda Ministry liked to portray in magazines and films."

Yet, born the son of a naval surgeon long stationed in Constantinople, Zschech was in truth an outsider who hankered to be an insider. He devoted himself to the sea, graduating from the Naval Academy in the "Olympic" Crew of 1936 as the youngest of its 560 officers—no more of the small, select classes of Loewe's day—and was brought into Dönitz's elite fold in August 1941.

Placed as Second Watch Officer (third-in-command) on *U-124* under Georg-Wilhelm Schulz, Zschech was clearly intended for greater things. One of the most famous boats in the Navy, *U-124* (which would ultimately destroy forty-six merchant ships and two warships) was Schulz's submarine school for promising officers. If he had approved Zschech's assignment, it meant the youngster was a highflier.

Schulz had mentored the *Drumbeat* veteran Reinhard Hardegen of *U-123*, Werner Henke of *U-515*, and most recently Johann Mohr—who succeeded Schulz a few weeks after Zschech's arrival. Uniquely, Hardegen, Henke, and Mohr would all receive command of their own U-boats; all would be designated as "aces" (for sinking more than 50,000 tons' worth of shipping); and all would be awarded the *Ritterkreuz*—the Knight's Cross—for exceeding the 100,000-ton benchmark. (Loewe, for the sake of comparison, had bagged around 37,000 tons before being sidelined.)

Zschech desperately wanted to be Schulz's next star—so much so that the men joked he suffered from *Halsschmerzen*, or "an itchy neck," caused by lusting after a Knight's Cross to hang from it. Now bestowed with a U-boat, Zschech was certainly odds-on to get his itch scratched.

And when he did, the men of *U-505* would proudly paint its emblem on the conning tower, for a Knight's Cross reflected not just the glory of a captain but the gallantry of a crew.

II

The reason why Loewe could never have dreamed of winning a Knight's Cross, Zschech believed, was because he'd run a lubberly ship. With the easygoing confidence garnered from long years at sea, Loewe had allowed his crew to dispense with their uniforms (pieces of British Army khaki captured during the invasion of France were popular items), required no saluting, and encouraged the lowliest seaman to talk to him almost as an equal. He had joked and bantered with the men, shared their hardships, and never had to raise his voice to be heard.

Loewe had always remembered that very few of the sailors on *U-505* were career Navy. They had been drafted into military service like everyone else in Hitler's warfare state, but they had *volunteered* for U-boat duty, regarded as among the most elite arms.

Even the Führer himself recognized that. In August, during one of his interminable lunchtime monologues to his assembled toadies, he'd talked of how "every war gives rise to a species of selectivity in reverse; the finest and fittest perish by the thousand. Even among the brave the choice of arm of the services constitutes a sort of super-selective process, the bravest of the brave going for Air Force and the submarine service."

The lads might not have appreciated the part concerning their perishing by the thousand, but if you had to die it was surely better to do so on a submarine—where, at least until the fatal moment, you were warm and received higher wages *and* hazard pay (unlike the conscripts sent to perish by the millions on the Eastern Front).

Whatever their reasons for signing up, the majority were unused to the smack of stern command. In their former lives, they had been metalworkers, auto mechanics, machinists, electricians, carpenters, bakers, and tailors—skilled working-class trades. Bellowing at such independently minded men like some parade-ground martinet, Loewe had known, was no way to forge a cohesive group.

The best captains punished as little as possible and listened to grumbles with a sympathetic ear. Zschech, the men soon found, was not one of those captains. Like any number of green officers, he'd mistaken his predecessor's relaxed nature for slackness: *U-505*'s crew, in fact, had been rigorously drilled. All Zschech saw, though, was a crew that had recently gotten so drunk in Lorient they couldn't be roused from their stupor to take shelter during an air raid. For this transgression, Loewe, who'd regarded the matter with urbane amusement, had merely struck two days off their shore leave.

Under Zschech, however, there would be no more slaps on the wrist.

III

The problems started within hours of *U-505* departing Lorient on October 4. German naval tradition dictated that Old King Neptune was offended by ships that dared carry flowers beyond sight of land. After leaving port, the men would therefore solemnly throw overboard the wreaths that decorated their conning tower. Everyone knew that ill fortune, either meteorological or mermaidic, would invariably accompany any failure on this account, so Loewe had encouraged the practice.

Zschech, by contrast, had no time for such nonsense on a ship of war. When *U-505* first submerged, he reasoned, the ridiculous wreaths would float away anyway, so why indulge such superstitions? To replace them, he invented new traditions, such as ordering the men to practice ground-combat tactics, for reasons never made clear.

The seeds of a high-seas human-resources fiasco were soon planted. Zschech's cool aloofness, which was actually sullen moodiness, hid an explosive temper. He also harbored a vicious resentment of petty or noncommissioned officers, especially the ones popular with the men. Machinist's Mate Karl Springer would later attribute Zschech's humiliating treatment of him and the others to his being bullied by petty officers at the Naval Academy.

Making matters worse was the fact that Zschech had replaced Loewe's executive officer, Herbert Nollau, with his friend Thilo Bode. All three—Nollau, Zschech, and Bode—had graduated in the same Class of 1936. The men had admired Nollau. Every bit as much, they loathed Bode, who, arrogant and contemptuous, barely acknowledged the crew.

Their dislike was magnified by Zschech and Bode's curiously close relationship. It was common knowledge, which is not necessarily the same as proven fact, that they spent hours alone together in the captain's tiny cubicle, shielded from onlookers by a green curtain, and had, it was said, been spotted holding hands.

Homosexuality on U-boats was extremely rare—lack of private space being one reason—and there was just a single known instance in which a skipper had been court-martialed for the act. In 1940, Kapitän-leutnant Helmut Franzke of *U-3* had been demoted to the ranks and assigned to a punishment battalion for dallying with some of the crew. That Zschech was *rumored* to be playing similar favorites with his deputy was not something that could be kept quiet on a boat only four train cars in length.

Zschech, in short, was soon running low on goodwill. Certainly it was a skipper's right to bring on his own people, but trouble ensued if those people weren't competent. *U-505*'s veteran chief engineering officer was the popular Fritz Förster, but Zschech elevated the "swaggering, baby-faced" (as one man put it) engineer Josef Hauser to lord it over him. It quickly became apparent to all that Oberleutnant Hauser was ignorant of even the most basic mechanical knowledge, and it was whispered that his Nazi Party membership had won him his overpromotion. Proving the point, on his very first crash-dive drill, Hauser almost drove *U-505*'s nose into the seabed; the boat was rescued only by Förster's last-second intervention.

The atmosphere aboard *U-505* worsened as she approached her assigned patrol zone in the Caribbean. Zschech succeeded in arranging Förster's transfer to *U-514* during a rendezvous, thereby ridding himself of the last senior officer remaining from Loewe's time. Dangerously, Hauser—now nicknamed "the Raccoon" for his deep-set eyes and comical preening of his facial hair—enjoyed no respect from the men, while Zschech and Bode became ever more hated and isolated.

Whereas Loewe hadn't cared who went where so long as the job was done, Zschech and Bode treated the wardroom as their private domain. Bode exploded at a sweating, soiled torpedoman who'd dared to pass through the officers' mess to get his "filthy carcass" outside. They ordered absurdly fancy meals, often returned to the galley with a complaint that they were unsatisfactory. Crewmen working as stewards were made to stand formally at attention during their dinners; if found to be slacking, they were dispatched to clean out the bilges as punishment.

Zschech mostly shouted at people—to avoid provoking a rage, the men soon learned never to mention Loewe's name—but Bode was the more sadistic, the one more eager to humiliate and belittle. He would demand that a random crewman, asleep in his bunk after a long shift, wake up and bring him coffee on the bridge. If the coffee was not brewed to his liking, he'd pour it over the crewman's head as he descended the ladder to make more. Another favorite was to order a youngster to haul a

300-pound bag the length of the boat, the lad's inability to do so making him a target for Bode's abuse. Zschech thought it hilarious, but no one else was laughing.

From Zschech and Bode's perspective, they were simply trying to instill the order and discipline they believed had been lost under Loewe's gentle hand. Officers were expected to be the men's unquestioned leaders, not their friends. That view had long been German military tradition, of course, but the Nazi preoccupation with authority induced Zschech and Bode to impose it where it did not belong: in the pressure-cooker atmosphere of a U-boat.

IV

In the unique world of the submarine, where up to sixty men lived cheek by jowl and died shoulder to shoulder, only his traditional white cap outwardly distinguished a captain from his crew after a month at sea. That the still-bright brass badge on Zschech's cap lacked the telltale verdigris encrustation marking the salty veteran from the first-timer only amplified his youthful feeling of insecurity toward the older petty officers and specialists.

Zschech's harshness and impulse to control might soon have been forgiven and forgotten had *U-505* been crowned with success. But his maiden patrol was shaping up to be a dud. Not until November 7, more than a month in, did Zschech belatedly find his first target.

The *Ocean Justice* was a British freighter imperturbably sailing a straight course. Unfortunately for the hunters, she was 1,600 yards, or nearly a mile, away when *U-505* caught sight of her—a long shot, literally, but one Zschech was desperate to make. He launched two eels at a 90-degree angle, which was too sharp; both of them missed. Zschech turned immediately for a second approach. This time, with a hard shot made harder by the range having widened to 2,200 yards, or a mile and a quarter, he loosed another two at a 110-degree angle to the target.

Technically, it was brilliant. After an anxious two minutes and thirty-seven seconds, the first torpedo hit forward of the mast; the second struck five seconds later, between the bridge and smokestack. Both were the ideal recommended locations for a successful attack; as much as the crew disliked him, Zschech had at a stroke proved both his own proficiency and the importance of drill and discipline. The *Ocean Justice* went down in minutes, her back achingly broken as twin columns of thick black smoke swirled upward. (All fifty-six crewmen aboard the freighter abandoned ship safely.)

The kill had blooded Zschech as a U-boat captain, and seemed to suggest that his "itchy neck" would soon be soothed by a Knight's Cross hanging around it. But any optimism on Zschech's part was soon dispelled. Their cumbersome new "Metox" device—which warned of aircraft-radar pings—led to stressful crash-dives two or three times a day. The good news was that the alerts were usually accurate; the bad, that judging by the volume of warnings the Caribbean Sea was becoming an Allied lake lorded over by hungry bombers.

Indeed, on November 10, three days after sinking the *Ocean Justice*, *U-505* narrowly escaped being sunk herself.

V

Now stationed east of Trinidad—but so close the men could smell the sweet fragrance of tropical flowers wafting past, and the turquoise waters so idyllically calm they lapped gently against the hull—*U-505* was enjoying a break from the nerve-jangling, sleep-depriving series of crash-dives that had followed the sinking of the *Ocean Justice*.

Up above, Flight Sergeant Ronald Sillcock, an Australian aviator flying a twin-engine Lockheed Hudson bomber out of Trinidad's Edinburgh base, was carefully planning his attack. It was just *U-505*'s luck that she had drawn the best submarine hunter in the Caribbean. He'd been baiting this trap for a few days, and now it was time to spring it.

Sillcock, a former dairy farmer, had devised a crafty technique to catch U-boats napping. First he would search a given area where a submarine was known to be present, then he would ping the U-boat with his airborne radar to red-alert its Metox detector and provoke a crash-dive. But Sillcock would not attack. Instead, over subsequent days—and this would explain the spate of exhausting alarms since the *Ocean Justice*—he would repeat the process, each time wearing down the crew while they placed ever-greater faith in their Metox device to warn them of a threat.

Finally, as *U-505* unpleasantly discovered at 3:14 p.m., Sillcock would establish a visual sighting, turn his radar off, then silently swoop out of the clouds like a hawk, his engines feathered, to catch the watch off guard because the Metox had stayed dumb.

By the time the crew reacted, Sillcock had closed the range, restarted his engines, and was almost directly over them, dropping a stick of depth charges.

Inside *U-505*, Hans Goebeler knew something wicked was this way soon coming when he heard the sound of Sillcock's engines over that of the submarine's clattering diesels. That meant death had arrived. Then a deafening blast, a thousand times louder than a thunderclap, knocked everyone off their feet. Goebeler remembered that it felt as if "a giant fist had slammed the boat down into the water."

Three more blasts, louder even than the first, hit them. *U-505* reverberated with the shock of the concussions. One bomb destroyed the deck gun, seriously wounding two seamen and leaving two others nearly deaf. The other bombs dented the pressure hull, knocked one of the two diesel engines out of service, blew leaks in the oil tanks, and blocked exhaust valves and the cooling-water intake. Jets of seawater threatened to flood the engine room and drag *U-505* down into the depths as the air filled with acrid smoke.

Zschech rushed topside, took one horrified look at the deck damage—a wasteland of crumpled metal, contorted pipelines, and twisted steel—and shouted down to the control room to abandon ship. Then Chief Petty Officer Otto Fricke stormed over and declared that the captain could do as he wished, but his mechanics would be staying on board to repair the damage. A humiliated Zschech slunk away and busied himself pretending to take charge of the effort.

None of this would have mattered had Sillcock been able to make a second run at *U-505*. Bleeding oil into the water and unable to dive, the submarine never would have survived. Unfortunately, whereas lesser pilots often stayed too high, Sillcock had made sure of his target by coming in so low that shards of *U-505* had flown upward and shattered his own plane. From the conning tower, Zschech saw aircraft parts and broken glass littering his deck, then an explosion and a flash of light some distance off to starboard. A little later, some of the watch sighted bleeding bodies in life jackets, and a mutilated one lying spread-eagled on a wing. Sillcock and all his crew were dead—killed by the pilot's own expertise.

The Australian's fate didn't concern Zschech, who had gloomily realized that *U-505* was still in grave danger from any of Sillcock's friends who happened to come across them. Given a day or two of round-the-clock work by Fricke, *U-505* could be patched together just enough to allow her to submerge to about 100 feet—the minimum depth necessary to keep Allied bombers from spotting her as she crossed the Bay of Biscay—but there was no chance whatsoever of continuing the Caribbean patrol.

Zschech's temper turned ever more rotten as the days went by. His first patrol, and all he'd bagged was a single ship. Recklessly, he decided to try adding to his catch by sailing into Trinidad harbor in broad daylight and wreaking havoc. The entire crew thought he'd gone insane in his quest for a Knight's Cross—a posthumous one, presumably, since there was no way *U-505* would ever make it out.

Zschech's attention, thankfully, was diverted by a freighter that crossed their path. Ignoring the mechanics' pleas that firing torpedoes could endanger their damaged boat, Zschech flubbed the shot, but the attempt alerted the coastal squadrons that *U-505* hadn't died. Over the coming days, no fewer than five air patrols were launched. The submarine survived only because the arrival of bad weather subsequently grounded the planes.

Zschech still had not given up on the idea of inflating his score by sinking more freighters, but he was growing increasingly desperate as Lorient got closer. At one point he started firing torpedoes at a fast-vanishing ship 4,000 yards away—the eels' theoretical limit—with virtually no likelihood of a hit but every chance of an aircraft spotting them. Excellent shots like Werner Henke of *U-515*, by contrast, almost always fired from a distance of 600 to 1,000 yards; U-Boat Command itself recommended a range of 400 to 500. Every torpedo that Zschech launched further convinced the crew that their captain had descended into lunacy.

U-505 eventually managed to limp back to the Bay of Biscay on her remaining diesel engine, with Zschech exorcising his frustration and anger by immiserating the crew with nonstop make-work, sometimes for seventy-two-hour stretches. Neither did it pass without notice that Zschech never once expressed any interest in his wounded men's welfare.

On December 12, 1942, when *U-505* arrived in Lorient, she received an embarrassing welcome. Ahead of her in the line was a submarine flying six victory pennants—one for each ship sunk—which was greeted with cheers from the crowd on the dock. *U-505*, pathetically fluttering a single pennant from the bridge, was not.

Yet none could deny that *U-505* had come home with battle scars aplenty. When the chief engineer of the flotilla came on board to assess her seaworthiness, he couldn't believe that *U-505* had made it back. It was the most damaged U-boat ever to return to base, he said. Half her bridge had been torn away, the deck had been ripped up, and it looked as if a giant shark had taken a chomp out of her metal body, exposing her eviscerated innards. And that was just the stuff you could see.

Zschech would receive a commendation from Dönitz for his "tenacity" in salvaging his command and his "toughness" for "attack[ing] with the badly damaged boat." None of the men could understand it. And least of all Loewe, who noticed his successor's "sallow and unhealthy color" and worried whether he had the constitution to command a submarine.

Lost upon them was that Zschech, despite his madness and petty cruelties, was *exactly* the kind of captain Dönitz wanted. The submarine war was entering a new phase, and winning it would require commanders like Zschech: hungry, and carnivorous.

VI

When *U-505* returned to Lorient, Dönitz was in the midst of fighting his own war against Grand Admiral Erich Raeder, the head of the German Navy. His boss was a traditional Big Ship man, and had always considered U-boats to be a distraction.

In 1938, Raeder had pushed ahead with "Z Plan," which proposed building a colossal fleet of super battleships, powerful heavy cruisers, and aircraft carriers. To gain the Führer's approval, Raeder had played upon his weakness for naming large things after Great Germans by proposing that ships be christened *Bismarck, Tirpitz, Graf Zeppelin, Blücher,* and the like. But Dönitz could see as plain as anyone that the bloom had since come off Raeder's rose: No aircraft carrier had been built, the *Bismarck* had been scuttled, and *Blücher* had been sunk. Most importantly, Hitler was beginning to think that Raeder was a pompous stick-in-the-mud who lacked the proper aggressive spirit.

During the fall of 1942, Dönitz calculated that Hitler would soon, finally, come around to his view that a surface battle fleet was a waste of resources—especially if Dönitz circulated memoranda subtly reminding the Führer that building such an armada had been Raeder's idea.

On December 31, the tail-between-the-legs performance of a force of two heavy cruisers and six destroyers sealed Raeder's fate. As the Germans hounded a convoy on its way to Russia, they'd been sent packing by a small number of British escorts. This humiliation, coming on top of the German retreat in North Africa and the encirclement of the Sixth Army at Stalingrad, put Hitler in a black mood—made blacker by the fact that the BBC had gloatingly broadcast the bad news before he'd heard about it.

Raeder was summoned to the Führer's Wolf's Lair headquarters to explain what looked like a cover-up, but the naval staff successfully postponed the conference for five days to allow Hitler's fury to subside. All the same, when Raeder finally arrived on January 6, he was subjected to an hour-and-a-half-long harangue on the ignoble history of the German Navy.

The meeting minutes quietly noted that Raeder "rarely had the opportunity to comment" during this spluttering tirade as Admiral Theodor Krancke, the Navy representative, scribbled down the gist of it: "Ships were completely useless [and their] crews spent time lying around and were lacking in zeal," Hitler raged. "It was now his unalterable decision to get rid of these useless ships at last" and put "the good personnel [and] the good weapons" to better use.

Then came the mortal blow: "Submarines constituted the most important branch of the German Navy." And with that, Dönitz won his battle against Raeder, who was forced to resign the position he'd held since 1928. To mark his downfall, on January 30—the tenth anniversary of the Third Reich—Dönitz would be anointed his successor as Supreme Commander of the Navy and receive the rank of Grand Admiral.

Dönitz's ascension to the aery realm to join the other Nazi princes—Himmler, Göring, Goebbels, Speer—would bring him the sweets he had always coveted but could now enjoy. For decades he'd lived modestly on a naval salary, but after his elevation he would travel in his own armored train, be escorted by a dedicated SS honor guard, acquire an impressive (if stolen) art collection to decorate his splendid new palace outside Berlin, receive 300,000 marks as a cash gift, and be granted his own quarters near Hitler's in the Wolf's Lair.

Best of all, he could finally run the kind of war he'd long wanted. "The sea war is the U-boat war," Dönitz's very first directive to his staff ran. "All has to be subordinated to this main goal." Raeder's aged loyalists soon found themselves exiled to distant backwaters, with younger men from U-Boat Command appointed to replace them.

To welcome their fellow peer at Hitler's court, and to outflank the much-hated Hermann Göring at the Luftwaffe, Heinrich Himmler promised to put his SS scientists and concentration-camp slaves to work developing a new propulsion system for faster underwater travel. Minister of Armaments and War Production Albert Speer, for his part, pledged to build 2,400 submarines by 1948.

These fine words glowed and shone, it soon became apparent, like rotten wood. The SS knew nothing about naval technology, and to build his fantasy fleet Speer would need 150,000 additional skilled shipyard workers and to reallocate valuable materials from the Army. Given Germany's manpower shortages and the hundreds of thousands of tons of steel for tanks and munitions the Army demanded each month to fight the Soviets, the chances of Speer's diverting these resources to building such an armada were remote, to say the least.

Never mind that, though. The key thing was that Dönitz was a team player. On February 18, a little more than a fortnight after his promotion, Propaganda Minister Joseph Goebbels held a colossal rally at the Berlin *Sportpalast* to whip the crowd into a frenzy of support for the coming of Total War. Total perseverance, total sacrifice, total devotion—these would be expected of every German in order to defeat the malignant forces of Bolshevism, International Jewry, and Anarchic Capitalism. "The mood of the Volk is like wild mayhem," Goebbels back-pattingly observed of his handiwork that evening.

Understandably, Goebbels was pleased when the new grand admiral came to pay his respects two days after the great speech. Dönitz assured the propaganda minister that both he and his U-boat weapon were unswervingly dedicated to the struggle. It made such a nice change from Raeder's aristocratic wishy-washiness, thought Goebbels, who wrote in his diary that Dönitz was "especially anxious that the *Kriegsmarine* from now on is seen by the public as a National Socialist [one] and not as an atrophied Imperial force." And at that moment, the era of the "Kaiser's navy" ended.

VII

As well intended as they perhaps were, the promises of Himmler, Goebbels, and Speer illustrated a dire quandary facing Germany: With the bloody maw of Operation *Barbarossa* opening ever wider in the Soviet Union, the obstinate persistence of the British Empire, and the accelerating production capacity of the United States, Berlin's fear that the Allies would eventually possess an overwhelming numerical superiority was coming true.

Germany was supposed to have knocked the western Allies out of the war by now; that plan having failed, the only solution was for Berlin to develop weapons technology sufficiently advanced to offset the increasing weight of numbers confronting the Reich. The dilemma facing High Command, however, was that immediate battlefield needs—especially on the Eastern Front—dictated maximum production of *current* technology. The best-case scenario was that Himmler's legions would fight Germany's enemies to a standstill, buying time for Speer's industrial miracle-working to develop such war-winning "wonder weapons" as the atomic bomb, rocket engines, jet fighters, and, of course, the next generation of U-boats.

What all of this meant for Dönitz's Navy was that, for the moment, he had to keep relying on his fleet of Type VIIs and Type IXs while awaiting his proposed Type XXI. This successor to the VIIs and IXs would be a radical leap forward and shift the sea war decisively in his favor.

Unlike the aging VIIs and IXs, which were really surface-dwelling submersibles that dived only when necessary, the XXI would be, finally, a true *submarine*—a vessel whose natural environment was underwater. Its ability to stay hidden for long periods would negate Allied superiority in radar, sonar, destroyers, and aircraft. At long last, the inherent promise of the U-boat would be made manifest as Allied convoys were annihilated by these invisible gray sharks of the deep.

Time was the key factor. Dönitz was fully aware that the Type VIIs and IXs were already obsolete. The Type IX, for instance, had been conceived in 1935 not as a glamorous attack platform but as a workaday minelayer and long-range scout. They—U-505, for example—were being deployed to Africa and the Caribbean now only because Dönitz had nothing better to hand.

Given his druthers, Dönitz would have long since scrapped the entire class. As he pointed out, building a single Type IX required twice as many construction workers and double the amount of scarce copper as a Type VII. Yet despite a few upgrades in armament, speed, torpedo tubes, and range, the Type IX was not so very different from a U-boat built in 1915.

No matter. Pure, unrelenting Will—the superpower of National Socialism—would inspire his U-boat men to stave off the Allies until new technology arrived to secure victory for the Reich. As Dönitz had long predicted, the coming year, 1943, would be decisive.

It would be then that his existing Type VIIs and IXs, supplemented by nearly 300 new ones the Führer had recently approved, would ferociously engage the Allies in a murderous war of attrition, with the killing stroke administered the following year by an unstoppable onslaught of revolutionary Type XXIs. As the admiral told his staff, "We have to pursue this goal with fanatical devotion and the most ruthless determination to win."

U-505, now undergoing repairs to the stem-to-stern damage inflicted by Sillcock's attack, would be one of Dönitz's paladins in this showdown between his U-boats and their antagonists.

NINE

THE FUNHOUSE

I

In keeping with Admiral Dönitz's plan, the U-boats kept coming. In fact, there were more of them than ever as Dönitz took the helm, at last freed from the interfering hand of his predecessor, Admiral Raeder. Nearly seventy new boats had been commissioned in the last quarter of 1942, and more than twenty were coming off the slips every month. Somehow, even after years of Allied anti-submarine efforts incurred at vast cost in blood and treasure, U-boats were being built at a rate three times faster than they could be destroyed.

Month by month, their numerical edge widened in preparation for the final act. In January 1943, there were 212 submarines assigned to the Atlantic, with another 187 undergoing trials and training. Exactly one year earlier, at the onset of Operation *Drumbeat,* there had been just 65 Atlantic U-boats—and look at the devastation they'd unleashed.

Finally, Dönitz had the force he'd been clamoring for since the outbreak of war in September 1939. Back then, when he'd had just fifty-seven U-boats on hand, submarines were relegated so far behind capital ships in terms of priority and prestige that Dönitz had been only a commodore in charge of a single flotilla. Now he was a grand admiral, with twelve flotillas under his command.

With the new reinforcements, recalled Captain Herbert Werner of *U-230*, no longer did they have to patrol in bands of three or four; these days, packs of twenty to forty were becoming the norm. Gone, too, were the long, static lines resembling the trenches of the Great War, along which submarines had passively waited for their prey; thanks to the new arrivals, Dönitz shifted to a war of orchestrated movement. U-boat packs would materialize where the Allies were weakest, and vanish where they were strongest.

Commanders Winn and Knowles were both alarmed at this dangerous evolution of German strategy, and of course the accumulating weight of numbers was never far from their minds. The most troubling aspect was that, inexplicably, the U-boats now seemed able to *anticipate* their diverted convoys' new routes.

Initially, the pair of sub-hunters wrote it off as a fluke. In January, for instance, Wolf Pack *Delphin* was ordered to spread itself along a 180-mile-long line perfectly perpendicular to Convoy TM-1's course from Trinidad to Gibraltar, where it would unload aviation fuel for American forces in North Africa. In their tracking rooms in Washington and London, Knowles and Winn noticed the threat and rerouted the convoy south of the Azores. The change would have achieved its aim of avoiding *Delphin* had the convoy's escort commander not decided to go north instead, resulting in the loss of seven of TM-1's nine tankers and the deaths of ninety-seven men.

That was certainly a break for the U-boats. But how had they known TM-1's original course? Had it been luck?

Possibly. Or it might just have been the power of probability at work: With the Atlantic so saturated with U-boats, it was becoming difficult for Knowles and Winn to swing convoys around one line without running into another. Indeed, at the end of January, they did exactly that by directing Convoy HX-224 away from a wolf pack in the western Atlantic—and straight into the jaws of a second that had recently deployed to the southeast. Thankfully, the convoy escaped with just two ships lost, but only because the second group hadn't expected such a bounty to fall into its lap so soon.

Because they had been surprised, it followed that the Germans could not have known the convoy's route in advance; ergo HX-224 must have been merely a random victim in a crowded ocean. That was one explanation, sure. But, Knowles and Winn now asked themselves, how had *both* packs been stationed so perfectly in the first place?

II

By March 1943, Knowles and Winn could see that strange things were definitely happening on the charts in front of them. The two January convoys could be chalked up to accident, but during February Dönitz started maneuvering his submarines in a peculiar fashion. Whenever their ships changed course, so did his—with eerily good timing. U-boats were intercepting convoys they should never have been able to catch. In short, the Germans were doing all the things *they* (Knowles and Winn) had been doing, but as a mirror image—as if Dönitz was playing the game by exploiting their own rules.

Their suspicions were borne out by an intelligence analysis that compared the evasive course corrections of an American convoy returning from Africa against an intercepted signal from U-Boat Command to its Caribbean wolf pack. Almost exactly, and *impossibly*, their movements shadowed each other. The U-boats had been told how fast the convoy was traveling, the coordinates where it would change course, and when it would arrive in Trinidad so they could lay an ambush.

Dönitz *knew*. But how?

The culprit was eventually traced to a British code known as Naval Cypher No. 3, which was shared by the Royal, Canadian, and U.S. Navies in coordinating their convoy operations. As the Allies had been trying to keep their ships safe, the Germans had been listening in.

That was bad enough—but it got worse. Investigators forensically examining transmissions and trying to match them to German movements discovered that as far back as February 1942, Wilhelm Tranow—head of the English section of the *B-Dienst,* the cryptanalysis department of German Naval Intelligence—had broken Cypher No. 3. As a result, Tranow and his team had merrily read up to 80 percent of No. 3 traffic until December 15 of that year, when a minor change in British security procedures brought a two-month near-blackout. Then in late January or early February 1943, B-Dienst succeeded in repenetrating Cypher No. 3—hence Dönitz's amazingly maestro-like orchestration of U-boat attacks after the New Year.

The Allies would have identified the Cypher No. 3 breach much, much earlier but for the sheer coincidence that the B-Dienst had cracked it at the same time that Dönitz introduced the upgraded Enigma M4 machine to the U-boat fleet. The M4's diabolical complexity had shut out the British codebreakers at Bletchley Park until mid-December 1942, thereby leaving the less spectacular Cypher No. 3 break-in to go undetected.

Then, two days after Bletchley Park resumed reading the U-boat Enigma on December 13, the Germans were themselves locked out temporarily from Cypher No. 3 when, as mentioned above, the British happened to upgrade their security as a precaution. Almost literally, two ships had passed in the night because neither side had noticed the other's penetration of its signals.

Only now, during the postmortem investigation into the Cypher No. 3 debacle, did the British and the Americans realize how lucky they had been in 1942, despite their horrific losses: Dönitz's shortage of submarines had prevented him from fully exploiting his codebreaking advantage, but just as important, thanks to their security-consciousness, Allied commanders had never mentioned the shibbolethic word *Enigma* in any radio message that could have been overheard by the Germans. So secret was Bletchley Park's penetration of it that neither Winn nor Knowles was permitted to see the raw U-boat intercepts—not that they could have made head or tail of the gobbledygook. Even within the most trusted precincts of Room 41 and F-21, the term *Enigma* was never said, just in case loose lips sunk ships. Instead, Winn and Knowles talked vaguely only of *special intelligence* or *Ultra* (the name for the plain-English intelligence derived from broken Enigma).

As a consequence, whenever Winn and Knowles had rerouted a convoy, the radioed instructions in Cypher No. 3 from London and Washington had always been carefully sanitized to cite only plausible reasons for the diversion. An incoming storm, a delay in port, a need to refuel escort vessels, a new rendezvous point—all these were given as rationales to explain the course change to convoy and escort commanders, who might otherwise blab the secret (if captured) or divulge it by accident.

This meant that, despite intercepting hundreds of No. 3 signals, U-Boat Command never twigged that they were reacting to their *own* Enigma transmissions—and the Allied reactions to those reactions. Decades later, an American spy chief would describe his country's intelligence competition with the Soviet Union as "a wilderness of mirrors." Make those mirrors the distorting funhouse variety, and it would go some way to describing the situation in the North Atlantic in 1942 and early 1943.

Following the revelation that Cypher No. 3 had been an open book, the breach was soon plugged by replacing it with the impregnable

A convoy battles a typical winter storm in the North Atlantic.

Cypher No. 5. But it didn't seem to matter: Dönitz's endless supply of new U-boats come 1943 was proving that quantity has its own deadly quality. Whereas January's convoy losses had been relatively modest (just over 203,000 tons in the Atlantic), February's nearly doubled to 359,000 tons, and March's hit 627,000—more than triple January's. By any measure, the Germans were once again winning the U-boat war.

III

On the cold morning of Monday, March 1, 1943, Admiral King addressed the Atlantic Convoy Conference at the impressive Federal Reserve Board Building a couple of blocks away from Main Navy. Among the hundred or so senior American, British, and Canadian officials present, the tone was somber; the mood, black. It was like attending a funeral.

In December, when Bletchley Park had rebroken *Triton*—the naval version of Enigma—after ten and a half months, they had been cock-a-hoop that the defeat of the U-boats was nigh. Since then, the Battle of the Atlantic had become the supreme crisis among crises. The war's outcome now partly hinged on victory against Dönitz's U-boats.

Allied shipping needs were ballooning. They were now fighting a truly global war, and convoys had to be sent across the Atlantic, into the Mediterranean, through the Arctic to the Soviets, and to India and Southeast Asia for the campaigns against the Japanese.

The Pacific theater, in particular, demanded ships, as the American island-hopping strategy required stupendous quantities of manpower, equipment, ammunition, and supplies: The 500-vessel task force that would be assembled for the assault on Iwo Jima, for instance, would haul 4,100,000 barrels of black oil, 595,000 barrels of diesel oil, 33,775,000 gallons of aviation fuel, and 6,703,000 gallons of motor gasoline. Over the course of a single month of fighting, ammunition totaling the weight of 237 Boeing 747s would be expended. And not forgetting that the Marine 5th Division alone was allotted 100 million cigarettes.

It was easy to see how continuing U-boat attacks would create logistical bottlenecks and hamper military operations throughout the world.

That was concerning, of course, but the *immediate* threat of the submarines lay in their power to persuade Stalin, with his reptilian eyes and mind pathologically alert to weakness, that it might be time to betray Roosevelt and Churchill, collapsing the united Allied effort.

That dreadful possibility had been uppermost in their minds since the Casablanca Conference in late January, when the two western leaders had announced that they would accept nothing less than an "Unconditional Surrender" from the Axis states. To end this second world war, there would be no armistice—regarded as the original sin of 1918 that had brought them to this calvary.

The "Unconditional Surrender" pledge had been primarily inspired by Stalin's complaint that the Soviet Union had been wading through blood since the summer of 1941 fighting Germany while the Anglo-Americans slept peacefully in their beds. This wasn't an entirely accurate summary of the state of play, but his point was nevertheless a fair one. After all, the reason why the Red Emperor had not come to sunny Casablanca was because *he* was overseeing the extermination of the German Sixth Army at Stalingrad while his two comrades dickered over some North African sideshow.

Roosevelt and Churchill were secretly relieved that Stalin had sent his regrets. As Churchill told the president, if he'd come all he would have done is ask two questions: "How many Germans did you kill in 1942? And how many do you intend to kill in 1943?"

"And what would the two of us have been able to say?" Churchill added. Only seven months earlier, the British prime minister had assured Stalin that a major invasion of Europe was being planned for 1943; more recently, however, he and FDR had decided to postpone the operation until 1944. They both dreaded Stalin's reaction to *that* news.

Something, then, had to be done in Casablanca to placate their Soviet ally; otherwise, Stalin's paranoia might convince him that the perfidious Anglo-Saxons were postponing their invasion in order to negotiate a separate peace with Hitler, leaving the USSR to face the fury of the Wehrmacht alone. As Stalin put it, the capitalist running dogs "find nothing sweeter than to trick their allies…Churchill is the kind who, if you don't watch him, will slip a kopeck out of your pocket. Roosevelt is not like that. He dips in his hand only for bigger coins."

All of which meant that if Roosevelt and Churchill didn't pledge to fight to the bitter end alongside their Soviet comrades, well, what was to stop *Stalin* from arranging his own deal with Berlin? With their bottomless cynicism, Stalin and Hitler had signed such a pact before, in 1939; why not again?

If that happened, Churchill remarked, the nightmare of blood-drenched Nazi armies being released from the Eastern Front and ferociously pointed at the western Allies was too awful to contemplate. At that very moment, about 8 German divisions were proving a very difficult nut to crack in North Africa; in Russia, there were 175.

The "Unconditional Surrender" gambit had, fortunately, worked wonders. "Of course, it's just the thing for the Russians," FDR bragged. It was such a handy phrase that "Uncle Joe [Stalin] might have made it up himself."

Still, Stalin's goodwill would not last forever. If he accepted that the western Allies could not land in France this year, then they had damn well better do it in 1944. And if they didn't, well, perhaps the Red Army would crush the Wehrmacht and roll into Berlin, then perhaps keep rolling until Russian tanks clanked down Paris's Champs-Élysées.

From Roosevelt's perspective, however, the United States could not send thousands of GIs across the Atlantic for *Overlord*—the cover name for the planned invasion of France—without a guarantee to their mothers they would not all ingloriously drown on the way over.

From February 3 to 7 alone, U-boats had sunk the *Henry R. Mallory* and the *Dorchester,* exchanging the lives of nearly a thousand American soldiers for a couple of torpedoes. One of the young army officers on *Mallory* had written to his new bride that "there have been a lot of explosions and firing tonight, and we don't know what is going on. We are all pretty frightened." It was found in his pocket, unfinished, a few hours later when his body was fished out of the ocean. If anything could weaken the American determination to finish the fight against Germany, it was letters like that being circulated at home.

Until the U-boats were vanquished, then, the liberation of Europe was off the cards—and if it stayed off for much longer, then a Nazi-Soviet peace or a Soviet victory would surely be on them.

IV

As the Atlantic Convoy Conference progressed, the admirals gingerly sipped Federal Reserve coffee, which was depressing enough, and attended presentations on the situation, each more dire than the last.

From March 6 to 10, in the midst of the proceedings, Convoy SC-121—sixty-nine freighters, nine escorts—was ravaged by a pack of twenty-seven U-boats. Thirteen merchant vessels were sunk, but not a single submarine. A week or so later, forty U-boats formed into three wolf packs swarmed Convoys HX-229 and SC-122, losing just one of their number to twenty-one freighters over the course of a three-day struggle. Three hundred sailors' lives were lost, as well as 150,000 tons of steel, ores, oil, and grain. "This is the greatest success ever achieved in a convoy battle," boasted a communiqué from Dönitz to his captains.

Among the conference attendees, the Great Unsayable was being said, if sotto voce: *Convoys are failing as a system of defense.* By the end of that month, after all, eighty-five ships had been sunk, of which sixty-seven were part of a convoy. It was actually safer, it appeared, to hazard a solo run these days.

As the British grimly said of these disasters, "evasive routing"—the specialty of Winn and Knowles—could no longer be counted on. The scale of future attacks would therefore "increase progressively as more and more U-boats are concentrated against our convoys." There was no other recourse, Admiral Sir Dudley Pound, the First Sea Lord, gloomily told King, than "to fight the convoys through them."

Regrettably, that was *exactly* what Dönitz had been hoping for—the convoys coming to him rather than him having to find them. In the first three weeks of March, consequently, every single Allied convoy that attempted to cross the Atlantic westward would be sighted by U-boats, and over half of them would be attacked. Owing to the extra effort required of the escorts to patrol and chase, fuel became a problem for the

Allies; not so for the U-boats, which could now lie in wait with engines mumbling happily. After a thousand-mile running fight, for example, one escort managed to limp into port only after her crew emptied 120 gallons of mineral and gunnery oil into the fuel tank.

Understandably, then, at the conference King was even more dour than usual. With no good news to impart, he was humbler—less bumptious—than he once had been. "Anti-submarine warfare for the remainder of 1943, at least, must concern itself primarily with the escort of convoys," he announced.

To his listeners, this sound-the-retreat and circle-the-wagons language came across as uncharacteristically defensive, even defeatist, especially considering how charge-ahead and damn-the-torpedoes King had been in 1942.

All the fire seemed to have gone out of him.

TEN

BLACK MAY

I

If, as they say, a week is a long time in politics, then two months is an eternity in war. By the end of April, Admiral King was back in good form and as gung ho as ever. Much had changed since the end of the Atlantic Convoy Conference, and while the Allies certainly weren't out of the woods they had found the path.

True, the first three weeks of March 1943 had been ghastly, but the fourth had brought an Atlantic hurricane that paused attacks. April then ushered in clear weather and longer days—making it easier to spot U-boats and allowing electronic detection equipment to function more effectively.

Most important, however, was that superior Allied industrial power and technological expertise was at last being brought to bear on the submarine problem, while German deficiencies were beginning to tell.

Not that Admiral Dönitz acknowledged the problem. He genuinely believed the enemy was on his knees, and that just one more push would topple him over. He was, alas, completely deluded.

A year earlier, in May 1942, U-Boat Command had calculated that the Allies would build 10.3 million tons of shipping in 1943. Based on that figure, Dönitz had argued at the time that if 700,000 tons could be sunk each month, the Allies would suffocate as their growing requirements exceeded their capacity to supply them. Seven hundred thousand was a lot, admittedly, but the Luftwaffe and the Japanese Navy assured him that they would considerably augment the U-boats' tally.

Actual tonnage built in 1943, however, would turn out to be 14.59 million tons—an incomprehensible 40 percent increase over Dönitz's own worst-case estimate, with nearly all of it (85 percent) coming from American shipyards churning out standardized, prefabricated Liberty freighters and T-series tankers. That year alone, more than 1,200 of the former and 185 of the latter would roll down the slips.

Yet Dönitz's only solution to this looming problem was to attack, and to keep attacking even when losing. And losing he was. As one senior planner later conceded, in assuming that 700,000 tons could be sunk monthly to ensure victory, they "had failed to make allowance for the exaggerated claims" of Göring and Tokyo. Since 1942, as it had turned out, the Luftwaffe had done nothing tangible (as Dönitz repeatedly complained to Hitler), while a beleaguered Japan after the Battle of Midway had been more hindrance than help. As a result, Dönitz had recently, and quietly, increased his estimate to *900,000* tons per month as the bare minimum needed to break Allied shipping, with the burden of it *all* now falling on the shoulders of U-Boat Command.

Another blind spot only belatedly realized as such was that Dönitz had never considered the possibility that one lost ship did not necessarily equal another. "The enemy's shipping constitutes one single, great entity," he decreed in April 1942. "It is therefore immaterial where a ship is sunk—for in the final analysis, it has to be replaced by a new ship."

This kind of one-dimensional thinking was typical of Dönitz. Convinced that only the single metric of what he called "Integral

TOP LEFT—Day 1: Birth of a Liberty ship.
BOTTOM LEFT—Day 14.

TOP RIGHT—The same ship on Day 6.
BOTTOM RIGHT—Day 24.

Tonnage"—tonnage sunk, essentially—was important, Dönitz ignored any advice to concentrate his U-boat attacks on the loaded convoys sailing east from the United States to Britain in order to destroy both the ship *and* its valuable cargo at the same time. Instead of massing his resources on a single critical point, he ordered his submarines to attack whenever and wherever they found a convoy. Whether it was empty and heading west was irrelevant.

Neither did he understand, because to him a ship was a ship was a ship, that heedlessly attacking every possible target was only compounding his woes. All things being equal, his U-boats tended to kill off the older, slower vessels—the very ones now being replaced by their modern, faster successors. The more successful his submarines were, in other words, the more Sisyphean Dönitz's job became.

In short, given that the average monthly loss for the Allies during the very bad year of 1942 had been 522,185 tons, there was no conceivable way that Dönitz could routinely destroy 700,000 tons (let alone 900,000) each month of 1943, even with the winds gusting in his favor.

But April's, in any case, were blowing heavily against him—and a dark storm was coming.

II

From late March and throughout April, Allied anti-submarine forces had been fortified by the arrival of new weapons, equipment, and personnel. They had been a long time coming, but at last they were here.

The initial cohort of convoy escorts in 1942 had been underarmed, undermanned, underpowered, and underwater half the time due to their inability to handle the Atlantic's waves. But from late January onward, they began to be supplemented by the introduction of a new class of boats called destroyer escorts (DEs). By the end of April, fifteen of these

A destroyer escort and convoy.

versatile ships were on active duty, with another thirty-three arriving in May alone as production ramped up.

The U.S. Navy planned to build no fewer than 1,005 of them. Across the country, fourteen shipyards, federal and private, made destroyer-escort construction their second priority (after aircraft carriers).

Destroyer escorts—King had forbidden calling them *frigates*, seeing the term as too British—were expressly designed for Atlantic anti-submarine work and convoy protection. Supremely agile, if prone to rolling and bucking in stormy seas (journalist Ernie Pyle, traveling on one, noted that even the ashtrays were tied down), they were dramatically different from the Pacific's "fleet destroyers," which were much larger, more heavily armed and armored, and far faster—and nearly twice as costly to build.

Unlike their jerry-rigged predecessors or the repurposed World War I antiques of 1942, these "baby destroyers" mounted an impressive array of the latest anti-submarine weapons and detection gear, all coordinated through an onboard Combat Information Center (CIC) that received, assessed, and plotted incoming information for the captain. Inside that nerve center, newly developed compact Huff Duff sets had been installed that could pick up gabby U-boat radio transmissions fifteen miles away, providing ample warning of the direction of an imminent attack.

But more dangerous, because it defeated even the strictest radio silence with an unsleeping electronic eye, was centimetric (10-centimeter) radar, which used short pulses to see objects far smaller than had ever before been detectable. Not until early February 1943 had the Germans realized that such microwave radar was even *possible,* let alone already a tangible reality, when a British Stirling bomber carrying one of the sets was shot down near Rotterdam.

After Luftwaffe crash experts discovered this strange device in the wreckage, Dönitz was alarmed to hear that centimetric radar was so sensitive it could pick up a metal periscope in calm waters at night or in fog at up to twelve miles' distance. U-boats had for some time been equipped with Metox sets that warned of incoming pings, but they had been designed for use against longer wavelengths—those from 1.4 to 1.8 meters. Against centimetric radar, the Metox was mute.

As Dönitz advised, the only defense against this new technology was to dive whenever an airplane was seen and to stay quietly underwater for half an hour. Such passivity was alien to the aggressive ethos he himself encouraged, but there was nothing else for it until a more advanced radar-warning set was developed.

Detection was half the game, destruction the other. Being spotted was quickly becoming a death knell. Escorts and airplanes now carried improved, heavier depth charges, but two new weapons proved especially deadly.

The first was the Hedgehog, which launched a fusillade of twenty-four light mortars *forward* of the destroyer in a circular pattern. Unlike rear-fired depth charges, which were set with bathymetric fuses and relied on pressure waves to damage a submarine, Hedgehog projectiles detonated on contact with a hull, blasting a hole right through it. After a hit, a giant white mushroom of water would swell to the surface, giving the escort commander near-instant feedback. Because depth charges auto-exploded at set depths, hunters had formerly been forced to wait for flotsam to surface before they could know if they'd scored a hit, giving the U-boat time to escape.

A report after the war concluded that depth charges resulted in a kill only once every sixty times, but a well-trained Hedgehog crew inflicted one for every six attempts. The reason: When a destroyer tailed a submarine too closely—about 150 to 200 yards—it lost sonar contact as the pulse and its echo merged. U-boat captains then exploited their temporary invisibility by undertaking evasive maneuvers such as fast diving and sharp turns. In the meantime, the destroyer was throwing depth charges behind it where it guessed the submarine probably was—and rarely guessed correctly. A Hedgehog cluster landed sufficiently ahead of the ship, by contrast, that sonar could still see the fugitive submarine.

The second weapon was alternately called Zombie or Wandering Annie, but the nickname that stuck was Fido. It was an air-launched acoustic-homing torpedo seven feet long and weighing 700 pounds, whose warhead was made of Torpex—an explosive 50 percent more powerful than TNT. At its nose were four hydrophones that listened for submarine-propeller noise and angled the torpedo's rudders accordingly (up/down, left/right). To confirm that these were working, a mechanic used to scratch one of Fido's cute "ears" and check whether its tail, a rudder, wagged.

When a patrolling pilot spotted a U-boat's telltale eddy after a crash-dive, he slowed to 125 knots and unleashed Fido at an altitude of 200 feet. The torpedo, powered by an electric motor, would circle in the water at 12 knots—much faster than a submerged U-boat—until it picked up the sound of a propeller, then steer toward the target. If it missed, Fido would sniff around until it heard the propeller wash again, then resume the chase for another fifteen minutes before exhausting its battery. During the war, American planes would drop 142 Fidos, racking up 31 kills and 15 damaged submarines for an astounding hit rate of one in three.

III

Underscoring Fido's success was the rise of airpower, and more specifically, of air-sea coordination in the form of the Navy's newest innovation: the escort carrier, designated *CVE*.

Ugly and ungainly, CVEs (which according to some stood for *Combustible, Vulnerable, Expendable*) were junior aircraft carriers quickly constructed by slapping a flight deck on top of a standard merchant-ship hull. Intended as bare-bones landing strips for convoy protection, they bore only a cousinly resemblance to the more familiar giant fleet carriers of the Pacific. A contemporary *Essex*-class carrier there, such as *Hornet* or *Intrepid,* was encased in up to 8 inches of armor, had a complement of 90 planes, sailed at 33 knots, was 875 feet long, and had 3,448 men aboard. A standard Atlantic CVE, by contrast, had no armor, carried 18 to 21 airplanes, steamed at about 19 knots, was nearly 450 feet long, and had a crew of 850.

Because the Pacific fleet had dibs on the newest airplanes, the Atlantic CVEs received its castoffs. Crammed aboard a ship whose flight deck was about one-fifth longer and four-fifths narrower than a football field, the CVEs' complement of nine to twelve Avenger torpedo bombers may have been up to scratch, but Pacific pilots had long disliked the Grumman Wildcat fighter, the other type of aircraft that the CVEs carried. They were slow, both in speed and rate of climb, and markedly inferior to the Japanese Zero in maneuverability. No wonder they were being replaced by the upgraded Hellcat.

For the Atlantic, however, the Wildcats proved ideal. Being a little ponderous was no disadvantage when on patrol trying to spot submarines or to strafe a conning tower, and it was actually a distinct advantage when landing on a short flight deck. As for agility, it was not as if they were tangling with Japanese aces or dogfighting German Messerschmitts.

The CVE, in short, may not have been one of the Great Ships of history, but it was a Good Enough Ship to do the job required of it. And that job was to close the Air Gap, colloquially known as the "Black Pit."

Land-based aircraft at the time, such as Dan Gallery's Catalinas in Iceland, had only limited range. To allow them sufficient patrol time at sea, their radius extended to just 400 to 600 miles from bases studded along the rim of the Atlantic: on the East Coast, and in Britain, Iceland,

and Newfoundland. Powerful headwinds or thick fog further reduced their effective range, but even under clear skies there remained a sizable gap in mid-ocean where there was no air coverage at all.

Until 1943, when there had been relatively few U-boats, that hadn't been very important—but now it was. Always on the lookout for vulnerabilities, Dönitz had begun to concentrate his forces within this 500-mile-wide Air Gap, where they could strike convoys en masse and overwhelm their escorts. Accordingly, the vast majority of sinkings were now occurring in mid-ocean rather than closer to coastlines.

CVEs—mobile airports, really—would help close the Gap. By flying patrols ahead of the convoy, guarding its flanks, and scanning for any trailing U-boat being used by others as a homing beacon, CVEs would force submarines to stay underwater, making it much harder for them to coordinate attacks.

Despite their cool, scary names, the CVEs' Avengers and Wildcats were domesticated creatures that rarely wandered far from the comforts of home. Their role was entirely defensive, intended to deter U-boats from attacking by their mere presence overhead. To be clear, the Avengers and Wildcats were not expected to range far and wide, aggressively pursuing German submarines. They were sheepdogs, not wolfhounds.

All the same, they quickly proved their worth. On March 6, the U.S. Navy's only active CVE, USS *Bogue*, joined the eastbound convoy HX-228. Four days later an Avenger spotted its first submarine, cruising two miles away. As the U-boat crash-dived, Ensign Alexander McAuslan raced to hit it with depth charges, but his bomb rack malfunctioned and they could not be released.

An inauspicious start from the looks of things, but more important was that the U-boat had been caught on the surface unawares. Startled by the unexpected appearance of an airplane so deep in the Gap, the submarine had fled the scene. *Bogue* had done its job of frightening off the enemy. The proof? Only *after* the CVE departed the convoy early—its fuel had run low—did a lurking wolf pack attack HX-228. Four ships and a British destroyer were lost in the fight.

Dönitz had a blind spot of long standing when it came to the deadly potential of airpower—he'd once remarked that "the aircraft can no more eliminate the U-boat than a crow can fight a mole"—but even he was beginning to recognize the risk that CVEs might pose.

For that reason, on March 26, Dönitz signaled Wolf Pack *Seeteufel* (Sea Devil) that "the sinking of the aircraft carrier [*Bogue*] is particularly important for the progress of the convoy operation." But then he added, "Do not on that account, however, let any other chances slip."

As Knowles commented of this intercepted message, the admiral "did not seem unduly alarmed"—but then there was little reason for him to be duly alarmed. There was but a single CVE currently in the Atlantic, and thus far *Bogue* had hampered U-boat operations only mildly. For Dönitz, sinking the pest still came a distant second in priority to hitting merchant ships.

In concluding that CVEs were probably more bark than bite, he had blundered, badly.

IV

In May 1943—or "Black May," as the U-boat men called it in contrast to an earlier Golden Time—all these long-gestating improvements together birthed a lethal anti-submarine counterstrike.

No silver bullet or bolt from the blue broke Dönitz's grip over the convoys; victory was the result of multiple layers of weapons, tactics, research, production, and experience converging simultaneously on a single, very murderous point in time. It could have happened sooner, it could have happened later, but the miracle is that when it did happen it happened so quickly that no one expected it.

May *should* have been a massacre to put Herod to shame. In preparation for the campaign, on April 29 the U-boat Atlantic fleet reached its wartime maximum of 159 submarines at sea simultaneously. That same day, Convoy ONS-5 departed Britain for New York—seeming for all intents and purposes like a lamb being led to slaughter.

The course of many great battles can be delineated by their landmarks. There is the Redoubt at Bunker Hill; there is Little Round Top at Gettysburg; and there is Mount Suribachi on Iwo Jima. The ebb and flow of the long fight for ONS-5, however, was traced within a featureless grid of invisible latitudes and longitudes. Yet in hindsight it was the moment when an eventual Allied victory in the Battle of the Atlantic became much more likely than not.

Initially forty-three merchant ships strong, and guarded by seven escorts under Commander Peter Gretton, ONS-5 was attacked by Wolf Packs *Star* and *Finke,* together mustering forty-two U-boats. For a week, day and night, the submarines ravaged and harried the convoy through a Force 10 gale, icebergs, and dense fogs. Owing to the appalling weather, ONS-5 lacked air cover for the most part; this was a duel between ships and submarines.

And the ships won. For the loss of thirteen merchant vessels, Gretton's destroyers sank an incredible six U-boats (another was destroyed early on by a Canadian B-17 Flying Fortress), severely mauled another five, and damaged a dozen others. Shipborne centimetric radar sets and Huff Duff arrays detected U-boats some 5,000 yards away, sonar pinged them at 800 yards, and depth charges and Hedgehogs finished them off before the submarines even knew their killers were close.

Dönitz had never witnessed anything like it. Over the radio he could hear his own captains' plaintive messages to headquarters: "Have been rammed—Unable to dive...Request Aid" (*U-125*) or "Surprised by destroyer coming out of fog. Shellfire and D/C [depth charges]" (*U-264*). Often these transmissions were their last ones. More than 300 veteran

U-boat crewmen went down in their submarines or were left to die in the water as the battle raged. Stunned by the losses, Dönitz called off the attack on May 6.

The admiral accurately observed that the Allies had robbed the U-boats of their power of undetectability. The North Atlantic was becoming too hot for hunting.

V

Any illusions that the ONS-5 debacle had been a fluke were soon dispelled. About two weeks later, on the full-mooned evening of May 18, eastbound convoy SC-130, comprising thirty-seven ships and an eight-strong escort, again under Commander Gretton, intersected a U-boat patrol line. The convoy was quickly surrounded by a pack of twenty-five submarines; Gretton recalled that he could see two ahead and at least one on each side shadowing them. Reinforcements, he was told, were on the way, but in the meantime he would have to defend his flock.

That night, Gretton's escort group proactively ran down every radar hit and chased the stalkers away, only to see them replaced by fresh ones. Meanwhile, the U-boats were signaling headquarters with updates as they gathered, like sharks circling blood in the water.

What would once have been a slaughter fizzled out on May 20, when Dönitz ordered a withdrawal beginning at midday. German losses had not been heavy—just three U-boats, but one of them had been special: U-954's final signal during the battle would be the last time anyone heard from Peter Dönitz, the admiral's youngest son, who was serving as a watch officer on his first war patrol.

The patriarch showed not a scintilla of emotion, just as he never lost his iron self-control when assessing the mounting U-boat losses. He did eventually bend enough, however, to give his wife, Ingeborg, a drop of hope by telling her that Peter might have survived. After the war, she could be seen pathetically checking the registers of POWs being held in the United States and Canada.

His son's death, however, was not what prompted Dönitz to call off the attack; it was the shock of realizing that despite multiple, determined assaults by twenty-five U-boats, SC-130 had lost neither a single ship, a single ton of cargo, nor a single man.

While Dönitz grieved silently, Commander Gretton was exultant. Before the attack, he had told Captain Forsythe, the commodore of the convoy, that he'd appreciate it if SC-130 could hurry things along. After all, he was getting married two days after they were scheduled to come into port, and he'd like to make it to the church on time to avoid disappointing the future Mrs. Gretton. Forsythe said he'd do his best: He in fact had a golf game booked that very same day, and he was loath to miss it on account of some impertinent German submarines.

SC-130 steamed into port twelve hours early, delayed only a little by powerful headwinds and the U-boats' impotent attack. No longer, judging by Gretton and Forsythe's sangfroid, were the wolf packs to be feared. Henceforth they could be considered a mere nuisance.

VI

On May 24, Dönitz suspended North Atlantic operations. During a conference at the *Berghof,* Hitler's retreat in the Bavarian Alps, Dönitz explained to the Führer that Allied advantages had so eroded the U-boats' effectiveness that in May alone thirty-eight U-boats had been destroyed—nearly one-third of the current operational fleet. Their crews were all lost, all gone, all dead, and for the rest, their life expectancy had fallen to a single patrol.

And in exchange for nothing. In the two weeks from May 10 to

24, just three ships had been sunk out of 370 that had sailed in ten convoys.

A year earlier, in the first halcyon half of 1942, Dönitz had lost one U-boat for every 220,000 tons of shipping sent to the bottom. Keeping in mind that 100,000 tons was enough to garner a captain a Knight's Cross, the risk to life had been more than offset by the potential reward. These days, though, it was one U-boat killed for every 5,600 tons—about half a single Liberty ship's worth of cargo—putting acedom out of reach for all but the boldest, the craziest, or the luckiest of skippers.

With medals so scarce, to cheer up his despondent men Dönitz had on May 13 approved Himmler's thoughtful suggestion that 3,000 gold watches and 2,000 beautiful fountain pens be awarded to returning crews. The SS chief didn't tell the admiral that the gifts had been stripped from Jews arriving at his extermination camps, and Dönitz, as conveniently incurious about such things as Speer, didn't think to enquire into their provenance—despite knowing, in his heart, the answer.

Neither did Dönitz believe that he had been *defeated* in the North Atlantic. By "suspending" operations—the admiral was too proud to admit they had ended—he was not bowing to the inevitable, nor had his will been broken. Rest assured, he told his loyal submariners, that "even if the U-boat war does not sink more than the enemy is building, we have to go on with it." For Dönitz, attack was the eternal imperative—even if the enemy was, by his own definition, unbeatable.

This was the kind of fighting spirit the Führer liked to see. "There can be no talk of a let-up in submarine warfare," Hitler confirmed to his acolyte. "The Atlantic is my first line of defense in the West, and even if I have to fight a defensive battle there, that is preferable to waiting to defend myself on the coast of Europe."

Now that convoy attacks were a busted flush, Hitler and Dönitz agreed that the U-boats' new mission would be to act as a guerrilla force opportunistically sinking Allied troopships and hampering supply lines in the lead-up to an expected landing in France. Dönitz even extracted permission from the boss to order Minister Speer to increase U-boat production from thirty to forty per month.

The problem, as Speer later said, was that when dealing with Hitler "one was always at a loss, because he was not stable enough in projecting things. When Dönitz was telling him, 'The U-boat needs top priority' he would agree...Then along came Guderian [Inspector General of Armor] who would say, 'We are really at the end with our tanks, and if we haven't first priority we're finished.' So he signed [that order instead]."

Needless to say, even thirty, let alone forty, submarines a month was a fantasy whether or not Hitler changed his mind according to whoever last spoke to him. Assailed on all sides, Germany lacked the raw resources and manpower to produce that quantity of U-boats alongside all the other competing munitions demands pressing on Speer. Just in terms of torpedoes, for instance, Dönitz had requested 2,000 but received only 1,170—just over half.

To make matters worse, even in a perfect world, forty was beginning to look like it would not be enough. On the very day that Dönitz ordered the North Atlantic withdrawal, Rodger Winn concluded that May marked the first time in the war that more U-boats had been sunk than built.

Dönitz didn't care. He saw the U-boats that had been lost as too old to serve in the coming phase of the struggle, so good riddance. "Shortly the day will come when, with new and sharper weapons, you will be superior to your opponent," he promised his remaining commanders. Admittedly, "the year 43 was a hard nut to crack," Dönitz added before cheerily boasting that "the years 44, 45, 46, 47 will be better."

Dönitz may have correctly concluded that the struggle could no longer be pursued using a World War I platform against World War II technology, but he remained locked inside a Nazi obsession with developing wonder weapons (such as the Type XXI) that would vanquish Allied superiority and provide the miraculous salvation Hitler promised.

After the war, Heinz Schäffer, a veteran officer who had served aboard *U-148* and *U-977*, spoke for many of his fellow submariners and countrymen in emphasizing the universal faith at the time that "the production of new and decisive weapons would save us from defeat." Goebbels's Propaganda Ministry circulated these rumors "in a really masterly fashion," selectively buttressing them with impressive-looking technical articles and photographs of guided missiles and jet-engined aircraft to instill confidence.

Schäffer often sat next to Dönitz when the latter visited his U-boat base. Blessed with cast-iron fealty to the regime, the admiral never once betrayed a hint of cynicism that he was selling a lie. Instead, he always came across as a "reliable and energetic man perfectly confident that final victory *would* be achieved" and repeatedly made "short, clipped references to ultra-modern U-boats that could do quite fabulous things."

Until their advent, the admiral declared, the survivors of the current generation of Type VIIs and Type IXs would marshal their strength in "areas less endangered by aircraft [such as] the Caribbean Sea, the area off Trinidad, [and] the area off the Brazilian and West African coasts." The Middle Atlantic, in other words.

Cynics might have dubbed this a retreat, but Dönitz insisted that the fleet was deploying there only to regroup. After their respite, the older U-boats would depart the warm south to resume the battle with "hardness and determination" in the cold north alongside their new and fearsome Type XXI brethren. "The glorious day of revenge is imminent," he told his diminished cadre of captains.

Little did Dönitz know, however, that the Middle Atlantic was *exactly* where Kenneth Knowles wanted him.

ELEVEN

THE PHANTOM FLEET

I

By fate or perhaps just coincidence, at exactly the same time on the same day (12 p.m. on May 20, 1943) that Admiral Karl Dönitz ordered his U-boats to break off the attack on Convoy SC-130 following his son's death, Admiral Ernest King magicked an entire fleet into being.

Because news of its birth was borne only by the tersest of messages from King to the Joint Chiefs of Staff, very few people knew "Tenth Fleet" now existed. Fewer still believed it.

Provided with but a single clue—its name—insiders could hazard only that this phantom fleet had something to do with the Atlantic. In March, King had reorganized the numbering rules so that Pacific fleets were odds and Atlantics evens. Even so, while there was a Fourth Fleet off Brazil, an Eighth in the Mediterranean, and a Twelfth soon to be activated in European waters, to which operational area was the Tenth assigned?

The answer was: *the entire Atlantic.* The Tenth was unique in the annals of naval history in being a fleet that contained no ships and yet controlled them all.

II

The Tenth's Chief of Staff—its de facto head—was Rear Admiral Francis Low, an inspired choice. He'd worked closely with King before, was unperturbed by the boss's "effortless" propensity to become "exceedingly angry," and, most importantly, understood his way of thinking.

King, Low said, always "knew precisely what he wanted accomplished." He would tell subordinates when he wanted it to happen, where he wanted it, and why he wanted it—but never *how* to do it.

What King wanted accomplished right now was simple. Black May had bloodily demonstrated that convoys had become virtually impregnable. The time had come, said King, to take as many carriers, aircraft, and escorts as could be spared off defense duty and reassign them to attacking U-boats.

He had long wanted to train his sheepdogs to become wolves themselves, but only now had it become feasible. Tenth Fleet's brief founding document uncompromisingly reflected this radical change: Its overriding priority was the "destruction of enemy submarines," with convoy protection falling to second place.

The *how* of beating a shield into a sword fell on Low. Known as "Frog" since his Naval Academy days—either for his large head and bulbous eyes or (maybe *and*) his ribbety baritone voice—Low was smart, logical, driven, and loyal. He had a knack for boiling down complex subjects, such as the art and science of anti-submarine warfare, to their essentials.

Two years earlier and before

Francis "Frog" Low of Tenth Fleet.

anyone else had even thought about it, for instance, Low had cut through the confusion besetting Main Navy during Operation *Drumbeat* by warning that "our [anti-submarine] organization was basically wrong and that we should have a completely separate organization to deal with the U-boats." His recommendation had now come to pass.

Low placed Commander Kenneth Knowles and F-21 (the Submarine Tracking Room) at the heart of Tenth Fleet, a decision that surprised Knowles as much as it did the other stridently autonomous departments and units that suddenly found themselves answerable to the mild-mannered, nearsighted Wisconsinite in the small room down the hall.

Knowles had always worked long hours, but henceforth he'd work longer ones still. After the creation of Tenth Fleet, he took to leaving his home in Arlington before 6 a.m. and not returning until midnight, seven days a week. Just once in this period would he stick his head outside his door, and that only because he heard a commotion in the corridor. A crowd of people were walking past, chattering excitedly. Knowles thought they might be evacuating due to an air raid, but then he noticed the time: It was 5 p.m. on a Friday, and everyone was heading out for dates, drinks, and dancing. He'd completely forgotten that other people lived regular lives.

III

When the British learned that King was dedicating this so-called "Tenth Fleet" to a purely offensive campaign, they had a fit. Their reaction was understandable: The most tempting method of hunting U-boats in their native habitat was to use *Ultra*, the intelligence derived from breaking the Enigma, to pinpoint their locations.

Ultra, in short, was much more precise than employing the Working

Fiction method—but it had to be used sparingly and extremely carefully to avoid alerting U-Boat Command that its communications had been compromised.

Enigma had always been a particular source of tension between the Admiralty and the U.S. Navy. From the very beginning, the British had believed the Americans were too lackadaisical, too sloppy, to be entrusted with the Koh-i-Noor of their intelligence crown. When it came to the codebreaking business, a British liaison in Washington once wrote home, the Yanks were like "kids playing at 'Office.'" Despite the patronizing tone, he was right.

Security around Washington before Pearl Harbor had been astoundingly lax. There were far too many leaks to the press for comfort. Poorly encrypted U.S. diplomatic cables were an open book for the Germans. Alumni magazines proudly published the names of university graduates who had joined the most secretive units. And copies of confidential memoranda were habitually disseminated around departments that had nothing do with intelligence. How long could it be before rumors that the Brits had penetrated Enigma reached Dönitz's ears?

Even after Churchill directed the Admiralty to establish closer ties with their opposite numbers at Main Navy in 1941, British Naval Intelligence refused to hand over complete *Ultra* decrypts. Instead, they provided only what they regarded as relevant translated highlights, meaning it was in this form—that of a cryptological *Reader's Digest*—that Admiral Adolphus "Dolly" Andrews had been warned by Winn in January 1942 that the Germans were about to launch *Drumbeat*.

For obvious reasons, this haughty policy had annoyed King, who demanded to see the full, unexpurgated *Ultra* intercepts after Bletchley Park again broke into *Triton* on December 13, 1942, after having been locked out since February. For his pains, he received a condescending note reminding him to apply "the care necessary in making use of this information to prevent suspicion being aroused [in Germany] as to its source."

To the British, this was merely sage advice to ensure that *Ultra* was cleansed of potentially identifying information before it was radioed to uncleared personnel—a precaution that would prove its worth during the Naval Cypher No. 3 breach. To King, however, it confirmed his determination to get off the British teat and build his own Enigma-breaking capability.

That would take time, of course, so for the interim he had to make do with a British pledge to send him all the *Ultra* they had.

The Admiralty was as good as its word, and King for his part accepted the need to improve high-level security. To that end, Knowles added a windowless, stuffy office, not much more spacious than a large wardrobe, at the back of F-21. It was kept locked at all times. Aside from Knowles, his deputy John Parsons, and a couple of trusted assistants, nobody had the key or knew what it contained.

The only people even allowed to knock on the door were the armed Navy messengers who regularly arrived bearing the sealed double pouches containing the latest *Ultra* decrypts. With Parsons put in charge of filtering this confusing stream of U-boat messages, on December 27, 1942, the nook was officially designated *F-211*—an anodyne name for the most secret room in the United States.

Since then, the British had been assuming that an acceptable compromise had been found between London and Washington. Hence their shocked response to the revelation in late May 1943 that Tenth Fleet was going to leverage the precious *Ultra* to hunt and kill U-boats.

From the Admiralty's perspective, by wantonly exploiting *Ultra*'s privileged information, King threatened to destroy everything they had built—and at such terrible cost. One mistake too many, one suspicion not explained away, one overly coincidental rendezvous between a destroyer and a U-boat in the middle of nowhere—that might be all it would take for Dönitz to realize that naval *Triton* was blown.

These were valid fears, for breaking Enigma was by no means a sure thing. Already, several Enigma versions defied penetration. Both *Neptun*, the German Navy's highest-level signal for fleet operations, and *TGD*, the Gestapo's cipher, would remain black boxes until war's end. If, because King gave the game away, the Germans junked *Triton* as compromised, its successor would inevitably be much tougher to crack than its current iteration. Most frightening of all, what if Dönitz opted at the same time to upgrade the Enigma M4 machine—which used four rotors to encrypt messages—to, God help us, an M5?

To British minds, if King threw away the Enigma advantage on pursuing wild-goose chases, the U-boats might regain their encrypted cloak of invisibility, setting back the prosecution of the war to the most desperate days of 1942.

From the American point of view, the British were being ridiculously cautious. Operation *Overlord* was coming next year—everyone knew that—but there would likely be no *Overlord* at all unless the U-boats were destroyed. Enigma or not, the Germans would swarm the English Channel, picking off the invasion force as it sailed for France. But now, handed a golden opportunity to mete out an early death blow, what did the British want to do? Protect what they had when it was time to *act*, not *react*.

As King, a cardplayer himself, might have said—echoing the great gamesman Edmond Hoyle—*When in doubt, don't husband your trumps; take the trick.*

IV

Knowles's old friend Rodger Winn was particularly upset by the news of King's decision, and disappointed that Knowles was part of it—indeed, central to it. From the perspective of Room 41, what Knowles was doing was a betrayal of Winn's principles—the very same ones he had imparted to the budding wizard who had once been his apprentice.

Outwardly the two men remained collegial—they had worked together for too long to fight—but the relationship had cooled. They were like a once-married couple, amicably separated, with joint custody of their child, who was more important than their individual needs. The tone in their communications was courteous, but it was no longer intimate.

Privately, Knowles warned Tenth Fleet Chief of Staff Low that there was "a marked divergence of opinion" between himself and Winn. His friend, Knowles said, was keeping to the traditional "divert-and-avoid" methods: There was, unfortunately, "a decided reluctance on the part of the British to go out of their way to engage the enemy offensively."

Ultimately, the issue at stake was whether to be "clever" or "daring" when it came to exploiting *Ultra*. Winn wanted to be clever, but Knowles, being "younger at the game," was determined to use "*Ultra* more aggressively" than those old sticks-in-the-mud in London.

So, daring it was to be.

V

Like a freshly minted superhero, Knowles was eager to try out his newfound powers. The first priority was to see whether working autonomously from Room 41 was even viable. A betting man might have said no.

Winn possessed a formidable reputation. He had invented the art of submarine tracking. He was the storyteller *sans pareil* of the Working Fiction. He was the man who could prize open the heads of Dönitz and his captains to learn what they were thinking before they thought it.

And here was the upstart Kenneth Knowles of Milwaukee, Wisconsin, former editor of *Our Navy* magazine, who had attended neither the finest colleges in the realm nor argued cases in barrister's wig and court dress, having the temerity to challenge him on his own ground.

The test that would decide the matter began unobtrusively enough on May 24, just a few days after Tenth Fleet opened for business. At the time, no one was aware of Dönitz's plan to withdraw from the North to the Middle Atlantic; all that was known was that on May 20 he had broken off attacks. What the U-boats would do next was a mystery.

To try to solve it, Knowles was riffling through that day's *Ultra* messages when he came across one from Dönitz to his beleaguered fleet in the North Atlantic. Sixteen U-boats—nearly all that remained of the current operational attack force—were directed to make for "Square 87 of the large square west of TT."

Oh no—the Naval Grid. This had always been the toughest part of submarine tracking, the factor most liable to error. In Enigma messages, U-boats' longitudinal and latitudinal coordinates, expressed in degrees and minutes, were *never* transmitted in the clear; instead, the numerals themselves were *super*-coded. Encryption on encryption, in other words, a fallback line of defense against cryptanalytical attack. Dönitz's thinking was that even if they somehow broke *Triton,* an obviously absurd scenario, the Allies would still have no idea where his submarines were, let alone their destinations.

Much of his system remained opaque. Winn and Knowles had so far worked out that the Germans' oceanic map was divided into a grid of large squares, known as quadrants, each enclosing an area of 236,000 square nautical miles—larger than France. Measuring 486 nautical miles per side and denoted by a bigram (a group of two letters), every quadrant was divided, redivided, and subdivided into a matrix of smaller and smaller squares, like a giant Sudoku puzzle, each denoted by a color and given a unique numerical identifier. The tiniest of them were just 6 miles by 6 miles, making for a relatively minute area of 36 square miles of featureless water.

These bigrams, colors, and numbers were changed, often monthly, so that in March the bigram *AE* might, for instance, be in the Caribbean and in April, off Iceland. The key to knowing each square's new location after one of these changeovers was contained in a pamphlet called the "Address Book," which was kept in every captain's safe. Adding an extra layer of security was that each entry was a phony address (*"Gottfried Becker, Blücherplatz 30"*) that disguised the formula the captain used to calculate the fresh coordinates. In this example, for the new bigram GB, switch from the Green grid layout to Blue and add 30 to each number.

The sole weakness in the system was that while the "addresses" of the squares in the Address Book changed frequently, the Address Book itself—because U-boats stayed out for a long time but always needed the most up-to-date grid references to confirm new orders—did not. It therefore necessarily contained the changing keys to the Naval Grid for a year or more into the future.

The obvious danger here was that an Address Book might fall into enemy hands. But Dönitz deemed that an impossibility. Drummed into every captain' s head was what to do if he risked being captured: His first priority—more important than saving the crew's lives—was to destroy the Address Book. As an additional fail-safe, its ink was water-soluble; even if a sinking U-boat was somehow refloated, all that could be recovered would be a soggy, blank pamphlet.

Lacking a current Address Book, Winn and Knowles had traditionally filled in much of the empty space in their replicated version of Dönitz's map table using intuition, guesswork, and logic. Usually the two men would agree that a certain piece should be put in a particular place in Dönitz's giant jigsaw, but the May 24 message presented a head-scratcher.

Where on earth was "TT"?

VI

Winn argued that the bigram referred to a pinch point "south of Sable Island (about 200 miles east of Nova Scotia)." In other words, Dönitz was shifting his forces closer to Canada and the American East Coast. Over the coming days, accumulating radio-traffic evidence showed Winn to be right. U-boat commanders were busily sending signals mentioning that particular spot. Winn believed that a pack of some twenty U-boats was congregating there.

For the first time, Knowles stridently disagreed. Excepting the radio traffic, every signal he had recently seen indicated that Dönitz was preparing to quit the North Atlantic, not double down on it.

Given the lethality of U.S. and Canadian airpower so close to the coastline, Knowles thought, ordering a wolf pack there would be madness on Dönitz's part. And since when did Dönitz permit so much easygoing radio chatter?

The move, in short, was out of character for the player across the board. Knowles took a huge risk in saying that the radio traffic, which so conveniently pointed to Sable Island as the rendezvous point, was in fact a deception operation.

Knowles insisted that "Square 87 of the large square west of TT"— the mystery location where the U-boats were to meet—was nowhere near Sable Island; instead it was "600 miles southwest of the Azores." More precisely, Square 87—a box 54 miles to a side—was centered on 34° latitude north, 42° longitude west.

That spot was a safe distance from land-based air patrols, had previously served as a favored hunting ground for Dönitz, and was an ideal place to lay out a patrol line to jump American convoys steaming to and from the Mediterranean and Africa. The only reason for Dönitz to order the bulk of his remaining North Atlantic fleet there would be to seek respite from the massacres of May while setting up a counterattack.

For this leap of faith, Knowles's lone piece of evidence, if one could even call it that, was a curious incident that had transpired more than a month earlier: On April 16, a Captain Uphoff of *U-84* had broadcast several nonsensical signals. A clumsy mistake by a novice radio operator? Navy cryptanalysts weren't sure, noting at the time that the messages might just as easily be intended "to draw attention and, if so, to withdraw attention from elsewhere."

Nothing had come of it, but to Knowles the meaning of these signals had since become clear: Uphoff must have been conducting an early test of the deception system. As it would turn out, the busy radio traffic that had convinced Winn that Sable Island was the destination had in fact been generated by just two U-boats directed by the cunning Dönitz to stay behind, sail around, and mislead the Allies with dummy transmissions while the rest escaped.

Winn had fallen for the ruse, but Knowles had not. The pupil had surpassed his mentor.

VII

While Dönitz's intelligence experts chortled that "it remains to be seen whether [the enemy] will soon discover the present absence of U-boats in the North Atlantic," Knowles now chose to focus on a message from Dönitz that had been decrypted on June 4. It ordered the sixteen or seventeen recently departed U-boats to form a pack named *Trutz* (Defiance) and establish a 400-mile north-south patrol line roughly fifty miles due west of Knowles's amazingly precise fix of Square 87. "Do not let yourselves be seen," Dönitz exhorted his captains. "Transmit only if you have been observed."

The admiral intended the *Trutz* line to be a trap, sprung by the arrival of no fewer than three Allied convoys scheduled to cross it in the next several days. These were: UGS-9, an American convoy heading eastbound for Gibraltar; GUS-7A, a convoy traveling in the opposite direction; and Flight 10, a collection of nineteen newly built LCIs (Landing Craft Infantry) intended for amphibious assaults on Italy and France. With no air cover that far out, the trio was intensely vulnerable to a deadly coordinated attack—a fact that Dönitz understood far too well.

The Winn-recommended thing for Knowles to have done to avoid a massacre would have been to divert the three convoys well away from the *Trutz* line. And Knowles did, in fact, route GUS-7A southward, bypassing the U-boats, but only because the convoy was due to arrive first, and he was not yet ready to spring his own trap.

His chosen bait was instead Flight 10 and UGS-9. Of these, UGS-9, which was running a day behind Flight 10, was the real prize. Knowles was aware that Dönitz had directed his U-boats not to waste their torpedoes on sinking Flight 10's easily replaceable 250-ton LCIs. No, they were to lie in wait for UGS-9.

Accordingly, on June 4 Knowles directed Flight 10 and UGS-9 to stick to their assigned routes, taking them on a seemingly suicidal interception course with the southernmost U-boats. But he *also* directed the newly formed Task Group 21.12—comprising the escort carrier *Bogue* and four destroyers—to hide itself behind Flight 10, now placidly crossing the German patrol line.

As Knowles wrote in an analysis of the gambit, Dönitz had repeatedly underestimated the risk posed by "carrier-borne airpower"; this was "one of the essential weaknesses of his conduct," and Tenth Fleet was about to exploit it.

The waiting U-boats had no idea that aircraft were even in the area until 6:42 p.m., when two of *Bogue*'s Avengers sighted *U-228* and dropped eight depth charges. The submarine managed to escape, as did *U-603* when another patrolling Avenger attacked her twenty-seven minutes later. A minute after *U-603* crash-dived in the wake of fighting off her attacker with antiaircraft guns, yet another Avenger caught *U-641* by surprise; this submarine, too, got away—proof that U-boats intent on fiercely defending themselves were not exactly sitting ducks.

The Germans' luck ran out the next morning, though, when *Bogue* recommenced its sweeping patrols. In a ferocious fight, a Wildcat teamed with an Avenger destroyed *U-217*—*Bogue*'s first kill, and a conclusive demonstration that sending American forces out to hunt rather than waiting for a convoy to be attacked was a deadly strategy.

VIII

With her southern end scattered, *Trutz* was disbanded on the evening of June 5, roughly twenty-four hours after the battle had commenced, with two U-boats damaged badly enough to have to return home while the rest dispersed until Dönitz could issue new orders. Never again would Atlantic U-boats attack in wolf packs; henceforth, Dönitz would reprise his early-war strategy of allowing individual submarine captains to use their own initiative. U-boats acting singly would sink seven ships (38,000 tons) in June, rising to 127,000 tons in July in the Atlantic and the Arctic. But for the Allies these were minor losses, easily shrugged off.

Even as Tenth Fleet celebrated its win, Knowles was seeking a fresh opportunity to strike. He didn't have long to wait. On June 11, a decrypted signal from U-Boat Command ordered *Korvettenkapitän*

USS Bogue *attacks* U-118. *Note bullet splashes, depth-charge explosions, and the evasive trail behind the target.*

Czygan of *U-118* to search for the damaged *U-758* and gave its position. In reply, Czygan had sent a short transmission confirming his current location. Now that he had fixed *U-118*'s whereabouts and her destination, Knowles directed *Bogue* to return westward immediately and put every plane she had in the air.

At around 2 p.m. on June 12, *U-118* was swarmed by an overwhelming force of nine Avengers and Wildcats. Czygan's desperate efforts to avoid being hit were doomed; he and his boat went to the bottom, leaving behind just seventeen survivors who had jumped overboard. The water was so clear, pilots remembered, that they could see the submarine falling and flailing to her death.

Explaining Knowles's urgency was that *U-118* was no ordinary boat. She was a precious "milk cow"—a Type XB, a monster U-tanker that refueled, repaired, and reprovisioned other U-boats at sea.

The Type VII, for example—workhorse of the fleet—carried about

46,500 gallons of fuel. Of this, at least 8,000 gallons had to be reserved for the voyage home. Normal operations may have sipped only about 800 gallons per day, but combat and evasion burned fuel prodigiously: When in contact with a convoy, daily consumption averaged 2,000 gallons; when sailing at full surface speed in pursuit or escape, between 3,200 and 4,000 gallons.

Given these figures, one can see why Dönitz relied so heavily on the six U-tankers he then had in service. One-third longer than the typical combat submarine and displacing more than twice as much, each U-tanker carried 300,000 gallons of fuel, 50 tons of food, a doctor, replacement crewmen for the wounded, and spare parts for broken anti-radar detectors and the like.

While acting as a major force multiplier for the diminished U-boat fleet, the U-tankers were also highly vulnerable. Dönitz may have taken every precaution to minimize their communications and to camouflage their coordinates, but when they called, the other U-boats had to flock to a prearranged time and place. Which meant that, if they could be hit hard as they waited at the rendezvous, it might be possible to kill two birds, maybe more, with one stone.

Knowles had first come up with this bold idea back in January. About a month after setting up F-21, he'd written a memorandum to King pointing out that, thanks to breaking *Triton* and the resulting stream of *Ultra* intelligence, "we are now able to determine up to a week or ten days in advance the exact position of the refuelling area." Ambushing the handful of existing U-tankers would reduce the other U-boats' "effectiveness out of all proportion to the number involved."

Knowles's insight was prescient, but premature. No escort carriers had been available in early 1943 to intercept the U-tankers, which were invariably stationed in the Air Gap. By the summer of that year, however, the situation was very different. With the destruction of *U-118* providing proof of concept, Knowles gained the enthusiastic backing of King and

Low to devote Tenth Fleet's efforts to sinking as many of Dönitz's refuelers as he could.

Knowles at last also had the wherewithal to do it. The solitary *Bogue* was soon to be joined by three more escort carriers: *Core*, *Card*, and *Santee*.

Core drew first blood on July 13, when, after Knowles moved her to the right square of the oceanic chessboard on the heels of an *Ultra* refueling signal, a fighter-bomber team spotted the telltale wake of *U-487*, a new Type XIV tanker. That it was her maiden war patrol certainly showed: Her antiaircraft guns were unmanned, and most of the crew were caught sunbathing on the deck.

Nevertheless, their good training kicked in and a Wildcat was shot down, killing the pilot, but not before the accompanying Avenger had straddled the boat with four depth charges. A second Wildcat-Avenger team dropped another four, which blasted *U-487* out of the water and broke her in half. A few moments later she sank beneath the waves, taking her captain and half the crew down with her. (The sunbathers and gunners, most of whom managed to leap away, were later rescued.)

Next, after Knowles picked up a signal ordering the tanker *U-117* to a rendezvous, his invisible hand guided *Card* to intercept her as she was refueling *U-66* on August 7. An Avenger dropped depth charges between the two boats, damaging *U-117* and forcing *U-66* to crash-dive. The Avenger then loosed a Fido, but it missed *U-66*. In the meantime, a newly arrived quartet of Avengers and Wildcats strafed and attacked the lumbering *U-117*. She submerged but was hit by another Fido and went down with all hands.

On October 4 *Card* struck again, launching her Avengers while the tanker *U-460* was serving as a gas station for *U-264*, *U-422*, and *U-455*. Confusion reigned among the four submarines: *Who should dive first? Who should fend off the attack?*

Kapitänleutnant Hartwig Looks, commanding *U-264*, wrote that he watched his counterpart on *U-460*, Ebe Schnoor, "shrug his shoulders and gesticulate as though not knowing what to do." Looks dived along with his fellow captains and later heard "underwater bomb detonations…and noises as if a U-boat were endeavoring to blow tanks" to come up. What he was in fact hearing was Schnoor and his men dying as a Fido got them just below the surface.

Dönitz's striking power and operating radius contracted every time he lost another U-tanker to Knowles. These specialized vessels were to have served as the guylines and poles of the reinvigorated Atlantic campaign; with each one cut or uprooted, the tent sagged a little more. By October 1943, out of fourteen that had been built, thirteen had been destroyed.

Every tanker eradicated meant that more combat submarines were forced to curtail their patrols and risk traversing the Bay of Biscay, where they could be picked off by long-range British patrol bombers. At the end of July there had been seventy-one U-boats either on patrols, undergoing trials, or in transit; a month later there were forty, many going home early with near-dry fuel tanks.

If in 1942 the Americans had been at sixes and sevens in the struggle against the U-boat, it was partly due to Knowles that they had since become aces.

IX

To keep the British happy, or at least to keep them pretending to be happy, King had promised that Tenth Fleet would carefully cover its *Ultra* tracks so that the U-boats' "destruction might be accomplished without trace." There would *always* be a cover story, he said, to give the Germans good reason to believe that the Enigma remained sacrosanct.

Knowles kept to the deal as best he could, but his repeated successes tried Winn's goodwill. If anyone knew how thin the ice Knowles was skating on when, as Dönitz put it, "high-flying carrier-borne aircraft" miraculously happened to stumble upon U-tankers at their secret rendezvous points over and over again, it was Winn. True, Knowles had gotten away with it several times, but that was due to luck, not skill, his old mentor believed. Above all, Winn thought Knowles was getting sloppy with *Ultra*. After *Card* sank *U-117* on August 7, Winn had had enough; he bitingly rebuked his former student that the fix had been "too true to be good."

By that he meant the interception was so eerily coincidental that U-Boat Command was liable to notice—and if it did, and changed the Enigma settings, then Knowles would be responsible for blacking out Bletchley Park *and* jeopardizing the coming invasion of Europe.

But Knowles wasn't listening. Because he didn't have to.

X

Bletchley Park's cryptological dominance had always hinged on its monopoly of what were called "bombes." These were letter-crunching machines—not computers, because they lacked a memory—that eliminated tens of millions of impossible solutions to the daily Enigma key, thereby enabling codebreakers to focus their human brainpower on a manageable number of possible ones.

In 1941, an American team of Army and Navy cryptanalysts had been the first outsiders permitted to see these electromechanical monsters, six and a half feet high and seven wide, whose eleven miles of wiring and million soldered contacts enabled them to mimic thirty-six Enigma M3s spinning simultaneously at high speed. As their motors and gears spun, all that could be heard was the racket of what seemed to be hundreds of knitters maniacally tickety-clicketing their needles. The distinctive ticking sound from the first such device had prompted its Polish inventor, Marian Rejewski, to nickname the machine a *bomba*.

In late 1942, at the height of King's fury that the British were rationing his *Ultra* portions, he had authorized *AAA* status—the same priority as the Manhattan Project—to develop domestic versions of Bletchley's bombes.

If he was going to build his own Enigma-breaking factory, he wouldn't do things by halves. The British, it was clear, were running out of steam. In September 1942 they had operated thirty-two bombes, each one painstakingly hand-built by the British Tabulating Machine Company. By December the number of bombes had risen to forty-nine, but in a worrying sign that the beleaguered country was growing short on manufacturing capacity, some basic components had to be assembled by volunteers in local village halls. By March 1943, production had slowed to such an extent that Bletchley Park had just sixty bombes, all of them last-generation models designed to emulate the old Enigma M3 machines.

Sensing an opportunity to get the jump on his ally, King then approved manufacturing up to 336 M4-grade bombes. The pharaonic grandiosity of the project was incomprehensible to the hard-pressed British. Its cost was astronomical, its scale astounding, its timetable astonishing. As early as September, just several months after King's green light, the first half-dozen American-developed bombes were loaded into mammoth, sealed crates on a special train at a dedicated loading dock in Dayton, Ohio. They had been assembled in the mysterious Building 26, owned by the National Cash Register Company (NCR) and equipped with steel-reinforced concrete floors, air-conditioning, and fireproofing—wise precautions to protect two-ton machines that generated desertlike heat and shot out sparks if overtaxed.

Guarded by armed Navy midshipmen all the way, they were transported to the former Mount Vernon Seminary for Girls on Nebraska Avenue in Washington, D.C., the new headquarters for the secretive

A WAVE works alongside an American bombe.

unit known as OP-20-G, which handled naval cryptography and signals intelligence.

These new bombes differed markedly from their British counterparts. They proved so powerful that 120 would serve just as satisfactorily as the originally contracted 336 because they could penetrate *Triton* in an average of thirty-six hours—thrice as fast as the Bletchley Park machines. Even when compared with the very latest British M4-capable machines, the American bombes were at least 30 percent quicker. And King possessed many more of them: around eighty by mid-November, for an incredible production rate of one per day.

Their arrival marked the moment when the U.S. Navy began to take over from Bletchley Park virtually all naval Enigma intercepts and decrypts. The effects were soon seen.

When Knowles first set up F-21 in December 1942 and began compiling a database of 5-by-8 sub cards cataloguing hull numbers, captains' names, and similar information, he used red ink to indicate intelligence that came courtesy of Winn and black ink for intelligence sourced from OP-20-G. Initially, the cards had been covered in red ink. Nine months later they were becoming a sea of black ink, with only an occasional splash of red.

These days, as far as Knowles was concerned, despite Winn's objections he could use homegrown *Ultra* any way he liked.

XI

The shift of power from Winn to Knowles reflected a greater truth about the evolving Anglo-American alliance: that it was a marriage, but not of equals.

The relationship was, in fact, becoming ever *more* unequal. In 1939, the Royal Navy's surface fleet had been the largest in the world: 7 carriers, 12 mighty battleships, 56 cruisers, and more than 180 destroyers conscientiously accumulated over the decades. In 1943 alone, however, the U.S. Navy commissioned 6 fleet carriers, 9 light carriers, 24 escort carriers, 2 battleships, 11 cruisers, and 128 destroyers. By 1945 it would be nearly twice as large in terms of warship tonnage as the British, German, Italian, Russian, French, and Japanese navies combined.

The old empire that had so recently spanned a quarter of the globe still had life in it, but its financial sinews were strained and torn by the hard audit of war. The trappings of power of course remained, but underneath the gilded crown and the silver scepter the tin was beginning to show.

When, for instance, Churchill had flown to the Casablanca Conference, indomitably masquerading as Roosevelt's peer, his personal B-24 Liberator may have borne a proud RAF roundel—but it was a donated American plane.

And whereas Winn's single plotting table in Room 41 crabbedly focused on a map of the Atlantic, F-21's huge wall charts ambitiously covered all the world's oceans—which, once *the* King's, now belonged to Admiral King.

Centuries earlier, Churchill's kinsman the Duke of Marlborough had said that "in every alliance one party wears boots and spurs while the other wears a saddle." In 1943 that prophecy had come to fruition, just not in the way his descendant had anticipated. Earlier in the war, the Americans had been obliged to let the British be the plumed rider, but King was now not only firmly in the saddle but he also owned the horse, the carriage, the highway, and the footmen.

Churchill understood, if he did not quite accept, that the age of majesty into which he had been born was approaching its final, and finest, hours. The purple once of Augustus was to pass to a Barbaric new emperor from far across the Rubicon. After the war "you will have the greatest navy in the world," he conceded to Roosevelt. "You will have...the greatest air force. You will have the greatest trade. You have all the gold."

XII

That fall of 1943, as he sat alone in the Secret Room, Knowles, the new master of the Great Game, pored over OP-20-G's intercepted messages, radio-direction fixes, transcripts of POW interrogations, and analyses of German radio operators' unique "fists." The U-tanker phase of the battle was reaching its conclusion, and he had begun to focus on the task of finding and killing individual U-boats.

One U-boat in particular attracted his curiosity. She would leave her pen, mosey around a bit, then return home. Not just once, but six or seven times. No other U-boat had ever behaved so strangely.

Knowles checked his sub cards. It was *U-505*.

THE SUICIDE STRETCH

I

Knowles had almost completely forgotten about *U-505*, once the most damaged boat in the fleet following her catastrophic encounter with Sillcock's stricken airplane. Ever since returning to Lorient for repairs on December 12, 1942, not a single radio transmission had been intercepted from, to, or about her until early July—more than seven months later.

U-505 had been so long in dry dock that Knowles likely assumed she'd been cannibalized for parts, her crew dispersed, her captain reassigned. But no, *U-505* had somehow survived a long series of surgeries and had returned to active duty come the summer.

While she'd been recuperating, *U-505* had missed not only the last grand hurrah of the wolf packs in March 1943 but also the devastating massacre of Black May. As of July 1943, she was entering a new and alien world from the one she had left in December.

Physically gone, for instance, was her traditional 105mm deck gun, once so useful for finishing off ships during surface attacks. Nowadays that would be madness. Taking its place was a four-barrel flak gun and two twin-barreled 20mms for antiaircraft work.

Mentally, the crew's morale remained high, but it was showing indications of precariousness. Peter Zschech, still in command, had made no attempt to endear himself to anyone during the many months on land. He continued to be disliked by all but his diminishing coterie of favorites. That he had recently been promoted to Kapitänleutnant signaled to everyone else that he was the type who failed upward and bullied downward.

There were occasional incidents of what had once been completely unthinkable among the Praetorians of the submarine service: desertion. Hans Goebeler, a *U-505* crewman, was approached by one of his comrades, Willi, who'd obtained false papers and planned to run to Switzerland with his French paramour. Did Hans want to come with him? Goebeler refused, and even considered reporting Willi—which would have resulted in his execution—but in the end persuaded him not to go. Willi stayed and served honorably, but Goebeler was never close to him again.

Winn had first noticed incipient signs of a decline in morale among U-boat men in February. By April, he had confirmed it. The clues lay in the little things. An uptick in the number of missions aborted owing to inexplicable equipment malfunctions. That fewer captains were boldly pressing home their attacks. A general reprimand from Dönitz saying that he wanted to see more "healthy warrior and hunter instincts" among his commanders.

But there were also practical giveaways that U-boats as a whole were becoming timid of encountering destroyers and aircraft. Whereas an angry Zschech had been an outlier when he fired those torpedoes from 4,000 yards in late 1942, a Tenth Fleet memorandum remarked that in these post–Black May days "commanders somehow seem reluctant to report distances." And no wonder: Many U-boat captains now regarded

3,000 yards as the minimum safe distance, and a few launched their eels at an absurd 5,000 or even 6,000 yards just for an excuse to withdraw. What had once been an isolated act of desperation had become, it seems, standard procedure.

II

Commander Robert Lee Norden of the U.S. Navy enthusiastically exploited this psychologically vulnerable moment among the U-boat men. In excellent but slightly American-inflected German, from January 1943 onward he regularly broadcast the latest news in six-minute clips to his secret fans at sea. In them he talked omnisciently of such things as Nazi Party sex scandals and the comfortable treatment of prisoners of war in America.

One subject Commander Norden repeatedly returned to was the real number of submarine losses as opposed to Dönitz's official, and ludicrous, estimate that just twelve U-boats had been lost since September 1939. To substantiate his assertions, Norden read out the lost captains' names and their associated hull numbers.

On the other side of the ledger, Norden dismissed stories of the U-boats' supposedly vast success against Allied shipping. Yes, we had lost some ships, he granted, but the most spectacular claims—such as sinking aircraft carriers and endless numbers of destroyers—were exaggerations put out by medal-seeking captains.

Speaking of flashy medals, why had no enlisted man or noncommissioned officer ever received a Knight's Cross? If the mortal risk was the same to all, Norden pointed out, then why did only officers get them? It was as if there was one rule for them and another for the rest of us. So why are *you* dying for *their* glory?

Another Norden favorite was to poke fun at the unexplained differences between what Dönitz said then and now. Why had he claimed in

1940 that "the true nature of the U-boat lies in its invisibility," whereas nowadays he was ordering U-boats to stay on the surface and fight off aircraft with their guns? Especially since he'd once dismissed air attacks as posing no danger at all?

Norden also made sure to undermine the crews' faith in their superiors by making merry sport of the enormous number of admirals being appointed ("That makes a total now of two grand admirals, five general admirals, [and] more than 150 admirals") while the common man drowned in a hellish sea. Thanks to this *Admiralinflation*, "Germany now possesses about ten times as many admirals as torpedo boats, destroyers, and cruisers combined," the commander remarked. "And 300 times more admirals than battleships." But most devastating was a line much quoted among submariners when their officers weren't around: "In April there were actually more admirals launched than U-boats."

To those tuning in or gossiping about the latest news, this Norden character was, it seems, frighteningly well-informed about the innermost workings of U-Boat Command.

But Commander Robert Lee Norden never existed.

He was the invention of a journalist named Ladislas Farago. Hungarian by birth and Jewish by descent, Farago was a typical émigré of the era. He had fled 1930s Europe, washing up like so many others in America. Intelligent and very creative (in the sense that he delighted in creating facts to enhance a good story), Farago maintained ties with various secret services and retained a romantic love of cloak and dagger—especially when it came to Nazis.

Before Pearl Harbor, he had enterprisingly produced a book titled *German Psychological Warfare*, which claimed to expose the weaknesses inherent in the steely Teutonic mind for an American audience. A former obstetrician, Lieutenant Commander Cecil Coggins, read it and was impressed. He had recently been made head of the Navy's psychological-warfare branch, OP-16-W, and thought this Farago was just the fellow to help him undermine U-boat morale.

Farago's recruitment made a nicely melodramatic scene. When Coggins, an intense man with no sense of humor, visited Farago in August 1942, he skipped the small talk: "Be in Washington on December 4. Go straight from Union Station to the Fairfax Hotel. Don't register, but go directly to Room 307 and enter without knocking. The door will be unlocked. Be there at 5 p.m. sharp." Then he vanished as quickly as he had appeared, at least according to Farago's recollection.

After joining OP-16-W, whose headquarters was a makeshift building near the Lincoln Memorial, Farago hit upon the idea of a fake American officer equipped with a cynical sense of humor and well-placed informants who hosted his own radio show. Unlike the British, who preferred "black" propaganda—their broadcasts purported to be German in origin—OP-16-W specialized in "white" propaganda: "Commander Norden" made no bones that he spoke on behalf of the United States Navy.

For that reason, Farago chose his name carefully: *Robert Lee Norden* was "indigenously American with a slight touch of Confederate chauvinism, yet easily understandable and pronounceable by the Germans." Same with his rank: As a commander, he was senior enough for his authority to be respected, yet not so much as to alienate junior officers and enlisted men.

Farago, creative juices aflow, went so far as to compose what would be called in Hollywood a "character bible" for Norden that described his parents, his schooling, his hobbies, his pets, and his family. This thirty-page biography was the scriptural truth of his forged life and could be consulted to keep contradictions and inconsistencies from making it onto the air. Farago even took the time to apply for Norden to be listed in the Naval Register of Commissioned Officers—he failed, red tape proving more than a match for the black arts—but he did get an address for him at the central Mail Room in case German agents tried to make contact.

Now he had to make the commander spring to life. An international lawyer with a ramrod-straight back and a British-style clipped mustache named Ralph Gerhart Albrecht served admirably as Norden's radio "voice." At the time, he was a Naval Reserve lieutenant commander working in OP-16-W's equally secretive sister department, OP-16-Z, which handled POW interrogations and closely liaised with Knowles at F-21. But he had perfect German, though to native ears he sounded as if he'd imbibed it growing up in an expatriate community, which he in fact had. It was perfect, though, for maintaining the pretense that Norden had learned his German from a textbook.

In order to further demonstrate Norden's authoritative credentials, Knowles helped supply Farago with highly classified intelligence, albeit appropriately downgraded and scoured of any potential *Ultra* giveaways. That was how "Commander Norden" knew so much about U-boat losses, the admirals, and medal awards.

After the war, U-boat crewmen claimed that the Norden broadcasts had no influence on them, but that was their pride and poor memory talking. At the time, Albrecht's 309 broadcasts worked wonders—perhaps not quite as marvelous as Farago later boasted about, but really not bad nonetheless.

Captain Heinz-Eberhard Müller, for instance, was one of three survivors picked up from *U-662*, sunk off Brazil in late July 1943, who turned out to be a huge fan. According to the interrogator's report, during his debriefing he "spoke of 'Commander Norden' and expressed a desire to meet him, if possible." Albrecht was duly brought in—an extra stripe temporarily decorating his sleeve to bump him up from a lieutenant commander—and happily chatted with the starstruck prisoner.

Müller told Albrecht that he and his officers used to listen eagerly to "Bob," as they fondly called him, and "never missed the Norden talk if they could avoid it." No one fully believed what Norden said, of course, knowing as they did that it was propaganda. Still, said Müller, they found the broadcasts "highly entertaining by reason of the manner in which they were presented, particularly the use of irony by the speaker and the occasional 'barbed shafts' directed at particular personalities"—the various brass, presumably.

But the most interesting question that Müller answered was the perennial one: Were the U-boat men aware of the scale of their own losses? Dönitz minimized them as much as possible, but even he couldn't forever disguise the emptied bars and brothels.

It turned out that the officers, at least, knew of fatalities within their circle. As Müller explained, the officers of each year's Naval Academy graduating class kept closely in touch with one another. Müller's was the "Olympic Crew" of 1936—the same as Zschech's, as it happened. When asked by Albrecht to estimate how many of his fellows had been lost, Müller said "a few less than thirty."

He was almost right. Of the 153 members of the Crew of 1936, exactly 31 had been killed since the war's outbreak to the time Müller was captured in late July 1943. He couldn't know it at the time, of course, but between then and the end of October another 10 would die.

Given the horrendous fatality rate among their dearest comrades, it would surely have been surprising for U-boat commanders *not* to have been affected emotionally. Müller himself said that as he departed on his final patrol he experienced, for the first time in his career, a "premonition of disaster."

Meanwhile, his brother-in-arms, Peter Zschech of U-505, already mentally delicate, was soon to experience a disaster of his own.

III

At a little after 10:30 a.m. on July 1, 1943—a foggy, drizzly day—U-505's crew arrived at her pen in Lorient and began preparing her for departure.

The torpedoes were wrestled aboard, followed by truckloads of provisions in their sacks, bottles, and crates, and finally came the ammunition: boxes and boxes of 20mm rounds. Then the boat's hatches and valves were shut, and *U-505* was filled with compressed air to check for sneaky leaks. After that, the entire length of the ship was demagnetized—to protect her, it was hoped, from the floating mines the British liked to drop in the Bay of Biscay.

The leave-taking lacked the razzmatazz of earlier years. There were no more oompah bands bashing out a brassy march, only a few accordion players humming traditional sea shanties. There were a handful of flotilla officers there to shake hands and exchange salutes, plus around fifty well-wishers gathered to see off *U-505* and the other four submarines traveling with her. The truth is, there weren't many people in Lorient anymore. Much of the place was a blackened pyre or flattened rubble, courtesy of repeated visits from RAF Bomber Command and the Eighth Air Force, both vainly determined to destroy the U-boat pens. The latter had been reinforced by thick concrete; the town had not.

U-boats sailed in companies these days across the bay, darkly known among submariners as the "Suicide Stretch." Once upon a time they had traveled submerged to avoid detection by B-24 Liberators, but not anymore: Because the Liberators could find them above or below water, U-boats, accompanied by a team of minesweepers, formed their own, mutually protective escort groups, their bristling collective array of machine guns capable of driving off any aerial interlopers.

Little did Zschech or his fellow captains know that virtually every message they sent and received was being read in Washington and London. In the Suicide Stretch, there was no such thing as a serendipitous interception by a Liberator. Despite appearances, there were no accidents, no such coincidences, in Knowles's world. In *U-505*'s case, albeit with some gaps, Knowles was aware of when she had left, where she was going, and when she was returning—often in almost real time.

IV

As they crossed the Bay of Biscay, each U-boat looked like church on Sunday morning. Only six men nowadays remained inside the boats during this part of the journey, with the rest kneeling, and perhaps praying, beside each other on the deck. If the submarine hit a mine, bloody research had shown that jumping overboard was the best way of saving as many of the crew as possible. Of course, there was instead the risk of aircraft swooping from out of the sun and strafing the deck crowded with human targets, but dying instantly in the sunlight by bullet was regarded as preferable to drowning by inches as a holed submarine descended into watery darkness.

Early the next day, having cleared the bay, the U-boats reached their scheduled departure point into the Atlantic and split up. For most, having safely run the gauntlet, waving farewell came as a relief. But for Captain Zschech and his crew, a new agony was beginning.

U-505 would undertake a deep test-dive for the first time since coming out of repair.

At a depth of 120 feet all seemed well, but then the starboard propeller shaft began to jet water inside. Zschech wanted to push on regardless, but his engineer cautioned him that it would only get worse. A very unhappy Zschech ordered a return to Lorient to fix the problem.

On July 3, U-505, with an even smaller crowd on the dock than two days before, again pushed off. This time the trial dive went well, but then the Metox radar detector went on the fritz, followed by the hydrophone set. Without any way of detecting aircraft or destroyers in the vicinity, this would definitely be a one-way mission.

Zschech nevertheless ordered U-505 to continue—at least until July 8, when, predictably, an undetected aircraft dropped six bombs. Thankfully none were fatal, but one opened a small crack in an external fuel tank. Once more Zschech set a course home for the necessary repairs, yet not until he peeked through the periscope did he realize *U-505* was leaving a shimmering trail of diesel oil in her wake.

Royal Navy destroyers were shortly on the hunt, following the slick like bloodhounds. With the Metox and hydrophone now at least patched up, Zschech managed to evade them by means of high-speed nighttime surface runs and slow, daytime underwater travel. On July 13, *U-505* limped back into her pen for repairs.

It was during a subsequent maintenance check that dock engineers discovered that most of *U-505*'s rubber seals—those attached to her emergency valves, air-relief valves, and fuel tanks—had been corroded by what some said was battery acid. The responsible officials claimed that the parts they'd been sent from the factory were defective, but many among the crew hissed that the acid had been deliberately poured over them.

As they waited to be recalled into service, the crew had plenty of time to indulge in gossip. The subject of much talk was Zschech's odd behavior during one of the depth-charge attacks they had experienced on their last outing.

When depth charges are raining down, as anyone who's seen a submarine movie will attest, actors dramatically look up as they wait for the delayed explosion—even though, in reality, the most dangerous depth charges were the ones that blew up *beneath* the submarine. Zschech, however, had not looked up or down at all. Among the crew, there were furtive whispers that their captain had been utterly expressionless during this episode, as if he were in another world. *Did Zschech have a death wish?*, they wondered.

Two weeks later, on August 1, *U-505* set out again, the men's hearts full of hope that a ship would cross their path so they could break the curse and bring the captain back to life. Alas, it was not to be. Soon after setting out and descending to 150 feet, mysterious creaks and loud cracks echoed through the boat. Then at 180 feet a crash was heard, followed by loud gurgling noises from the pressure hull. Even Zschech realized the impossibility of continuing. By midnight, they were back where they had started that morning.

His superiors and a few fellow captains greeted this latest mechanical malady with skepticism. Every commander had his share of problems, but Zschech was experiencing a suspiciously large number of them. Questions, and eyebrows, were beginning to be raised about his commitment to the cause.

Zschech, however, was given a pass when inspectors found a potentially fatal defect in the plates on the repaired pressure hull: Rather than being solidly welded together, the plates had been caulked using oakum (a kind of oil-soaked rope) before being thinly covered with solder. Had Zschech descended any deeper, U-505 would have torn herself apart.

After another two weeks in dry dock, U-505 cast off her lines on August 14. Not far out, and again at 180 feet below, there came a thunderous crack, then the now-familiar gurgling. This time, an air-intake valve began vibrating madly. Zschech was livid. U-505 would have to return to Lorient immediately.

A week later U-505 was yet again pronounced seaworthy. During the subsequent test-dive, U-505 passed with flying colors and the crew was giddy that finally they could begin their war patrol. Then they heard Zschech's curses from the conning tower and the peculiar, sinister tone his voice took on when trouble was brewing. U-505 was again leaving an oil slick in her wake.

Upon her return, engineers would discover a small hole in a fuel tank, which the crew attributed to someone having purposely drilled it.

That was a tiny thing; a far larger thing was that the detested bully Thilo Bode, Zschech's deputy and his dear friend from the Crew of 1936, was suddenly reassigned to command his own U-boat. His departure left Zschech isolated. A gray cloud accompanied even the welcome news that the Second Watch Officer, Oberleutnant Paul Meyer, had been promoted to replace Bode. Zschech disliked Meyer and was intensely jealous of his popularity with the crew. The captain retreated more and more often to his bunk, leaving Meyer to give the orders and run the boat.

On September 18, *U-505* again put out to sea. Each man had earnestly knocked on wood for luck before entering the boat, but during the test-dive water gushed in from the starboard diesel exhaust. Then an electric motor shorted out after *U-505* dived to evade an airplane. But this time Zschech refused to concede. He stubbornly drove on for another five days on the surface as the submarine shipped water through her necessarily open hatches. To make matters worse, no sooner had the motor been repaired than water seeped into the electrical switchboard and the main bilge pump failed. Staying out any longer was clearly impossible; on September 30, *U-505* was again ignominiously placed in dry dock.

The new flotilla chief, Ernst Kals, tried to comfort the distraught Zschech, to little avail. Nothing had been his fault, but rumors spread that Zschech was not made for a military career. There had been too many aborted missions; too many complaints about his command style; too many evenings onshore when he retreated to his billet and refused to dine with his fellow officers. Dönitz, he was told, had grown "suspicious" of his behavior.

The word *coward* was never openly uttered. Zschech heard it nevertheless, at least in his own mind, over and over again. But the truth was worse than that.

Thirteen

THE LEMON

I

No matter how heartily they disliked him, none of his men believed Zschech was yellow. Everyone knew the real issue afflicting *U-505* was *sabotage*.

As shocking as it sounded, the charge was surely incontestable: How else to explain the weird propeller-shaft leak, the oakum stuffed between the hull plates, the battery acid poured on the rubber seals, the failures of the Metox and hydrophone, the hole in the fuel tank, the malfunctioning motor, engine, and bilge pump?

Allied propaganda specialists had long encouraged crews to self-sabotage their boats to avoid being killed. The British, for instance, produced a leaflet that was air-dropped over Lorient and other bases. It gave simple instructions on how to cause a ballast tank to split at sea by turning off the valve that regulated its air pressure. "No one can prove who has done it," the leaflet promised, but one thing was certain: The boat would have to return and the entire crew would get "six weeks' leave" during the repairs.

These Allied efforts weren't very productive. No matter what they said, the risk of getting caught was too high and the submarine service still prided itself on recruiting only the best, not blackguards who turned off valves to stay home. Even when the scuttlebutt around Lorient was, according to one German POW rescued from *U-172*, that Zschech was a "shrewd and able master of sabotage," his crew defended him from the sneer, partly because it would have reflected so poorly on *them* but mostly because there was a much more obvious culprit.

The true enemy, the crew just knew, were the French auxiliary workers at Lorient. It was they who attracted the greatest ire and the bitterest fury. Until late 1942, relations with them had been "calm," according to *U-505*'s former captain, Loewe, but he had nevertheless always maintained guards on board. He had never suffered a case of sabotage, so far as he knew. But by mid-1943, by which time Loewe had been kicked upstairs to headquarters, the French had turned less hospitable, especially after the Allied bombings of their town persuaded them to hold their occupiers "responsible for the destruction of life and property."

Blaming the locals for the breakdowns was a natural consequence. Previously quiescent workers were now suspected of being secret members of the French Resistance, and obvious instances of carelessness were chalked up to their diabolical cunning.

After *U-557* once got stuck on the seabed, said Herbert Werner, a junior officer at the time, a search turned up "a wrench [that] was jammed in the outboard air induction valve." That a tool might have accidentally fallen in and gotten stuck, not been purposefully "jammed," did not cross his mind. Even ludicrous allegations were given credence: A consignment of sailors' shirts, for example, was once impregnated at the laundry with an itching powder so debilitating that a U-boat was forced to surrender—or so the cartoonish story ran.

Also falling under suspicion were the imported ethnic Germans from Poland and other Eastern European countries, known as *Volks-deutsche,* who had been dragooned into the Organization Todt, the giant state civil-engineering concern that had built not only the U-boat pens but also the Atlantic Wall to withstand the expected Allied invasion. Among them were certainly a number of leftist political opponents of the Reich, mused Peter Cremer of *U-333.*

Hostility toward the Todt construction workers was common at the time. While the U-boat men were risking their lives, these yokelish ingrates were living it up in comfortable accommodations and taking it easy on the weekends, or so the whispers had it. The ugly contempt that front-line soldiers can have for rear-area civilian personnel soon made its appearance. *U-505*'s Hans Goebeler, drinking by himself in a Lorient restaurant, once got into a fistfight with a Todt dockyard worker he claimed had said, "We'll make sure that [*U-505* doesn't] get very far in the future."

The alleged saboteur, later heard singing in French, was soon arrested. Much to Goebeler's disgust, he was pardoned "because he had five children and had received a good recommendation from his supervisor." This liberal and tolerant attitude sounds somewhat atypical of the German military police. More usually, a saboteur—kids or recommendation notwithstanding—would have been shot without so much as a pro forma trial.

As Goebeler's confused story indicates, it's hard to discern fact from gossip in these tales. His fellow *U-505* crewman Hans Decker, for instance, said that in late August 1943 enginemen discovered sugar mixed in with the lubricating oil. Goebeler, however, heard that the sugar-in-the-oil incident happened on a different submarine. For good measure, he added that a dead dog had been found in the drinking-water tank of yet another U-boat, and that contracting botulism from improperly canned food had become common thanks to the nefarious practices of French chefs.

Some of these horror stories resemble old sailors' tales told to scare the youngsters aboard, while others, such as the botulism one, might more realistically be attributed to, well, improperly canned food rotting for months in a damp, unhygienic environment. But it was easier for the U-boat men to blame an invisible enemy than the system itself.

II

Despite their unswerving belief in a wide-ranging conspiracy against them, reality was more prosaic. For one thing, despite Captain Loewe's contention to the contrary, Frenchmen were not allowed aboard U-boats or in the heavily guarded pens, making sabotaging internal equipment such as gaskets and valves a difficult trick to pull off, let alone heaving dead dogs into water tanks or pouring bags of (severely rationed) sugar into the oil supply. Still, even granting the possible occasional instance of opportunistic sabotage at the yards, U-505's series of malfunctions and breakdowns was much more likely the result of poor workmanship, overly strict quotas, and shoddy materials.

The Todt workers were hardly the world's greatest or most motivated craftsmen, and many of the more skilled ones had in any case been assigned to shore up the Eastern Front. Trained, native manpower in the Reich had run seriously low by 1943, and French civilians were increasingly liable to be hauled off to Germany to serve as forced labor. For their part, Todt workers who had been sent the opposite way to France were expected to slave at all hours to repair increasing numbers of crippled U-boats following encounters with Allied forces.

The pace was punishing, so corners were cut. Making matters worse was the variable quality of the materials they worked with. Minister of Armaments and War Production Albert Speer's all-out drive to produce unparalleled amounts of iron and steel was bound to result in poor product.

Speer was also under pressure to accelerate production by switching from traditional methods of shipyard construction to the kind of prefabricated sectional and sub-assembly processes pioneered by the Americans to speed-build their Liberty ships, destroyers, and carriers. This was no easy feat, and it was made harder still by Allied bombing raids on the factories and railways necessary to keep the system running.

With good reason, then, U-boats constructed before 1942, when time and resources were lavish, experienced relatively few technical and quality problems. Those built or repaired in 1943, by contrast, when charges of sabotage first began to be heard, suffered myriad problems. From July to September of that year, more than 40 percent of all U-boat departures were plagued by such issues as gaps between hull plates, sloppy welding, loose valves, and rattling pipes.

Before *U-505* left port on a trial run, for instance, crewman Aloysius Hasselberg noticed that a workman had tightened several valve-fastening bolts just a single turn and lazily painted over empty screw holes. Had a depth charge detonated anywhere near them, the valve would have shaken free and flooded the boat. Even after those problems were fixed, the trial itself ended abruptly when water leaked in through "incorrectly welded...cable-holes for the underwater listening telephone."

U-505 was a pre-1942 U-boat, originally built with high-grade workmanship and first-rate materials. But the shocking degree of damage that had been inflicted on her by Sillcock's airplane obviated those advantages. During her time in dry dock, pipes and valves and gauges and intakes and exhausts and tanks had been beaten back into shape, and engines and motors renovated. No less than 36 square yards of twisted plating had had to be replaced, re-bolted, and resoldered together.

Much of this work had been performed carelessly or quickly using low-quality material and lesser-skilled labor—a formula guaranteed to make *U-505* even creakier and more vulnerable than her less-damaged sisters.

There comes a point when an insurer simply writes off even the most beautifully made car that's been in a bad accident. Even if fixed at vast expense, it will never drive the same as it once did. In retrospect, given all that followed, it would have been better if the German Navy had done the same and scrapped *U-505* there and then.

III

During *U-505*'s mechanical travails, Knowles and Winn had noticed her erratic performance. It was difficult not to: From July 1 to September 30, *U-505* had cumulatively logged just 3,293 nautical miles, nearly 20 percent of them submerged to hide from predators in the Bay of Biscay. By comparison, a routine war patrol would normally log around 13,300 nautical miles, with only 4 percent of those miles traveled underwater.

With that in mind, in an October memorandum he shared with Knowles, Winn broke down the number of "false starts due to defects" among the Biscay U-boat fleet. The upshot was that since Black May a large number of U-boats had experienced a false start of some kind.

Most of the time these were one-off instances: A bit of hammering here or a replacement part there patched the problem. There were eight U-boats, however, that made two false starts, three that made three, and one that made four. These were indications of deeper issues. If these submarines had been cars, they'd have been called lemons.

But even among the lemons, one stood out for its sourness: By Commander Winn's reckoning, *U-505* had made no fewer than *seven* false starts. Ironically, the very attributes that earned such negative attention from the German side would in time make *U-505* extremely attractive to the other.

IV

In attributing this dubious record to *U-505*, Winn had miscounted, but only slightly. As of the end of September, *U-505* had in fact left Lorient six times. Her seventh attempt, however, would prove the most eventful.

On the same day, October 9, that Winn sent his false-starts memorandum to Knowles, Zschech set out once more. This time the voyage went surprisingly well, aside from a broken piston in one of the diesels. This occurrence was common enough that no one bothered to blame it on saboteurs.

Strangely, instead of his usual bluster and bullying, Zschech was exceedingly cautious and quiet. He took forever to cross the Bay of Biscay and insisted on traveling every mile safely underwater. Throughout, he was particularly "pale and nervous-looking," according to one crewman, who also thought the captain was showing signs of "deep depression." Among the men, there was hushed talk that Zschech had lost his nerve and couldn't perform even routine operations.

On October 24, matters came to a head when the hydrophone man picked up sounds of distant depth charges. The noises paused before starting up again—closer than before.

Zschech disappeared into his curtained bunk. At 7:48 p.m., a crewman dared to enter his lair to tell him that they were now also hearing the worrying sound of propellers churning the water. The enemy destroyers were coming closer.

Without acknowledging the report, Zschech walked zombiedly past the messenger—but instead of heading for the control room, he climbed the ladder to the conning tower. The control-room crew looked at each other in wonderment. What was Zschech doing up there? The only time the conning tower was used was when the captain wanted to look through the periscope, but they were presently 300 feet down.

Then they heard the distinctive *pings* of Allied sonar, reaching out for them in the dark. These sounds were horror-movie terrifying. From a distance, the men would hear the creepy *tick-tick* of fingernails being run over a comb. Then, as the hunters approached, a sound reminiscent of dry peas rattling in a can. And finally, when mortal danger was imminent, there was a deafening screech like an ancient train taking a curve too fast.

Immediately after that came the explosions. *U-505* rocked crazily as depth charges threw her side to side. In the control room, bulbs shattered, lights flickered, and objects flew as the men seized hold of anything solid to keep them upright. With her rudders useless, the boat became a bobbing cork at the mercy of the next concussive wave.

Now Zschech descended the ladder and entered the control room. His face was expressionless, lit only by the fluorescent paint of the dials and air ducts. Wordlessly, he shuffled through to the radio room. Hans Goebeler "could see his wide-open, unblinking eyes shine in the half-light."

Two more explosions broke Goebeler's stare and sent him sprawling. When he recovered, Goebeler looked over and saw Zschech slowly leaning over; perhaps he was concussed.

There was another *boom,* and Goebeler waited for the rush of water that heralded their doom. Instead there was only silence; the destroyers were reloading.

Now Goebeler saw Zschech lying face down on the deck, a shiny pool of blood encircling his head. He had shot himself with his pistol during the depth-charge attack. The captain had never relayed his reasons, but they were easy enough to guess.

Whereas the bulk of the crew rarely mused on the fates of their comrades on other U-boats—the assumption that "it'll happen to the other guy" is immutable in military history—Zschech was personally sensitive to the devastating scale of the losses among his peers. While the crew from one boat rarely associated with another one, so did not miss them much, Zschech had kept abreast of his fellow Olympians in the Class of 1936. That month alone, four of his friends had died.

Zschech may have had a foreboding that this time he was going to be "the other guy." His number was up, as it had already been for so many of his brothers-in-arms from the academy.

And why, if the end was at hand, should he endure the horror of their deaths? Unlike other captains, who interacted and socialized with the men—Meyer, his deputy, used to drink with them onshore—Zschech was isolated and friendless, especially after Thilo Bode's departure. He had no loyalty to his men, and they none anymore to him. The captain felt humiliated and embarrassed, too, by *U-505*'s inaction in the months when he wanted to be out there, like his comrades, fighting the enemy at a time of crisis. So when caught in an otherwise survivable fusillade of depth charges, he quit his men, his ship, and his life.

Zschech wasn't the first captain to have cracked: Heinrich Bleichrodt of *U-109*, an ace, had had to cut a mission short in January 1943 for what were gently called "psychological" reasons. And there were certainly other instances, such as Loewe's after the *Roamar* killings, that were covered up. In Zschech's case, however, he was desperate to avoid being relieved of duty or subjected to a court-martial. He was on thin enough ice as it was; a rumor that he had been unmanned by a depth-charge attack would have been the end of him.

By shooting himself, perhaps Zschech thought no one would ever know he hadn't died heroically as the boat entombed them all within an iron coffin. Instead he wound up being recorded as the only German U-boat commander known to have committed suicide at sea.

That's not quite accurate, though. He had only *tried* to end his own life—for Zschech was still alive.

The captain was carried to his bunk. Blood was spurting from a small bullet hole in his temple onto the thin mattress.

Zschech was groaning—and doing so loudly enough to attract attention from a keen-eared destroyer. He had to be quieted. Someone performed the necessary murder of suffocating him with a pillow.

V

Now in command, Zschech's executive officer, Paul Meyer, sprang into action. Despite ejecting two *Bold* capsules—countermeasures that released a cloud of bubbles and metal pieces to simulate a dead submarine—the destroyer captain above wasn't fooled by the ruse and launched another spread of depth charges.

These came close to finishing off *U-505*. But by running as silently as possible over the next hour, Meyer succeeded in extricating his boat from the killing field. At 9:29 p.m., he finally had time to enter the terse entry, "Kommandant dead," in the war diary.

Not until dawn, after evading their more dogged pursuers, did Meyer feel sufficiently confident to surface and recharge the batteries. At that point, Zschech's corpse was wrapped in a hammock, a weight was placed inside, and it was sewn up tight. Nobody in the control room saluted as it was borne upstairs to the bridge. Toward their old captain, the men felt nothing but anger—that, and a sense of betrayal for his abandoning them. Only decades later would those who had been there begin to feel an ounce of sorrow or a mite of pity for his demon-haunted soul.

Zschech was unceremoniously dumped overboard at 4:06 a.m., after which *U-505* turned for home. But her ordeal was hardly over. Through the coming days, with the enemy's blood up for the escaped submarine, *U-505* was hunted and depth-charged mercilessly. Those keeping count of the explosions lost track once they reached 300. Many times Meyer had no time to recharge the batteries fully; the men then had to lie motionless, conserving whatever meager reserves of oxygen were left.

Finally, after a horrible voyage, *U-505* entered the Suicide Stretch of Biscay on November 1. Even as they neared their pen, they were diverted to assist a stricken *U-123*.

Those aboard the battered *U-505* probably didn't realize it, but *U-123*, at the time under Reinhard Hardegen, had led the *Drumbeat* assault on

Harald Lange, third commander of U-505.

the United States in January 1942. Just twenty-three months earlier, the Allies had been at their feet. Now they were at their throat.

VI

The arrival of their new captain on November 18 gave the men of *U-505* something to cheer. The first impression they got of Harald Lange was that at six feet, he was taller by a head than any of them. The second was that at forty years old, Lange was close to double the age of most sub skippers these days—in fact, he was the oldest officer in the entire U-boat combat fleet. And the third, that he was a taller, older version of their beloved Captain Loewe.

Unlike Zschech, who expected unquestioning obedience, Captain Lange led by example and confidence, as Loewe had. He chain-smoked—not because he needed to relax, noted one crewman, but because he was already so relaxed that he could stylishly dangle a cigarette from his lip without drawing on it.

Lange was not a professional submariner, nor had he attended the Naval Academy full-time. But as a native of the port city of Hamburg, he was a natural mariner: In peacetime he'd gone to sea as a regular hand, rising to captain a "monsoon boat"—a merchant steamer that plied the tropical waters off West Africa and sailed the ancient trade routes of the Indian Ocean.

In the mid-1930s, Lange served as a Navy Reservist and an officer with the Hamburg-America Line. As a result, he was quite familiar with Americans and the United States. He often visited his best friend in Indiana and had met his future wife, a German immigrant, in New York.

When war erupted, he was posted for a time on a minesweeper and then a patrol boat before being transferred as executive officer to *U-180*, one of a handful of U-boats sent to the far reaches of the world.

On a secret mission in April 1943, *U-180* had transferred the Indian nationalist, Subhas Chandra Bose, to a Japanese submarine, which deposited him in Sumatra to train an anti-British army composed of Indian POWs. In exchange, *U-180* brought home two tons of gold ingots as payment for German weapons technology.

Such special operations were a far cry from taking command of *U-505*, but this time Dönitz had chosen well. If anyone could restore the crew's sagging morale, it was Lange, who had recently served for a month as captain of *U-180*.

But key for Dönitz, as well, was Lange's documented loyalty to the Reich. As Member No. 3,450,040, he had joined the Nazi Party on May 1, 1934—a mere fifteen months after Hitler's elevation to the chancellorship. So Lange wasn't one of the *Alte Kämpfer*—the bloodied "Old Fighters" who'd been with the Party in the 1920s—but neither was he a late-1930s entrant of the kind mocked as nothing but crass opportunists.

The timing of Lange's membership was important. In 1934, there had been a push for merchant mariners and Reservists to join either the paramilitary SA (the Brownshirts) or the Party in order to secure their jobs. Lange was just one among numerous Hamburg-American Line officers to sign up for the latter.

Lange doesn't seem to have been a very active Party member. Aboard *U-505*, few were even aware of his affiliation, possibly because, following Wehrmacht regulations then in effect, he may have surrendered it upon being activated for war duty. But membership, even former membership, nevertheless had its privileges.

In Lange's case, one of those perks was a mental check mark from his superiors that he was one of the good ones. In 1943–44, when the war was not going entirely to Germany's advantage, Dönitz had begun Nazifying the Navy in line with Goebbels's demand to prepare for Total War. In fact, the grand admiral himself would dispense with tradition and join the Party in February 1944. Outward allegiance to the Führer had become paramount, and would turn even more so after Colonel Claus von Stauffenberg's attempt on his life at the Wolf's Lair on July 20.

Dönitz's subordination of the Navy to Party imperatives—military salutes were replaced by arm-raised *Heil Hitlers* at this time to demonstrate loyalty—was soon readily apparent within the submarine corps. U-boat captains of Lange's "generation" were quite different from the two that had preceded them.

First had been the interwar professionals such as Loewe—traditionalist holdovers from the *ancien régime* Imperial Navy. Then had come the youthful, thrusting phalanx of Zschechs, bred if not born in the Nazi era.

The former had almost all retired, the latter were mostly dead, and now there were Langes as replacements: Solid loyalists of proven pedigree, the faithful old retainers of the Reich, they could be relied on to Hold the Fort and Die Draped in the Flag while Dönitz urgently developed the new U-boats that would allow the Führer to strike back against his enemies.

VII

For the third time in as many years, the skipper's sigil on the conning tower of *U-505* was scraped off and replaced. Long gone was Loewe's axe, and now so too were Zschech's Olympic rings. When *U-505* set off on her first patrol on Christmas Day 1943, she did so under Lange's painted-on seashell.

Three days later, as *U-505* slipped through the Bay of Biscay in a cold rain, she was ordered on a rescue mission: A group of German destroyers and patrol boats had been in a firefight with the British, and *U-505* and three of her sisters were diverted to pick up survivors. "Beware of enemy aircraft," U-Boat Command added in a perhaps unnecessary postscript.

Lange succeeded in fishing thirty-four half-frozen men of the torpedo boat *T-25* out of the choppy water. None had been on a submarine before, and nearly all of them devoted their next few hours to vomiting from the U-boat's violent yaw.

Lange had in the meantime received orders that *U-505*'s new home port was to be Brest. Lange arrived in the harbor on January 2, 1944. By now their guests had recovered their spirits and were describing the sensuous delights of the port to their new friends. As Lange maneuvered his way into the reassuringly huge and inviolate concrete pens, the crew and many of the survivors crowded the upper deck, waving and cheering when they saw that the Navy had done them proud.

For the first time in more than six months, there was a grand gathering ashore. Commanders of the U-Boat and Torpedo Boat flotillas were there, as well as newsmen and photographers and even a brass band. They were heroes.

Below, the remaining *T-25* survivors jostled to be the first to climb the ladder from the control room to the bridge. But one ascending sailor lost his footing and fell back down, happening to land on the helmsman's rudder control at the very moment when *U-505* was making her final approach to dock. The U-boat lurched to starboard; her right diving-plane fin ground sickeningly against the concrete and was torn off. Inside was felt only a momentary shudder, but 1,200 tons of metal mass had collided very slowly with an immovable object.

The damage was serious: Aside from the lost fin, its shaft had been bent and needed replacing. The nearest one was in Bordeaux, 400 miles away, and subject to ambushes as it was transported through Resistance-infested territory. Then, predictably, fixing the shaft took much longer than predicted: two and a half months, to be precise. Not until March 16—her departure delayed yet one more day to avoid the cursed Ides of March—was *U-505* able to depart on what would be her final patrol.

VIII

The crew certainly felt a twinge of apprehension about what lay in their future. A couple of weeks later, as they headed south toward Liberia, they rendezvoused with *U-154*, which had been on patrol for the last two months, to pass over the latest edition of the Enigma codebooks as well as a spare copy of the newest Address Book.

It was then, remembered Hans Decker, that their battle-scarred comrades told them "for the first time of the new Allied hunter-killer groups, composed of small aircraft carriers and destroyers, that were raising havoc with our U-boats."

FOURTEEN

THE CAN-DO KING

I

When Captain Dan Gallery was released from his Icelandic prison in June 1943, he felt that he was owed restitution. He had served his time and become a trusty, but had garnered few of that job's privileges. Instead, he had missed his chance to command destroyers during the Great U-Boat Hunt of May. Worse still, after being told that he was to take charge of one of the new escort carriers, USS *Guadalcanal*, he had assumed that he was to be sent to the Pacific, where most CVEs went—and where the real action was to be found.

But no, he was to take her from Astoria, Oregon, down the West Coast and through the Panama Canal to the Atlantic. Well, orders were orders. Gallery resolved to make the best of his situation during his ship's shakedown cruise.

The good thing about taking over a brand-new ship was that it came with a brand-new crew. Some captains would have despaired, but when Gallery discovered that 80 percent of his men had never seen saltwater, he rubbed his hands in glee.

Unlike old lags, green sailors don't know anything. This assortment of "young farmhands, shoe clerks, and high school boys" would do whatever you told them to do, Gallery said, no matter how crazy—because they assumed it was part of everyday routine.

Taking advantage of their naivete, Gallery invented a new exercise involving the stringing of heavy chains from *Guadalcanal's* stern to the bow of a trailing destroyer. In the U.S. Navy, he claimed, it was common for big ships to tow small ones; hence the need for practice. "I didn't say that the thing I had in mind here was eventually taking a U-boat in tow," recalled Gallery, who suspected that even newbies might have thought the idea *too* crazy.

But finally they were in Norfolk, Virginia, and ready to leave. There, four destroyers joined *Guadalcanal,* together forming what was being termed a "hunter-killer" task group.

These were essentially the brainchild of Knowles, who, fresh from his victory against the U-tankers, had proposed creating "super-killer groups" that would, as King had always dreamed, focus on "sweep[ing] areas of U-boat concentrations" *independently* of convoys.

Before then, carriers such as *Bogue* had been, at least nominally, attached to convoys for air protection; Knowles wanted to unchain them so they could roam freely, like maritime knights-errant set upon a quest. "Our little ships used to be a defensive arm; now they are an attack weapon," one CVE captain explained to a journalist. These days, "we try for kills." To that end, their commanders would operate on their own initiative during the hunting and killing phases, but they would be directed to the hot zone by Knowles himself.

II

Just before departure, Gallery distributed a memo to every man in his mini-fleet.

First, "the motto of this ship will be 'Can Do,' meaning that we will take any tough job that is given to us and run away with it. The tougher the job, the better we'll like it." And hence Gallery was instantly dubbed, or perhaps dubbed himself, "the Can-Do King."

Second, learn how to do your job. No excuses. "Pretty soon we will be out where it rains bombs and it will be too late to learn."

And third, most importantly: "This ship will be employed on dangerous duty. We will either sink the enemy or get sunk ourselves depending on how well we learn our jobs now and do our jobs later."

But he added, just in case: "Anyone who prefers safer duty see me and I will arrange to have him transferred."

No young American male, as Gallery well knew, would hazard inviting the shame and mockery that would accompany an admission that he just couldn't handle the red-blooded adventure that came with hunting subs on the high seas.

It was thus a happy Task Group, if "cocky and unproven," that embarked on its maiden voyage on January 5—three days after *U-505* had been damaged at Brest. As they got underway, Gallery insisted that the chaplain, Father Weldon, pronounce "a nonsectarian prayer to which Protestants, Catholics, Jews, and Moslems could all say 'Amen.'" Every man turned to face the bridge to murmur his profound gratitude to the Lord, and Dan Gallery, for allowing him to participate in the great battles to come.

III

Their prayers were answered less than two weeks later, albeit with Knowles's off-screen "hand of God" pointing them uncannily in the right direction. On January 16, as Gallery discreetly put it, he was given "reason to believe that in this particular area at this particular time, we might find something."

That particular area was a position 500 miles northwest of the Azores, that particular time was just before sundown, and that something they found was *U-544*, one of the very few tankers left after Knowles had finished with them. Gallery caught the milk cow on the surface, with *U-516* sucking on her hundred-foot-long rubber-hosed teat. Another submarine, *U-129*, patiently waited her turn nearby.

Gallery's bombers barged in "like a couple of hawks in a chicken-yard" and plastered the area with a new weapon—3.5-inch rockets—and depth charges. *U-129* managed to get away, but Gallery's Avengers killed the tanker and injured her calf. It was an excellent score for a first-timer.

Gallery, like all the other task-group commanders, was never told anything about the true source of what he called the "red-hot dope" he was sent each day from some unremarkable office designated "F-21" at Main Navy. All he knew was that there "was a Commander Ken Knowles in Washington who ran this submarine estimate thing," he recalled more than three decades later. "He was just a soothsayer. He could put himself in the position of a German skipper and just figure out what that guy was going to do, and where he would go. He was absolutely uncanny in his predictions."

Privately, Gallery suspected at the time that this obviously absurd tale of Knowles's Wizard of Oz–like omniscience was intended to disguise the fact that the Allies ran a huge network of secret agents in Occupied France that passed on top-grade information. That was probably, he assumed, the same source of Commander Robert Lee Norden's inside tips on U-boat gossip. So maybe, just maybe, this "Ken Knowles" was as imaginary as his colleague. Which meant the likeliest explanation, Gallery thought, was that the tip-off for the refueling location had come to Spymaster-General Knowles, if he even existed, via a "gal in Lorient who may have a lot of serious sins to answer for at the Last Judgment."

IV

After that bright start, U-boats made themselves scarce for the rest of *Guadalcanal*'s first cruise. In their off time, in keeping with his dedication to doing the unexpected to catch his opponent unawares, Gallery tried something new to Atlantic aircraft carriers: night flying.

This was the most dangerous type of operation, but it was critical to get right. Until then, air patrols had started at first light and the last plane had returned home, without fail, by sunset. The U-boats had gotten wise to that ritual and had begun to stay underwater all day, surfacing to recharge their batteries only at night. Gallery resolved to give them a surprise during his next cruise.

After *Guadalcanal* and her destroyers again departed Norfolk on March 7, 1944—a little more than a week before Lange's leaving Brest in the repaired *U-505*—Gallery ordered that beginning from the first full moon, and with *Guadalcanal* "lit up like a barroom on Saturday night," his Avengers would practice nighttime takeoffs and landings from a pitching carrier deck. The boys "were jittery and they made some of the wildest passes" Gallery had ever seen, but on each successive night, as he dimmed the lights and the moon waned a little more, they got a little better. Within a few weeks, they could fly in pitch-blackness.

This training would prove invaluable in the small hours of April 8, when, after being alerted by Knowles to a U-boat in the vicinity, Gallery sent up his squadron in the hope of catching the marauder unawares. The gamble paid off when Avengers spotted *U-515* on the surface, recharging beneath a full moon.

U-515 was a sister ship to *U-505*. Though about six months younger, she had more than made up for her lack of maturity. And unlike *U-505*, *U-515* had had only one captain—but what a captain he was.

Together with his comrade Peter Cremer of *U-333*, Kapitänleutnant Werner Henke was the very last of the Old Guard: They were the only two Atlantic veterans of 1941 still alive and fighting. Whenever they had a chance, they met to talk shop at the Hotel Claridge, the upscale hotel off Paris's Champs-Élysées that was reserved for generals and holders of the Knight's Cross. Henke and Cremer, of course, both had one.

Among the U-boat men, tales were told of Henke's legendary patrol in 1943, when over the course of a single night he had sunk seven ships. Now Henke was the one being hunted at night.

But this wolf wasn't going to be easy prey. Once Gallery's hunter-killer group arrived, Henke was driven down by the Avengers but evaded his pursuers over and over again in a masterly display of command skill. This happened, according to Gallery, three or four times. He'd never seen anything like it.

Losing patience, Captain Gallery ordered his destroyers to rush ahead and hound their quarry mercilessly. "OK, hop to it, Big Boy," he radioed them. "Bring us some prisoners." From seven in the morning until the early afternoon, they "were working this guy over" with depth charges and Hedgehogs. Henke, Gallery wasn't too grudging to admit, "was a hell of a sub skipper...He knew all the tricks of the trade. He was down at six hundred feet. He was squirming around and would do all sorts of tricks on us."

For every sonar *ping,* Henke released a bubble decoy; for every depth charge, he dived deeper; for every Hedgehog salvo, he sharply turned. But he couldn't escape the noose forever.

At about 2 p.m., with his batteries exhausted and having sustained damage to his ballast tanks and oil pipes, Henke threw in the towel. In great style, he surfaced right in the middle of the task group. As Henke peeked over the conning-tower hatch, he knew it was over. "All hands, abandon boat!" he shouted down.

According to Gallery, who was five miles away on *Guadalcanal,* "a deadly rattlesnake had just reared his head from the depths—ready to strike, as far as we knew! So we let him have it." The commander of the four destroyers on the scene shouted over the radio, "Sub! Sub is on the surface. Sink him. SINK HIM. Shoot everything you've got!"

And they did. "All destroyers opened up with everything they had in their lockers, depth charges, torpedoes, four-inch guns, and 20mm AA guns." Gallery feared that the U-boat might unleash a close-range salvo of six torpedoes, and in such circumstances "you don't count the number of men who pop out of the forward and after escape hatches and dive over the side before issuing the order to cease firing. You watch the snake to see if you have broken its neck."

As *U-515*'s crew struggled in the water, the shooting mercilessly continued for another four minutes. But as the flooding *U-515* slowly, inexorably disappeared beneath the waves, the firing died down, as if to pay respect.

Sixteen men were lost, but the rest—including Captain Henke—were picked up by the destroyers. Gallery's men had met a worthy adversary.

V

Following custom, Henke was kept separate from the rest of his crew, which was divided into a hierarchy of junior officers, petty officers, and seamen, with each group being allotted separate, walled-off cells in the brig. Officials back home at OP-16-Z—the branch of the U.S. Navy that handled POW interrogations—insisted on this arrangement: The aim was to prevent the crewmen from being menaced into silence by their superiors, while also hampering any efforts to coordinate stories among the upper ranks.

Well, OP-16-Z had its interests, and Gallery had his. The POW interrogators in the former sought to extract information that could be passed upstairs to Knowles, around the back to the cryptanalysts at OP-20-G, or sideways to OP-16-W—the psychological-warfare unit running the "Commander Norden" operation.

Gallery, however, wanted only to know how to prevent a submarine from sinking so that he could capture the next one. Nothing had changed since that late-night, raise-the-glass conversation with his Catalina pilots in Iceland in August 1942, when they had first conjured up the idea. He was still driven, like Custer or Nelson, by a thirst for glory, but in Gallery's case it was whetted by impatience. He had performed a valuable role in Iceland, but taking one for the team doesn't earn you immortality. In Gallery's mind, his career had stalled in Iceland; now, at last, he was going to seize the opportunity not just to catch up to his peers in the Pacific, but accelerate far past them—and have fun while he was doing it.

Gallery understood that he was under the gun. He certainly wasn't the only captain out there hunting for the ultimate scalp. He already knew that the British had captured *U-570*—he himself had toured her before heading to Iceland—but that had been back in the summer of 1941. And he had almost certainly heard that the Canadians and the British had taken *U-744* following an intense thirty-hour fight on March 6, just a month earlier.

He was *not* aware, though, that the Brits had also bagged *U-110* in May 1941, as well as *U-559* in October 1942. On both occasions, the Enigma machines they took from them had helped accomplish Bletchley Park's penetrations of the code. The reason Gallery (or virtually anyone else) knew nothing about *U-110* and *U-559* was that their capture had been kept strictly secret.

There were, however, two major differences between these successes and what Gallery wanted to do. First, none had involved Americans, which left the door wide-open for an ambitious patriot hankering to score a victory for the home side. And second, in every case but that of *U-570* (which was public knowledge, even to the Germans), *the submarines had sunk very soon after surrendering*; either they had sustained heavy damage, been scuttled, or a combination of both. Briefly "capturing" them, it seemed, was the relatively easy part. The seemingly impossible bit was to keep them afloat and make them yours.

Here, though, Gallery had been given at least a week with the prisoners before he had to hand them over for processing. That was plenty of time to get them relaxed enough to confirm the best ways of saving a stricken boat.

VI

It was the golden rule never to allow a U-boat to fall into enemy hands. Gallery—who'd been raised on the story of the valiant cry of the mortally wounded Captain James Lawrence in the War of 1812, "Don't give up the ship!"—naturally assumed that the Germans were as concerned as Americans with the dishonor of surrendering a vessel intact. And that was certainly true.

What he had no idea about was that to U-Boat Command, *nothing* was more important than ensuring that the priceless Enigma machine and its codebooks went down with the ship. Whenever a U-boat reported that it was facing death, Dönitz wanted to hear one last message in Morse—*YYY*—before the inevitable. This was the signal for confirming that "Confidential books, especially cipher material, have been destroyed."

Often, however, this was a problem that solved itself: Badly wounded U-boats ended up on the seabed, where their secrets lay well beyond any mortal's reach. Only if they surfaced to save the crew, however, might they require a helping destructive hand.

The approved technique for scuttling a U-boat was to detonate a string of fourteen five-pound explosive charges along the keel. Only senior engineers could perform this task, as the charges were hard to find in the dark and setting the timers demanded a cool nerve.

Most captains preferred to avoid this method, not least because the charges actually detonated only about half the time. If seawater had seeped in they would not work, and maintenance checks on their health were few and far between.

A surer method was to flood the boat's diving cells—large tanks filled with air located outside the pressure hull. Done forcefully, as happened during a crash-dive—but leaving the hatches open to allow tons of water to rush in—would sink a submarine in less than sixty seconds. But it also doomed any crewman not already swimming away from the wreck.

Finally, there was the tried-and-true technique of opening her sea-cocks. These were a couple of large, wheeled valves (Americans called them Kingston valves) that controlled the intake of seawater from outside. A pipe ran from each to a strainer (which filtered out sand, seaweed, and other gunk) before ending at a pump, which shunted the now-cleanish water to sinks, a freshwater distiller, and the engine room to cool the machinery.

The problem was that, unlike exploding charges or flooding the diving cells, the Kingston valves took time to work. Owing to their small diameter and the necessity of opening as many fittings as possible the length of the boat, water did not gush in—it trickled. In a crisis when minutes counted, an hour would be needed to sink the vessel.

None of this was exactly a state secret, and for the crewmen of *U-515* it seemed harmless enough information to divulge in exchange for a pack of Lucky Strikes or an American hamburger and fries.

But it was news to Gallery. And a mystery.

VII

Why hadn't Henke scuttled his command? Well, because he hadn't needed to. The ferocious barrage unleashed by the destroyers and aircraft *after* he surfaced had ensured a fast death for *U-515*. So, mused Gallery, "if we hadn't been quite so bloody minded about sinking her," *U-515* might very well have lingered on, injured but alive, while Henke and a few brave souls desperately flooded her as the rest of the crew jumped overboard.

Gallery had grasped something no one else had. "I was pretty familiar with the habits of submarines by this time," he said, "and I knew that when you got one cornered and hammered him with depth charges and punished him so much that he figured he was finished and going to sink, it was standard operational procedure for submarines to blow their tanks and come up and abandon ship, give the crew a chance to get overboard so they could be rescued, and [then] open the scuttling valves [seacocks] and sink the sub."

Blazingly clear in hindsight to Gallery was that Captain Henke had surfaced not to fight it out bloodied fang and claw, but because he wanted his crew to live.

But Henke had miscalculated. The depth charging may have wounded *U-515*, but by no means was she "finished." She still had a lot of life in her—as did, miraculously, any German submarine on her apparently last legs. They were tougher and meaner than they looked. During a recent attack on *U-744*, for instance, it had required the combined efforts of no fewer than seven ships to finally take her down. In *U-515*'s case, mused Gallery, "we had thrown everything but the galley ranges at [her] before she up-ended and sank."

Digging deeper, Gallery found that his destroyer *Chatelain*, for instance, had opened fire at 3:05 p.m., ceased four minutes later, and watched *U-515* disappear at 3:12.

If *Chatelain* (and all the others) hadn't shot up the submarine, he realized, there was every chance that *U-515* would have stayed afloat for a time even after Henke, a gold-star skipper, had abandoned her as a goner.

That seven-minute interval from 3:05 to 3:12 would have been critical to saving the patient. The paramedics in this case would have been a boarding party—trained, armed to the teeth, and prepared to go—that

Chatelain *attacks the ailing* U-515.

crossed over, entered the abandoned U-boat, and performed emergency surgery to plug any major leaks, empty diving cells, shut off Kingston valves, and disarm demolition charges.

Easier said than done, especially if there were pockets of Germans still on board willing to die for the Führer in a firefight. Gallery knew that U-boats kept a locker of small arms aboard, and since nobody wanted to be shooting guns at close quarters in a narrow metal tube, it would be a priority to induce any fanatics to leave of their own accord well before the boarding party arrived.

All the way back to Norfolk, recalled Gallery, "a fantastic idea kept thrusting itself forward and would not be swept under the rug."

VIII

Guadalcanal put into Norfolk on April 26, 1944. A week later, Gallery dropped by Main Navy to see an old friend, Captain Henri Smith-Hutton. The two men had served together on the *Idaho* years earlier, but the Lavatory Man wasn't there just to catch up on the good old days.

Smith-Hutton was currently Admiral Ernest King's Assistant Chief of Staff for Combat Intelligence. Gallery, he later said, ran his "capture a German submarine" idea by him, and much to his surprise Smith-Hutton didn't reject it outright as mad.

Instead, Smith-Hutton took Gallery to the Technical Intelligence Section (OP-16-PT), where they gave him the latest internal schematics of whatever was known about the Type VII and Type IX U-boats. Gallery had gleaned what he could about the inside of the submarines from his prisoners, but having a map would ease a boarding party's task as they rushed to shore up a listing submarine.

There was one other person whom Smith-Hutton thought Gallery should meet. First, though, he had to be, as Gallery put it, "processed," "briefed," "indoctrinated," and "duly checked to see if I was a good security risk." Only then could Smith-Hutton take him down the hall to F-21.

IX

As mentioned earlier, Gallery already knew Kenneth Knowles's name from the daily "red-hot dope" on U-boat positions that came straight, he quaintly believed, from America's web of secret agents and beguiling seductresses in France. In actuality the inside tips were sanitized *Ultra* intelligence, supplemented by Knowles's predictions. Gallery was probably surprised to discover that he was in fact a real person and that F-21 wasn't made-up.

No matter. After Smith-Hutton introduced the two, Gallery excitedly told Knowles about his grand plan to steal a U-boat. Knowles's reaction was not exactly enthusiastic. Quite the opposite, in fact: He was horrified. It was the worst idea he'd heard in a long time. It was the kind of thing that Action Men cheerfully propose while Brain Men recoil at the sheer folly on display.

Knowles was always willing to stretch *Ultra* to the limit, but at least he knew there *was* a limit. Despite his differences with Winn, he was generally as careful as his mentor in covering his tracks and making it appear as if the Americans had accidentally stumbled upon a U-tanker or had used easily attributable clues, such as radio direction-finding, to locate one.

Gallery, on the other hand, was ignorant of the ramifications of what he was asking and what was at stake. He was mystified as to why Knowles was so reluctant to tell him exactly where to find a random U-boat to heist. He'd assumed that it would be a simple request: Just give him the location, thankee very much, and he'd be on his merry way.

But it wasn't as straightforward as that.

X

Allied planners were at that moment putting the finishing touches on Operation *Overlord*, the invasion of Europe scheduled for early June—about a month away. Knowles knew, if Gallery didn't, that Admiral Dönitz would be relying on Enigma to coordinate defensive naval operations in the English Channel in an effort to sink troop transports and supply vessels.

What Gallery's proposed *Boy's Own* escapade threatened to do, however, was expose at the very worst possible time the Allied penetration of Dönitz's secure communications.

Berlin was bound to be hypersensitive at this moment. Dönitz would be watching for the slightest twitch upon the thread. If he felt even the merest suspicion that one of his boats had *not* been lost with all hands along with its Enigma machine and codebooks, he would instantly change the encryption settings for the entire U-boat fleet and introduce new security procedures—thereby blinding Allied intelligence on the very eve of D-Day.

In 1942, when Dönitz had switched to the M4 and *Triton*, he had virtually blacked out Bletchley Park for almost a year. Now, in 1944, the stakes were much higher. When *Overlord* finally kicked off, if Knowles did not know where all the U-boats were, the consequences would be devastating.

XI

But...

If Gallery managed to pull this stunt off, the potential payoff was surely worth the risk.

For one thing, the Americans would gain access to the latest Enigma machine, its most recent keys and documentation, and the super-encoded Naval Grid references right in the nick of time for *Overlord*. The American letter-crunching bombes could begin their work without delay. For the first time, they'd be not one but several steps ahead of U-Boat Command.

Another bonus: acquiring a U-boat equipped with the most modern radar and hydrophone gear, and the most up-to-date torpedoes. Research on countermeasures would be massively accelerated.

And so Knowles relented—with one stipulation. *Gallery could have the glory of storming his submarine, but no one could ever know about it.*

The U-boat had to disappear. And not just the boat, either.

If the survivors were brought to the United States, as the crew of *U-515* had been, they had rights accorded by the 1929 Geneva Convention on Prisoners of War. They were, among other things, permitted to send letters and cards, as well as receive packages of clothing, medicine, Bibles, musical instruments, and food.

All correspondence was subject to the censor's black marker, but that didn't matter. If a single postcard containing a single sentence from a single crewman hitherto assumed dead got through by accident to someone's aunt Gertrud in Germany, it would alert Dönitz that his "lost with all hands" U-boat might not be so lost after all.

So if Gallery did manage to "kill" a U-boat, he was made to promise, her entire crew would have to die with her.

XII

Gallery instantly agreed to the terms of the deal and returned to *Guadalcanal* to await Knowles's signal to give hot pursuit.

Fortunately, Knowles just happened to have the ideal candidate for a high-seas heist. Since March he had been watching a lone boat cautiously making her way out of the Bay of Biscay and hugging the African coast to the Monrovia (Liberia) and Freetown (Sierra Leone) area. Far enough off the beaten track, then, not to be immediately missed.

She was an interesting one, this *U-505*. There had been the quirky behavior the year before that had first brought her to his and Winn's attention: all those ins and outs, stops and starts, and back-and-forths. According to the Working Fiction, she was likely, then, to have once been the victim of a serious attack and had been suffering mechanical problems ever since. That supposition tallied with her unglamorous assignment to patrol the waters off West Africa: *U-505*, it was clear, was not a spry, crack combat submarine captained by an ace, but a near-retiree afflicted with the aches and pains of old age. Just as lions select not the strongest but the weakest gazelle to chase, *U-505*'s very creakiness made her a temptingly vulnerable target.

Equally intriguing was the disappearance of Captain Zschech. All Knowles had ever been able to glean came from an American intelligence report, based on sparse intercepts, which noted only that Zschech "did not return on *U-505* to Lorient, early Nov. '43. Missing from boat." U-boat captains did not just vanish into thin air. Something either very bad or very odd, or perhaps both, had happened on this submarine.

Still, despite the inexplicably prolonged interlude in Brest since January, *U-505* now seemed to have returned to the straight and narrow. Someone new had been put in charge—Lange was his name; no background on him—and she had embarked on her African voyage with no more of the interruptions that had cursed Zschech's command.

Even so, *U-505*'s bad luck continued to dog her. Six or seven weeks into her patrol, little had happened. Knowles felt Lange's frustration as he read his intercepted messages noting that he had "observed nothing except a few fishing boats" or that there had been "no traffic." An entire month elapsed in which not a single ship was seen. And when finally the dry spell was broken, it was by an untouchably neutral Portuguese passenger liner.

Just as bad, frequent air alarms set off by the radar detector had prevented Lange from fully recharging his batteries, meaning that he could spend less and less time underwater—which of course forced him to spend more and more time on the surface, where he became the target of ever more frequent air alarms. A vicious circle, all in all, for poor old Lange.

By mid-May, *U-505*'s captain realized that his had been a wasted patrol. Low on food and fuel, if not torpedoes, Lange reported to U-Boat Command on May 14 that he was off Freetown and "Returning

21/5"—May 21. Just five hours later, the naval intelligence analysts in OP-20-G informed Knowles that their bombes had decrypted the message.

The very next day, May 15, Gallery's *Guadalcanal* task group, designated 22.3, hurriedly departed for Africa.

May 21 was less than a week away. That would not give *Guadalcanal* enough time to cross the Atlantic before *U-505* turned for home. But if Knowles guided Gallery to her predicted track back to France, maybe she could be intercepted—without anyone in Berlin the wiser.

ACT 3

"BUSINESS IN GREAT WATERS"

(Psalm 107:23)

FIFTEEN

NINETEEN MINUTES

I

June 4 was an otherwise routine day aboard USS *Guadalcanal*. An inspection had found toilet seats "busted" in the forward head and a number of plugs inexplicably missing from the washbasins. An anonymous felon had left a bucketful of clothes on deck and someone else had failed to empty the trash cans.

For the men's cultural edification, Pharmacist's Mate 2nd Class Scherrebeck was to lecture on Gershwin's *Rhapsody in Blue* at 7 p.m., to be followed by a movie (title to be announced) at 8:30. For anyone who'd seen it before, there was always a poker or cribbage game going.

All of that was scrubbed when at 11:09 a.m. Raymond Watts, a sonarman on the destroyer *Chatelain*, heard an echo 800 yards away. The sound was so sharp it startled him, Watts thinking that "maybe what happened was they had let one of our own ships cross the bow." A minute later, "Frenchy"—*Chatelain's* call sign—radioed Captain Dan Gallery ("Bluejay") on the carrier: "Investigating possible sound contact."

Now, there were "possible sound contacts" all the time—whales were the usual culprits, and sometimes the unfortunate creatures were bombed by overeager pilots—but Gallery knew in his bones that this was *U-505*, the submarine his Task Group 22.3 had been playing cat and mouse with for weeks.

It had been a tiring hunt. Nearly three weeks earlier, Knowles had amazed him by "predicting" that *U-505* would be heading back to France as of May 21, and the Can-Do King had overexcitedly promised his destroyer skippers: WILL BE HOT ON TRAIL TOMORROW.

But the trail turned out to be cold. Neither hide nor hair of the wily *U-505* had been detected. By May 26, when his chief engineer, Earl Trosino, warned him that they were running low on fuel, Gallery had been forced to order his small fleet to operate on half-power to husband its reserves. At this rate, he'd be back at home before *U-505* was.

That same day, Captain Harald Lange received an alert from U-Boat Command to be "particularly cautious in the area within a radius of 500 miles around Square Green KO 180. Count on appearance of land and carrier based anti-submarine groups."

The signal was soon cracked by the American bombes and passed on to Knowles, who worked hard to estimate the location of the grid reference "Green KO 180" to forward to Gallery.

From these isolated clues and his honed intuition, Knowles succeeded in placing *U-505* within 267 miles of what would turn out to be her actual position. He had done the best he could under the circumstances. There were few radio-direction-finding stations in West Africa, the Naval Grid out there remained mostly a blank, and this Lange figure was not a carelessly chatty skipper.

In staying silent, Lange was acting out of an abundance of caution for good reason: He had, after all, been warned that a hunter-killer group was out there intent on hunting and killing him. Confirming his fears, the radar detector repeatedly shrieked warnings of nearby aircraft throughout the night of May 29–30. Ironically, though, those were not Gallery's birds: The *Guadalcanal* that day was steaming some 600 miles southwest of *U-505*. They were in fact harmless, unarmed American transport planes whose pilots would have been hard-pressed to recognize a U-boat up close.

The crash-dives nevertheless exhausted the crew. The first had been at 10:16 p.m. on May 29, the second at 12:02 a.m., then another exactly an hour later, a fourth at 3:12 a.m., and a fifth at 5:48 a.m. Enough was enough.

Convinced by the frequency of the alarms that *Guadalcanal* must be right on his tail, Lange, who was heading northwards, decided to make a sharp right and jog 84 miles due east toward the African coast to get away from her. He would do the opposite of what any carrier commander would expect him to do—keep to the sanctuary of open sea—and as an old Africa hand Lange knew those shallow littoral waters well.

For once, Knowles had been outwitted: His Working Fiction had turned out to be, well, a non-working one. Because Lange, with but a month's record as captain on an obscure Indian Ocean U-boat, was not the conventional product of a naval academy and possessed real-world experience of which Knowles was unaware, he'd been able to pull off the unpredictable.

On June 1, accordingly, Knowles sent Gallery his updated estimate that *U-505* was about 175 miles away and still proceeding north. The *Guadalcanal* group accordingly burned valuable fuel converging on that position as fast as possible.

Lange, however, was now actually far to Gallery's east and following the African coast some 60 miles out. Had he kept to that track, Task Group 22.3 and *U-505* would have continued north toward Europe unwittingly *parallel* to one another, and Lange's subterfuge would have succeeded. On June 2, for instance, Gallery was still 280 miles southwest of Lange, and none of his planes had even sniffed the U-boat.

Lady Luck (or Lady Misfortune, depending on one's perspective) intervened when, on June 3, Lange decided he was safe enough to arc west into the Atlantic Ocean. Gallery, however, continued along his original path. Lange's new heading had therefore set hunter and prey on an inadvertent collision course—at an intersection point almost exactly where Knowles had predicted, and only a day later than forecast.

The Working Fiction had, somehow, become Working Nonfiction.

II

It *must* have been Fate, even if, as Gallery had to admit, to impartial observers it certainly might look as if he and Lange had come together by a succession of "fantastically improbable" events, and what should not have happened had, in fact, happened.

But, as Gallery later pointed out, their meeting "was much too improbable to just happen that way as a result of pure chance." It was God, he surmised, who nudged the dice His creatures were rolling to make them come up the way He wanted.

The captain nevertheless continued to nurse the uncomfortable suspicion that perhaps the human factor was more important than he was willing to grant. Ultimately, his rendezvous with *U-505* had come down to a single decision that he, not He, had made at an afternoon conference on June 3.

It was then that Gallery had ruled, against all advice and evidence, that he would extend the search for one more day.

Years later, Gallery would say that these conferences, always held in the flagship's Combat Information Center (CIC), were the toughest part of his job.

Here, in this semi-darkened room with its never-ending pings and rings and dings, and barraged with conflicting opinions every which

Guadalcanal's *Combat Information Center (CIC) on June 3, 1944.*

way, the captain had to decide whether to chase an ambiguous blip emanating from what *might* be a U-boat—or, just as likely, a piece of flotsam or even an Allied submarine. In this case, Gallery didn't have even an ambiguous blip.

What he did have was a dozen pairs of eyes on him, awaiting an answer.

The sensible thing to do would have been to drop the pursuit. To that end, in the CIC meeting Chief Engineer Trosino had urgently warned Gallery that "we've *got* to quit fooling here and get in to Casablanca; I'm getting down near the safe limit of my fuel." Having to summon tugs to haul in a fleet that had needlessly run out of gas would mark the end of Gallery's career.

And not to forget that sticking around was a fool's errand *because there was no proof that U-505 was even out there.* No air patrol had picked up the faintest scent, let alone sighted the quarry. All Gallery had was the word of the soothsayer in Washington. Perhaps Knowles had gotten it wrong for once. Everyone made mistakes, after all.

In fact, Knowles had not erred in claiming that U-505 was on the run. But what he and Gallery *had* gotten wrong was to think the Germans incapable of playing their own assumptions back against them.

Lange, for instance, had outwitted Knowles by unpredictably heading toward Africa instead of staying in open sea, and he had recently noticed that *Guadalcanal's* aircraft patrolled actively only at night. Why? Because Gallery, who had devoted weeks to training his pilots to fly in the dark, had taken for granted that was when U-boats surfaced to recharge their batteries.

It was a sound assumption 99 percent of the time, but not this time. Lange had instead exploited the Americans' habit of sleeping in by surfacing briefly during the daytime. At one point, U-505 would spend an incredible forty-five of forty-eight hours submerged, coming up only when volts and oxygen were close to zero. Hence his magical invisibility.

The night of June 2–3 had been particularly frustrating for the Americans. The Wildcats and Avengers that Gallery sent up to scour an area of 100 miles east and west of him, and 250 ahead, had as usual found nothing. Since Gallery had ordered their searches "to overlap so that if the sub were running surfaced at night anywhere in that area, we would be bound to find him," he was flummoxed by U-505's vanishing trick.

And yet at that June 3 afternoon conference in the CIC, something compelled, or persuaded, him to pause and continue searching for another day. But what was that something?

He once confessed that everyone in the CIC used to think "I was logically analyzing the various factors and arriving at a shrewd and penetrating answer," but really, "what I was doing was mentally flipping a nickel."

What he meant was that he was assessing a situation in which there might or might not be a submarine nearby. It was not a matter of learned disputations and hard facts, nor of spins of the wheel of fortune, nor of waiting for divine inspiration to show him the way. Ultimately, it all came down to his gut instinct.

And Captain Gallery had that in spades. Just as Ahab had sensed his White Whale was close thanks to his innate understanding of the Season on the Line, Gallery, having tangled with the best of the best and blooded by his long Icelandic tour, was preternaturally wise to the ways of the U-boat. Despite all the evidence to the contrary, he could *feel* that *U-505* would be there, and that "one more night in the area would cook his goose."

Chief Engineer Trosino, a Can-Do kinda guy of Italian extraction who thought Gallery had a touch of Irish madness to him, promised that he would scrounge the necessary fuel from somewhere. But he warned Gallery that the entire task group would literally stop moving if it stayed out any longer than another twenty-four hours.

"Beyond that, you're finished," Trosino said.

Gallery nodded. "Good. I want another crack at that bastard."

It would be a close-run thing. And until that 11:09 a.m. "possible sound contact" report from *Chatelain* the next day, it looked as if Gallery's hunch had not paid off.

If *Chatelain* came up empty from checking out the lead, the understanding was that Gallery must call off the hunt. So it was a tense three minutes until, at 11:12, she confirmed that the contact was a submarine: By some miracle it had blundered, or had been guided, right into their arms.

III

In the moments before *Chatelain* confirmed *U-505*'s metallic *ping* and changed the trajectory of his life, Captain Harald Lange would later remember, he had been letting the men take turns peering through the periscope at a school of frolicking seahorses.

When the soundman subsequently reported that he could hear several faint propellers, recalled crewman Hans Goebeler, Lange optimistically believed that a convoy had crossed their path: It had "never occurred to any of us that the damned carrier task force might have accidentally intercepted us." Finally, *U-505*'s day of triumph had arrived!

Back on *Guadalcanal,* Gallery immediately ordered two "Friskies"— *Frisky 1* and *Frisky 7,* both Wildcats—to launch and "stand by to assist." Before they left, though, he reiterated to their young pilots, "Use no big stuff if the sub surfaces—chase the crew overboard with .50-caliber fire."

After that, he made sure that a sound-and-video team was ready. Before he'd left port, Gallery, determined to memorialize the grand feat of arms that he *knew* was to come, had brought on board audio-recording equipment and a stack of blank phonographic discs, as well as Koda-chrome color film and a movie camera.

It was only after readying his AV crew to capture the moment that Gallery directed Commander Frederick Hall, aboard *Pillsbury* ("Daisy") as head of the destroyer-escort screen, to divert *Jenks* ("Jumbo") to *Chate-lain*'s position as support. *No one,* Gallery repeated in case anyone hadn't understood, was to use armor-piercing shells.

Guadalcanal, meanwhile, followed protocol by steering well clear of the U-boat's position. Putting a carrier amid a submarine hunt, Gallery believed, was like being "an old lady in the middle of a barroom brawl." The primary danger was that the sub might loose a spread of torpedoes to panic the enemy, and the first thing it would aim at would naturally be the largest, slowest thing in sight.

During all this, Lange was whistling a peppy tune as he raised the periscope above the surface. Expecting to see a vulnerable convoy, he was unpleasantly surprised to find three American destroyers bearing down on them, with two Wildcats circling overhead.

They were dead men.

IV

Fortunately for the Germans, *Chatelain* was too close to make an attack and lost sonar contact with *U-505* at 100 yards. Her captain, Lieutenant Commander Dudley Knox, turned starboard to open the range to 700 yards—the ideal firing distance for a Hedgehog forward salvo.

The contact with *U-505* was repeatedly lost and found—sure indications that she was very close, moving fast, and staying shallow. It was recommended procedure when a U-boat was surrounded for her to ride out the first attack by remaining close to the surface. If the submarine did sustain damage, not having tons of sea pressure threatening to crush its hull was a distinct advantage. To avoid being hit in the first place, Lange ordered a series of violently evasive maneuvers and waited for the destroyers to have to reload before going deep.

When the Hedgehogs proved unsuccessful, Knox prepared depth charges, making sure they were set to the minimum twenty-five feet.

So clear was the water that at 11:16 a.m. Ensign John Cadle, Jr.— piloting *Frisky 1* at 2,500 feet altitude—could make out the spectral shape of *U-505*. To help *Chatelain*, at 11:17 he had a brilliant idea and sent a burst of machine-gun fire into the water to mark the submarine's location.

Inside *U-505*, the men heard a weird noise that sounded as if someone was scraping a metal cable along the deck. A few on board thought they had run into the mooring chain of a mine, but in fact it was just Cadle's bullets plinking against the hull. More terrifying was what came next: the distinctive screech of a hard sonar fix by an approaching destroyer.

In full red-alert mode, Lange ordered a deep dive.

Cadle lost sight of the U-boat at 11:18.

It didn't matter. Commander Knox knew where she was. He radioed *Jenks* at 11:21 that *Chatelain* was beginning her attack and laid down a depth-charge spread.

The Germans weren't used to these particular depth charges; they were the new 600-pound giants, one of which came close to proving *U-505*'s undoing when it punctured the outer hull about 180 feet down. The submarine "shuddered violently," remembered machinist Hans Decker, "the lights went out, and amid the din we heard the most dreaded of noises to submariners: water rushing in."

Someone bawled, "Ruptured hull in the control room!," and Decker assumed it was all over as the boat plunged toward the seabed.

V

Inside the control room, crewman Goebeler could see that the "ruptured hull" was, at least in this part of the vessel, only a high-pressure jet of water from a pipe—almost certainly fixable. But that didn't mean they were out of the woods.

No electrical equipment was working and a report came in that the rear torpedo compartment of the sub was flooding. Lange ordered everyone out of there and had the watertight hatch clamped shut.

Then he turned to trying to arrest their dive, only to find that the rudder was jammed and the diving planes stuck in the downward position. With *U-505* falling to near 700 feet—another 100-odd and they'd be at crush-depth—and any man who believed in the Lord murmuring his final prayers, Lange had only a few seconds left to act.

By now, speech was useless; the wall of noise caused by the depth charges and the inrushing water was deafening. Lange made the thumbs-up gesture to blow the ballast tanks.

VI

As *U-505* shot up like a cork, the crew still did not know what Lange would do next. At this point, assuming that *U-505* made it to the surface, Lange had the power to order "Battle stations" and mount a suicidal Last Stand on deck.

Thirty seconds later, Ensign Cadle in *Frisky 1* excitedly yelled over the radio, "You struck oil! All DEs, sub is surfacing!" His comrade, Lieutenant Wolffe Roberts in *Frisky 7*, loosed a burst of .50-caliber machine-gun fire, then urged everyone to "come in and have fun."

Cadle agreed: "Let's get the bastard."

"I wish I had 10,000 rounds," chorused Roberts.

Inside *U-505*, the men heard the bell-like clang of bullets hitting the conning tower.

Now came the decisive moment. When a damaged enemy submarine broke the surface, it was convention that every plane and ship in the vicinity opened fire with the big weapons, as had happened with *U-515*. But this time, Gallery made sure to intervene.

At 11:23 over the general radio circuit he urgently reminded all ships (and especially his enthusiastic Wildcat pilots) to use only enough firepower to persuade the crew to abandon ship in a hurry. "I would like to capture that bastard if possible!," he shouted, "I would like to capture that bastard if possible!"

Lange was first on deck, not because he was a coward but because it was a captain's duty to assess the danger before ushering the rest of the crew topside. He was followed by the executive officer, Paul Meyer (who had served as acting commander after Zschech's death), then by the rest of the bridge crew. Per Gallery's orders, they were greeted by a fusillade of bullets, albeit intended to avoid further damaging the prize or killing potentially valuable prisoners.

Lange was nevertheless peppered by shrapnel in the face and legs.

Crawling over to the hatch, he shouted down to the control-room crew to scuttle the ship. Then he fell unconscious.

Later, Hans Goebeler would remember that Josef Hauser, the much-loathed Zschech toady and chief engineering officer widely mocked as "the Raccoon," was standing next to him when Lange called out. Hauser panicked, wailing, "Out! Out! We're sinking!," which began a stampede up the ladder, led by said Raccoon.

As the men streamed onto the deck, *Jenks* reported at 11:24 that "they are all holding their hands up! They are surrendering!" Most, including the Raccoon, jumped overboard as soon as they could. Lange in the meantime had briefly come to, and he was relieved to see his crew abandoning the listing boat. A few of the men hustled him onto a makeshift raft.

Goebeler and some others from the control room had remained below, determined to carry out Lange's order. The main problem was that only three men knew how to set the scuttling charges—Lange, Meyer, and the Raccoon—and none of them were there. An engineering petty officer named Holdenreid, now the senior man aboard, immediately took charge.

They would flood the ballast tanks with water and let *U-505* sink, he said. Like any crash-dive, it would need thirty seconds—just barely enough time for them to scramble out and swim for it.

But Fate, or Fortune, had other plans.

VII

Everything was stuck fast. Try as they might, the men in the control room could not fill the ballast tanks.

There was nothing left for them to do except save themselves—and hope that *U-505* somehow sank of her own accord.

But then, as Goebeler climbed the ladder, he remembered the seacocks. Perhaps, just perhaps, they had been left open. If so, the nearby strainer that filtered the water flowing through their pipes could serve to flood the boat. Yes, its diameter was only six inches or so, but that was better than nothing. Goebeler jumped down, rushed over to the strainer, tore off its steel lid, and, "in a move that I would regret for the rest of my life," flung it into a corner.

By the time Goebeler popped his head above the top of the conning tower, the shooting had petered out. He couldn't know that at 11:27, everyone had been directed, "Cease firing! Cease firing! Cease firing until further word."

"Don't attack unless sub attempts to submerge," Gallery's voice boomed over the radio. And "don't forget pictures."

Even then, *Frisky 1*'s blood was up and he asked, hopefully, at 11:28, "Shall I stay up here or fire?"

"Cease firing," instantly came the no-nonsense reply.

To this Cadle and Roberts in the Friskies confirmed, "Roger," in what Gallery later said was "the most disgusted tone of voice I have ever heard."

A minute later, Gallery asked Commander Hall of the *Pillsbury*, "Do you think we can capture this guy?" But Hall was already preparing to send a boat across.

Jenks had asked permission to send a boarding party, but Hall wanted the glory for a capture and instead directed them at 11:32 to instead use their boat to "start picking up survivors." From above, the Wildcats confirmed that there wasn't "a damn one left" topside on *U-505*. Three minutes later, Roberts in *Frisky 7* circled back around to double-check.

"No one on it," he reported. "If they are, they're dead."

At 11:38 Hall gave the order he'd been dying to give—one that hadn't been heard in the United States Navy since the War of 1812 amid snapping sails and swinging cutlasses:

"Away boarding parties!"

Sixteen

THE BOARDING PARTY

I

Lieutenant Albert David's whaleboat dropped heavily into the water. He had eight men with him, plus three others to crew the craft. David, aged forty-two and a longtime Navy enlisted man who'd recently been promoted, had chosen his team carefully. They included a gunnery mate, a torpedoman, a signals man, a boatswain's mate, two machinists, a radioman, and an electrician. All had been selected for skills that might prove useful for mounting a submarine heist.

Nobody knew what awaited them. According to one, it was quiet on the boat on the trip over: "There wasn't nobody saying 'I go first' or 'Anything going to blow up' or 'What's going to happen?'" But, inevitably, a few wondered whether some Nazi diehards might be hiding inside *U-505*, planning to shoot it out or detonate their demolition charges and take a few Americans down with them. Just in case, all eight men were armed with Colt M1911 .45 pistols. One carried carried a Thompson submachine gun—the "Chicago Piano," useful for close-quarters combat—and another a brace of six hand and six tear-gas grenades.

Away Boarding Party! Pillsbury*'s pirates.*

David's pirates, most just nineteen or twenty years old, were the very picture of apple-pie ordinariness: They had high-school educations, played baseball, went to the movies, read the local papers. After the war they would become steelworkers, furnace installers, roofers, bar owners, and appliance-service managers. All were sons of toil, and six were sons of immigrants—from Lithuania, Ireland, and Poland, among other places.

Until that moment, as young, high-testosterone males embarked on a grand adventure with their best pals, it had never crossed their minds that the iron coffin across the way might become their own watery tomb. Some had volunteered for the boarding party weeks earlier; others were told only that they had *been* volunteered, and to be ready to leave their posts when summoned. As for David, he'd been selected for the role of *Pillsbury*'s commando chief because he'd once spent five months in the Submarine Repair Unit, making him the resident expert on U-boats—American ones, at any rate.

There had been little point in rehearsing detailed scenarios. All they had as guidance was a flyer distributed by Captain Gallery, laying out each man's tasks once he got aboard. The boatswain's mate, for instance, was to lash a thirty-foot-long chain to anything suitable on the U-boat's deck, tie the other end to a heavy toolbox, then throw it clattering down the open hatch, just as Gallery had conceived long ago in Iceland. That would keep the hatch from being shut while also taking care of any Germans sneakily hiding directly below. The next man down after David would be torpedoman Arthur Knispel, who was detailed as the muscle and entrusted with the tommy gun. He was to be "ready and prepared [to employ] all types of strong-arm methods" against recalcitrant Krauts and to look around for anything resembling an explosive charge. The gunner's mate, meanwhile, would help by lobbing grenades and firing a flare gun down the corridor to temporarily "blind any of the enemy" who might decide they wanted to enter Valhalla as heroes of the Reich.

It was fitting that the Americans were in what was called a whaleboat, for U-505 resembled nothing so much as a wounded whale. The men had been expecting a glamorously sinister black submarine full of menace, but this was a weather-beaten, steel-gray leviathan, moving at five or six knots in a lazy clockwise circle—a result of the stuck rudder and the fact that no one had shut down the engines before evacuating.

As their Nantucket forebears once had, David's party was guided toward the lolling creature by their coxswain for the day, Philip Trusheim, who usually manned a 40mm stern gun on the Pillsbury. He didn't want to chase the errant U-boat, so he cut across the circle and at 11:42 pulled up alongside starboard, as close as he could get to the conning tower.

U-505 was listing to the right, while her slippery deck sloped alarmingly. A gunner's mate named Chester Mocarski tried to leap across, but at that moment a wave roughly shoved the whaleboat almost *onto* the

David's boat, bottom right, approaches U-505.

submarine. For his troubles, he got his leg crushed—and much of their equipment was washed overboard.

No matter. Improvise, improvise, improvise. David managed to grab a handhold on the conning tower and scrambled up, closely tailed by torpedoman Knispel and radioman Stanley Wdowiak. When they got to the open hatch, lying at their feet was a corpse whose chest had been torn to pieces. He was radioman Gottfried Fischer, who had once confided to his diary that he wanted to smash a radio set and then fix it to relieve his boredom, and he would be, remarkably, the day's only fatality. He had been killed by shots fired by one of the Wildcats as he exited the tower.

Seeing nobody below, Lieutenant David clambered down the ladder, pistol at the ready, and became the first American to enter an enemy submarine. "Attaboy," Gallery exclaimed when he heard the news.

It was an exceedingly dangerous task, one for which he would be awarded the Medal of Honor—posthumously, not because he was killed in action but because he would die of a heart attack just a year later.

The good news: No bullets tore into him. The bad: A smell so malignant that every American who came on board that day would remember it more than five decades later. Scores of men living in close confinement for months had left behind a monstrous bucket of shit, its stench accentuated by an overpowering smell of mildew and *eau de diesel oil.*

At least the control room was deserted. David's men followed him down, while Knispel and Wdowiak swept through the U-boat to search for holdouts and dastardly saboteurs.

Thankfully, in the control room there was only about four to six inches of water—but it was rising. Zenon Lukosius, a machinist, spotted a telltale bubbling. They had sea strainers on ships, too, and he knew what he was looking for. He glanced around and saw the steel lid that Hans Goebeler had rashly thrown into a corner. Grabbing it, Lukosius reclamped it to the outlet. Seawater still came in—a gasket was missing—but it was more now a leak than a flow.

Still, none of them knew where else water might be getting in. As the men wandered down the cramped corridor and strove to avoid hitting their heads on unfamiliar pipes and valves sticking out at weird angles, they found no one aboard. They did, however, find warm cooktops in the galley and half-eaten lunches on a makeshift table, hastily abandoned when *Chatelain* had pinged her and Lange had called general quarters.

With *U-505* as eerily deserted as the *Mary Celeste,* David set about his second task: prying open two safes. From prisoner interrogations, it was known that one was located above the captain's bunk and the other built into a desk near the radio room. Locked inside these safes, he had been told, were certain "confidential publications" that someone in Washington *really* wanted.

Gallery himself was interested only in his submarine. But as part of his deal with Knowles, he had promised to recover any alien-looking machines they found and to take off every piece of paper, no matter how worthless-looking.

Once the safes were broken open—they were secured only by small locks—David left them to radioman Wdowiak and Wayne Pickels, Zenon Lukosius's *Pillsbury* buddy, to clear out. Wdowiak handled the radio room, while Pickels searched the captain's area. There he noticed a small cabinet above the desk and broke it open, followed by a drawer. Inside both were more papers, which he handed over to Wdowiak, though he kept Lange's rather nice Mont Blanc fountain pen for himself.

Wdowiak had in the meantime been busy grabbing codebooks and what would turn out to be the jackpot: the latest version of an Enigma M4 machine, as well as an older, broken M3. Pickels had no idea what they were but Wdowiak certainly thought they were important, so he carried them upstairs to the whaleboat along with the papers. The booty was soon transported back to the *Pillsbury* and given to her startled chief radioman, who made them vanish into a sailor's sea chest before anyone began asking questions.

II

By this time, the boarders had been joined on *U-505* by some new arrivals. This was a second whaleboat, led by Gallery's chief engineer, Earl Trosino, which had come over from the *Guadalcanal*. *U-505*'s precarious condition had been noticed, and Trosino had been sent with a team to see if Gallery's prize could still be salvaged.

As a former engineer on a Sun Oil tanker, Trosino had no experience with submarines, but he was a sound choice to lead the effort. "To him machinery [was] machinery," said Gallery, "no matter what kind of a craft it is installed in."

Outranking David, Trosino immediately took charge. After struggling to the top of the conning tower, he told signalman Don Carter to get permission from *Guadalcanal* to "deep-six this cadaver here"—referring to poor Fischer—and then descended into the submarine. Since everybody had conveniently turned a blind eye to the shit-bucket, Trosino manhandled it himself up top and got rid of it.

After that, the immediate priority was to suck out as much water as possible from the control and engine rooms—the latter awash by now in nearly two feet of seawater—using gas-powered portable pumps. While the pumps were hauled aboard, Trosino used his engineering smarts to fashion a temporary gasket out of his T-shirt for the capped but still-leaking sea strainer.

The second thing to do was stop the engines so that *U-505* stayed still. Trosino noticed that their shafts were turning and guessed that they were being powered by the electric motors. He sent Ensign Fred Middaugh and an electrician named Stein to check the batteries fore and aft. They were dry, the pair reported, and Trosino thanked the Lord for the break. (Had they been flooded, everyone aboard might soon be choking to death of chlorine gas.) Trosino managed to cut the power, then Chief Motor Machinist's Mate George Jacobson, who'd come over with the *Pillsbury* team, shut down the engines at 1:38 p.m.

And yet a third thing to do: work out what all the stuff did in the control room. Trosino had no idea how a submarine functioned but, as was the case with all sea vehicles, he knew the key thing was to keep it level—easier said than done when everything was labeled in German and turning a random valve or pulling the wrong lever might well fill the tanks with water and kill everyone, or fire a torpedo and kill someone else.

After getting everyone else off the boat, Trosino and David prepared an escape plan, just in case. They shut as many compartment hatches as they could to preserve some air pockets if *U-505* began to sink.

Then they gingerly experimented with righting the boat, using the time-honored engineering principle of *What happens if I do this?* Decades later, Trosino could still remember how his cap crept back on his head every time he flicked a switch or pressed a button; his hair was almost literally standing on end. (Trosino had always thought that was just a turn of phrase, but no—"Your scalp pulls and your hat goes up like that and you pull it down, it goes back up again.")

He and David looked at each other. It was a beautiful 70 degrees outside, but they had both broken out in a "cold, cold sweat." David's glasses were fogged and he had to repeatedly wipe them off on his shirt.

The lieutenant asked Trosino how he felt.

"I'm not gonna lie about it," the engineer replied. "I'm damn scared."

And then, amid the gray pipes and the black valves and the white gauges that controlled this armored, rusty industrial behemoth, Trosino added an incongruously rustic touch:

"What I wouldn't give to be under an apple tree anyplace in this world than to be right here."

David disconsolately nodded as he watched the water rising and lapping against the bulkhead.

"So would I."

The water was about a foot and a half deep now, and both Trosino and David urgently wanted to run, scramble up a ladder, and get outside. But they stayed, determined to do their duty for Captain Gallery. They'd give it another few minutes before abandoning the boat as lost.

As they watched anxiously, the water stopped rising inch by inch. By some miraculous combination of their twiddling and tweaking, Trosino and David had managed to bring *U-505* into temporary neutral buoyancy. They may not have been floating free and easy, but neither were they any longer sinking.

U-505 *slips perilously low in the water.*

"I think we got it," said Trosino, hesitantly. "Let's secure and get out of here."

III

There was a moment of panic when David climbed a ladder in the conning tower and opened a hatch partway, only to be drenched by seawater pouring down from the compartment above. Were they actually underwater? Just a few feet, or hundreds?

David descended to say goodbye. They'd come so close, but this was it. Trosino, however, wasn't ready to give up. Thanks to having closed the hatches, they still had plenty of air in the compartments around them.

What they needed to do was go up, releasing an air bubble from one compartment to the next to keep them breathing. If they really were 200 feet under, well, there'd be time enough to shake hands before the air ran out and the darkness fell. But if *U-505* was near the surface, they'd be able to swim out.

Trosino proposed shoving David into the upstairs compartment, with a pocket of air accompanying him. David would then shut the hatch while Trosino opened his own hatch below to let in another bubble. After that, he would join David upstairs and together they would try to reach the outside.

It was a good plan, but an unnecessary one as it turned out. When Trosino pushed David up, this time only a little water poured down and, odder still, they noticed that they could see daylight. The two of them erupted through the upper hatch at the same time and found themselves on the bridge outside. "Neither one of us could talk," recalled Trosino, and it took them a minute to realize what had happened.

U-505's stern was mostly underwater—so much so that the waves had come within a foot of the lip of the outer hatch. While they had been below, a good deal of water had sloshed through the opening—this is what had soaked David—but after that the compartment was more or less empty.

Soon afterward, a boat led by *Guadalcanal*'s Lieutenant D. E. Hampton landed her complement of seventeen men on *U-505*. Trosino needed the extra hands to help rig a 1.25-inch steel cable to *U-505*'s bow. Because the submarine was still taking on water here, there, and everywhere, eventually, inevitably, and inexorably she would sink.

Now that the engines had been turned off, Trosino realized that his prize needed, like a propelled airplane's wings generating lift, forward movement to keep her from sinking—at least until the leaks could be stopped and the water fully pumped out. *Guadalcanal* would serve admirably as an aquatic tow truck until he could get *U-505* running under her own steam. The fanciful towing exercise that Gallery had put his green sailors through a few months earlier now came in incredibly handy.

Beginning the tow.

At 2:23 p.m., carrier was attached umbilically to submarine, but forty minutes later Trosino told Gallery it would take at least another two days to drain *U-505*. He estimated that as much as 4,500 gallons of water—about eighteen tons' worth—could still be inside.

In case Trosino was wrong and there was no saving the submarine, Lieutenant Jack Dumford, a cryptology specialist, was dispatched with a few handpicked radiomen to scour the navigation and communications rooms for any documents and equipment that Pickels and Wdowiak might have missed in their rush.

There was quite a lot. Aside from charts, "we saw messages that had been decoded, tons of them," which Dumford and the others dumped into mailbags. Along with other documents they recovered, they filled nine or ten of them. Half an hour later, Dumford was heading back to

Guadalcanal, where all the confiscated material was moved to a locked room.

Gallery was adamant that secrecy remain paramount, especially since the operation was taking much longer than he'd expected and they were sitting exposed in open water. To make sure they remained safe from prying German eyes and opportunistic torpedoes, Gallery ordered his destroyers to establish a defensive screen, its perimeter patrolled by Wildcats and Avengers.

Throughout, he was updated on the submarine's status by means of flag semaphore sent by signalman Don Carter, standing on the bow. Since the capture, *Guadalacanal* had been coordinating operations via short-range radio transmissions, but to make absolutely sure that no passing U-boat picked them up and relayed the news to Dönitz, Gallery had returned to old-school methods.

For the same reason, the men were ordered to hand over any "souvenirs" they might have lifted from the submarine. The ancient practice of taking war trophies was generally tolerated, but not now. The last thing Gallery wanted was for trinkets from a U-boat that was supposed to have been lost without a trace being sent home or written up by excited reporters.

Even he was taken aback by the "mountain of stuff" that was subsequently turned in: Luger pistols, binoculars, clocks, cameras, and officers' caps piled up in his office. Despite the warnings of dreadful consequences, however, a few things were held back: Signalman Carter kept quiet about the packet of French cigarettes, deck of cards, and two pens that he'd filched, and he wasn't the only one.

IV

At 2:45 p.m., Gallery sent a flash message by high-security cipher to Rear Admiral Francis Low at Tenth Fleet, saying only: REQUEST IMMEDIATE ASSISTANCE TO TOW CAPTURED SUBMARINE.

No one answered. When the signal was received by communications officers at Main Navy, they scarcely believed that Gallery had "captured" a submarine; instead they assumed it was a careless decoding of an otherwise routine notice that a U-boat had been sunk. With the Normandy landings initially scheduled for the next day (June 5) and Main Navy otherwise preoccupied with the liberation of Europe from the Nazi jackboot, Gallery's message was put at the bottom of the pile.

An hour later Gallery sent another urgent message, this time providing more specifics to prove his bona fides, including: HAVE U-505 IN TOW.

This message got through to "Frog" Low, who rushed to Admiral King's office to tell him that Gallery "has captured *U-505* and he requests your desires as to her disposition." It was at that moment that Low, for the first and only time in his career, observed King turn "momentarily speechless."

SEVENTEEN

NEMO

I

At 5:40 p.m. that June 4, *Pillsbury* sent over to *Guadalcanal* the sea chest containing the Enigma machines and the "confidential communications" that Wdowiak and Pickels had found. Eight minutes later, *Jenks* "reported having 20 very important publications" en route that someone else had picked up.

Since his return to *Guadalcanal,* cryptology specialist Jack Dumford had been sorting through the sackfuls of messages and documents he'd found on *U-505,* trying to make some sense of them. The ship's navigator, helpfully, was of Dutch extraction and could read German. He quickly realized that Dumford's pile was mostly decoded dispatch orders from U-Boat Command to proceed to Point X at Y speed and be there at Z time. Some of them were very recent. Dumford realized, especially after the haul from *Pillsbury* and *Jenks* arrived, that he had something very special, and very important, here.

To give himself time to work out exactly what it was, Dumford decided to wait until the following day to tell Gallery, who was run off his feet anyway, about the secrets of *U-505.*

II

Over the course of the afternoon and into the evening, survivors from *U-505* who had been picked up by the destroyers were transferred to *Guadalcanal*. With the luckless Gottfried Fischer the sole fatality, that left fifty-eight prisoners. But only fifty-seven would be alive the next day, technically speaking.

The missing man was Ewald Felix, who had made himself known to the Americans when he and his crewmates were confined to a holding pen on *Guadalcanal*. He got to talking to one of the guards, a fellow named Leon Bednarczyk. The two chatted conspiratorially in a strange language—Polish, as it turned out.

Bednarczyk reported to Gallery that there was a possible friend among the prisoners, one who claimed that he could help keep *U-505* afloat. The Germans could see the submarine from their porthole, and it was clear to them that she would not last much longer, no matter how much salvaging the Americans tried to do.

Gallery called Felix in. He was twenty-one years old, a junior machinist, and one of the newest among the crew. He'd had little time to make friends on board, and it was clear that his crewmates did not count Felix as one of them. As an ethnic German from rural Poland, one of the *Volksdeutsche* looked down upon by the native-born *Reichsdeutsche*, Felix had been conscripted into the submarine service as a late replacement, making his loyalties to the boat and his brothers suspect.

Felix was an exception to the camaraderie that reigned on U-boats. He had no pals, and no one liked him. He was a lonely young man, and almost certainly bullied. He had no love for the Nazis—who, he claimed, had killed both his mother and his uncle. Understandably, Felix was motivated to help the Americans.

Next he was brought in to see Trosino, who noticed that Felix never lifted his head. Trosino told him that when he asked a question, he

U-505 *prisoners file aboard* Guadalcanal.

wanted the young man to look him in the eye. Felix refused, explaining that in his experience "if I looked in an officer's face, they would slap me." To which Trosino, in rousing *Four Freedoms* mode, patriotically replied, "You're [on] an American ship—we're a democracy. We don't do that. You are equal to me. I'm equal to you. Just because I got stripes here, that doesn't mean that I'm different."

Never had he witnessed such freedom, exclaimed Felix, who pleaded for permission to join the U.S. Navy. He would serve without pay for life, he said, if only they took him on. To demonstrate his loyalty to his new American friends, he then volunteered to help save *U-505*.

Trosino and Gallery were initially wary of the offer, not knowing whether Felix's intention was to get on board *U-505* and blow her up with some secret stash of dynamite. But they decided to trust him—to a degree: Felix would be shadowed by Bednarczyk, not only for translation but to shoot him if he so much as turned a valve without permission.

The last the German prisoners ever saw of Felix was him gathering his few things—toiletries the Americans had distributed to everyone—into a handkerchief and being escorted out. The next day, a Navy chaplain informed them that their shipmate had died of a sudden stomach ailment, and that he had been buried at sea. No one believed this ridiculous story, especially when they could plainly see *U-505* rising inch by inch, foot by foot, from the water.

Felix turned out to be a crucial addition to Trosino's efforts to keep *U-505* afloat. The engineer had performed miracles, but miracles wouldn't save the submarine during her coming voyage. The hemorrhaging had been stanched, but still she bled. Trosino needed practical guidance—the sort of hands-on knowledge that only a mechanic trained on U-boats like Felix could provide.

Together, Felix—now proudly outfitted in an American sailor's blue-dungaree uniform—and Trosino cleared debris, released the stuck rudder, figured out how to recharge the batteries, and got the pumps running. Felix also showed Trosino *U-505*'s darkest secret: He pulled back the mattress on the captain's bunk and pointed to a faded scarlet stain—Zschech's blood.

In short order *U-505*, which Trosino said had seemed to possess "a mind of its own," was tamed. He could confidently control her—not enough to attempt a dive, but to steer her on the surface like a ship was well within his command.

III

By the late morning of June 5, a replacement 2.25-inch steel cable securely tethered *U-505* to *Guadalcanal*, but Gallery did not yet know what King wanted him to do with his prize.

The answer came at 2:11 p.m., from the admiral himself. In one of his follow-up messages to Main Navy, Gallery had suggested heading to Dakar in Senegal, which was just 140 miles away and the only place he could reach on the snifter of fuel he had left. King replied that under no circumstances was he to do that: Dakar was riddled with German spies, and if *Guadalcanal* steamed in towing a U-boat, Berlin would know about it within hours.

No, Gallery was to bring *U-505* to Bermuda, some 2,000 miles away, where there was an American Naval Operating Base at Port Royal Bay. Given the extreme distance, he'd need to summon supreme seamanship skills, but King expected no less of his subordinates. To relieve the fuel situation, a tanker and tender were being sent to meet him. A fleet tug, too, would assist with the towing.

The next day, June 6, cryptologist Dumford finally managed to snatch a moment of Gallery's time. He had tried to see the captain five or six times already to tell him about the documents, only to be turned away. When he was finally admitted, Gallery was eating tomato soup and looking annoyed at his junior's impertinence, but he listened.

When Dumford was done, Gallery laughed.

"I know what's wrong with you," he told the lieutenant. "You want to be a secret agent."

But at least Gallery approved sending a message to Washington, classified *Top Secret Operational Priority,* stating that he had "material which should be examined by communications experts immediately."

Despite being rather busy—it was D-Day, after all—King's COMINCH headquarters replied within the hour. Dumford recalled that it was an "urgent message" ordering him to "get the material here" by the fastest means possible.

IV

At 5:45 p.m., Gallery the Great himself came over on a whaleboat to tour his trophy.

U-505 had been spruced up for his arrival. In homage to the Can-Do King, someone had daubed CAN-DO JUNIOR in red paint on the conning tower. Gallery grinned triumphantly for Chief Photographer's Mate Clifford Werlla atop the tower beneath two fluttering flags.

The improvised flagpole from which they flew was actually a boat hook that signalman Don Carter and some of the salvage team had bent into shape and propped up behind Gallery. The upper, larger flag was an American one; the lower, smaller one a German ensign known as the *Reichskriegsflagge,* or Imperial War Flag, designed by Hitler himself.

The armaments minister Speer once noted that the only two things the Führer devoted more loving care to designing than this flag were the Berghof and his personal standard as Chief of State. The great leader probably wouldn't have found it amusing, then, to learn that this particular version had been hurriedly sewn together by parachute repairers in

Gallery and Can-Do Junior.

Guadalcanal's sail loft because the original could not be found and Gallery insisted on having one to show off.

V

On the morning of June 7, the task group rendezvoused with the naval oiler *Kennebec* and the fleet tug, *Abnaki*, accompanied by the destroyer *Durik*, which had been diverted from the passing convoy UGS-43. None of them had been told why they were being dispatched at short notice to such a remote location. Their captains assumed it was to bring in a broken-down carrier.

As *Guadalcanal* began to gulp down 506,000 gallons of fuel, the towing cable was passed over to the *Abnaki* at 10:18 a.m. *U-505*'s stern was still dragging, so a salvaging party was sent over at 10:35 to pump the bilges, to empty any tanks of their remaining contents, and to jettison any unnecessary weight (including some torpedoes). By 8 p.m. she was assuredly afloat, and Gallery was finally confident that his prize was "in the bag."

It would take fully another day to complete refueling *Guadalcanal*, and she couldn't move before her escorts were likewise replenished. In any case, *U-505* still needed plenty of patching and fixing before the 2,000-mile voyage could be hazarded. Task Group 22.3 would not be going anywhere for a while.

But Jack Dumford was. King had granted his wish: He was going to be a secret agent. The destroyer *Jenks* had been reassigned from escort duty and was to rush Dumford directly to Bermuda as soon as she finished refueling. Dumford had already transferred the confidential material and Enigma machines from *U-505* to a safe room on *Jenks;* he himself was ferried over early on the morning of June 9, and *Jenks* was underway barely two hours later.

VI

By traveling at top speed, *Jenks* arrived in Bermuda in just four days. When he disembarked, Dumford was met by a Navy captain and commander, neither of whom gave their real names, and hustled onto a special plane bound for Washington. When the whirlwinded Dumford landed, "there were all kinds of [armored] cars around [and] they took all this stuff and put it in [a] panel truck and took me and the mailbags to…Naval Intelligence." There, an admiral insisted that Dumford sign a receipt acknowledging delivery of "nine mailbags and one sea chest [containing the Enigma machines] of top-secret material."

Dumford was then given a hasty tour of OP-20-G, where he heard a cryptanalyst exclaim, upon riffling through the stack of Enigma radio messages, "Hallelujah! We got the setups for today." Dumford was ignorant of Enigma and *Ultra,* and also of course the bombe project, so he didn't understand the excitement his haul had provoked. He just knew it was important.

In the aftermath of D-Day, the volume of German radio transmissions in Enigma tripled as the advancing Allies cut landline communications. To anticipate German movements, or to react to them quickly, reading *Ultra* decrypts in as close to real time as possible had become exponentially more important than before June 6.

Small wonder, then, that the cryptanalysts were astounded at the treasure Gallery had stolen. It glittered and gleamed beyond imagination. Some 1,100 pounds' worth of material, including at least one brand-new Enigma machine that finally allowed them to penetrate its mysterious workings and wirings.

Not all of the roughly 1,200 documents were graded *Top Secret.* The crew's personal letters were interesting but not important, for instance, and around 800 items were technical drawings and charts, which were important but not interesting. The rest, though, contained gold in the form of ciphers, signal books, manuals, logs, standing war orders, analyses of new technology such as acoustic torpedoes, and radio-navigation intelligence.

Commander Joseph Wenger, head of OP-20-G and a future founding father of the National Security Agency, explained in a memorandum how valuable the trove was a short time later. Throughout the key month of June, thanks to Gallery's haul, "we were able to read all messages in this cipher [*Triton*] as soon as the Germans were." As a result of their not having to strain to break *Triton*, some 13,000 bombe hours were saved in those weeks alone. Instead of lying fallow, then, the bombes were diverted into penetrating German Army and Air Force keys that otherwise would have taken too long to crack.

More exciting still was that Gallery had swiped updated bigram and short-signal ciphers that were scheduled to become effective in July/August and would probably remain active for a year. This meant that OP-20-G would be able to read ciphers laying out the Enigma machine's devilishly complex internal and rotor settings far into the future. Before Gallery's scoop, Allied cryptanalysts had no choice but to laboriously reconstruct these settings, causing delays of one to ten days. Now they had them laid out in front of them, pretty as you please.

For Kenneth Knowles in particular, the prize accession was the most recent, and pristine, edition of the Address Book, which solved the super-encoded Naval Grid problem until the end of the war. Never again would he or OP-20-G have to guess a U-boat's origin, position, or destination.

The British had to be told of the heist, of course, and they were—the morning after the capture. Almost immediately, the long-simmering Anglo-American tensions over Enigma flared up. Admiral Sir Andrew Cunningham, the First Sea Lord, antagonized King by high-handedly directing him to "maintain complete secrecy regarding the capture of

U-505." King replied testily that yes, thank you, he'd already taken matters in hand, and pointed out that if there were any leak it would come not from the Americans but from the British needlessly contacting him with patronizing instructions.

The British wisely backed off, only to infuriate their ally anew when Bletchley Park messaged OP-20-G with an order to send them the entire haul taken from *U-505.* This haughty reminder of their previous subservience to London came across as rather rich, considering that by this stage the Americans were doing much more codebreaking than the British.

When OP-20-G asked Knowles about how to handle the British demand, he replied, "We will do nothing in this regard until situation clarifies." It was only after the material had been examined that Knowles consented to give Bletchley the originals of a few of the less important documents. The rest were photographic copies.

VII

Admiral King, as jocular as ever.

After a night's stay at a hotel, Dumford was driven to Main Navy and escorted into the sanctum sanctorum: Admiral King's office at COMINCH headquarters. Flanking the Chief of Naval Operations were Admiral Royal Ingersoll (Commander, U.S. Atlantic Fleet) and Vice Admiral John S. McCain, Sr. (Deputy Chief of Naval Operations for Air).

Present, too, almost certainly, were Commander Knowles and Admiral Low.

All these nabobs and panjandrums had taken the time to come meet Dumford, self-described as "twenty-two years old [and] just barely familiar with the English language, being from Kentucky," who found himself asked to narrate the tale from beginning to end. "They were enthralled," he remembered. "They wanted all the details, what happened, how did it happen...and they asked a lot of questions." Afterward, with everyone happy, even King, they asked if he had a place to stay. Dumford's father happened to live nearby, so "I called my dad and he picked me up."

From then on, to preserve secrecy, the name *U-505* was scrubbed from any document or transmission. Neither would it ever appear in official U-boat statistics. Two favorites for her new cover name included *U-606* (but too easily guessable by German Naval Intelligence) and *Ark* (a nice callback to Noah's), but the oddest one to our contemporary ears was *Yehudi*—Hebrew for *Jew*.

At the time, however, it referred to a well-known sketch in which the great violinist Yehudi Menuhin had appeared on a radio show hosted by Bob Hope, whose sidekick kept repeating, "Who's Yehudi?," as if he wasn't there. This was regarded as a real rib-tickler and was soon being used as a catchphrase to describe a person who was mysteriously absent. Then had come a 1942 Warner Bros. cartoon, *Crazy Cruise,* that featured an invisible ship—dubbed, inevitably, the *Yehudi*—which no doubt inspired the suggested cover name. It's impossible to say now for sure, of course, but it bears the distinct hallmark of Gallery's sense of humor.

In short, a worthy comic effort by the Lavatory Man, who also liked to bestow on his destroyers and callsigns the names of characters from the *Blondie* newspaper strip. But it would be Knowles, a fan of Jules Verne, who came up with the winning handle, approved by King himself: *Nemo*—Latin for *no one*—after the submarine captain in *Twenty Thousand Leagues Under the Sea.*

VIII

On June 20, a long-range Douglas C-54 Skymaster, a military version of a civilian DC-4, took off from Washington National Airport and headed toward Bermuda. On board was a team of seventeen officers, all keen to see their first U-boat up close. Aside from three OP-16-Z interrogators and an OP-20-G cryptanalyst, there were anti-submarine warfare researchers, a radar expert, and representatives from the Bureau of Ships (the Submarine Design and Sonar sections) and the Bureau of Ordnance's Torpedo Design department.

Also present: one Kenneth Knowles.

The no-frills flight could not approach the luxurious surroundings of the Sikorsky VS-44 that he had traveled on nearly two years earlier after training with Commander Rodger Winn at The Citadel. But that was of no account. For Knowles, he was at last going to come face to face with one of the metal beasts he'd hunted from afar for so long.

A day before Knowles arrived, Gallery had pulled into port as inconspicuously as a carrier-led task group hauling a stolen German submarine could. For the duration of the voyage, *Guadalcanal's* destroyers had fanned out to intercept friendly ships, which were directed to change course and make way so the task group could pass without scrutiny. If any area was too crowded, the escorts had laid down a smoke screen around the *Abnaki* tug and her precious tow.

To preserve anonymity, Gallery ordered signalman Carter to haul down the two flags fluttering from *U-505's* conning tower when Task Group 22.3 got within a few days of Bermuda. Carter, assuming no one wanted the makeshift German ensign, stuffed it into his locker—only to be told by Gallery that he intended to present it to the Naval Academy. In exchange, he gave Carter *U-505's* flare gun.

Gallery had stressed the need for secrecy—not only once they arrived in port, but *forever*—multiple times to every man. This "can be one of the major turning points in World War number two *provided* repeat *provided* we keep our mouths shut about it," stated a notice distributed throughout the task group. "The enemy must not learn of this capture. I fully appreciate how nice it would be to be able to tell your friends about it when we get in, but you can depend on it that they will read about it eventually in the history books." Above all, remember that to "safeguard your own health as well as information which is vital to the national defense: KEEP YOUR BOWELS OPEN AND YOUR MOUTH SHUT."

In case that wasn't clear enough, all hands were mustered and told by Gallery that if anyone shot his mouth off, the Navy had "a way of finding out who it was," and that for the culprit there would be "no court-martial, we'll just shoot you at sunrise."

Afterward, everyone had to sign a nondisclosure agreement of sorts, obviously drafted by Gallery but supposed to sound terrifyingly legalistic. They swore an oath never to tell anyone, including "my closest relatives, friends, military or naval personnel—even an Admiral," what they had seen and done during their high-seas heist.

For the rest of the time, Gallery had been in good form, as well he might. A number of his officers highlighted a section in the maritime regulations stating that a crew which brought in a captured ship was owed prize money, as in Days of Yore when privateers roamed the foamy main for spoils and booty. Since *U-505* was worth, they imagined, several million dollars, fantasies swirled that they would all receive fat checks from the U.S. Treasury and buy Cadillacs. Sadly, someone belatedly discovered that the relevant section had been repealed three decades earlier by a few killjoy congressmen.

When they arrived at the Naval Operating Base at Port Royal Bay in Bermuda, Gallery handed over the prisoners to the custody of the provost marshal. The office boys could figure out what to do with them. Gallery had other business.

He was personally taking home a German war ensign and a souvenir picked up from Lange's bunk on *U-505*. The latter was a recent book titled *Der maßlose Kontinent: Roosevelts Kampf um die Weltherrschaft* (*The Excessive Continent: Roosevelt's Struggle for World Domination*) by the odious Nazi hack Giselher Wirsing. Gallery found it amusing enough to want to present to Admiral King.

Little did he know that King would forward it to the White House. A few months later, Gallery was surprised to receive a letter from President Franklin Roosevelt, signed *Commander in Chief*, thanking him for the gift and promising that he would add it to his personal library at Hyde Park. It would serve "as a lasting testimonial of the enterprise, valor, and determination of you and your fine task group."

The president was as good as his word. The book is still there.

IX

Captain Harald Lange had not reported to U-Boat Command since May 14, when he said that he'd be turning for home a week hence. Given the risks associated with radio transmissions, that was not so out of the ordinary; U-boats were delayed all the time.

And for a few more weeks, Berlin took no additional notice. Fortunately for Gallery, U-Boat Command was somewhat busy dealing with more important matters: Allied bombing had forced Dönitz to move his Berlin headquarters from the Hotel am Steinplatz to the suburb of Bernau on the night of June 5, the day after *U-505*'s capture. Then, in the early hours of June 6, the grand admiral was awakened by a phone call informing him that the long-anticipated Allied invasion of France had begun.

At 5:35 a.m., Dönitz ordered thirty-six U-boats to depart their bases and attack the Allies ruthlessly, but little of practical consequence was achieved. The U-boats were too easy to spot in the restricted confines of the English Channel, and enemy aircraft were patrolling everywhere overhead.

It was only on June 15 that U-Boat Command enjoyed a brief respite and sent a signal helpfully pre-authorizing *U-505* to approach Lorient. There was no reply.

Most other U-boats on operational duty had long since come in by July 13, a month later, when at 3:54 p.m. Lange was curtly directed to "report position at once." At 4:08 p.m., U-Boat Command followed up with one last, plaintive appeal: "Report position immediately."

But there was only silence. There was nothing more to be done for a single submarine when the life of the Reich lay on the line. On July 16, U-Boat Command briefly recorded that *"U-505* must be presumed lost… Nothing is known of date or cause of loss."

U-505 was officially dead.

X

There is a story, perhaps not entirely true, that the Greek philosopher Empedocles planned to astound his followers into believing him a re-incarnated god by vanishing off the face of the Earth, only to miracu-lously reappear before them later on. To this end, he secretly ascended Mount Etna one dark night and threw himself into the volcano. The foolproof ruse, disappointingly, was undone by his forgetting his distinc-tive sandals on its rim.

Similarly, Gallery had pulled off the greatest heist of the war by mak-ing a submarine disappear in broad daylight. But now it was imperative to maintain the illusion by *also* abracadabraing away her crew—and, unlike Empedocles, leaving behind no trace.

Eighteen

TOPSY-TURVY

I

For dead men, they were treated well. Under certain other regimes, the prisoners of *U-505* might well have been dropped overboard on the way to Bermuda to guarantee their silence. They were lucky that their captors were civilized Americans who wanted the enemy only to *think* they were dead until the war was over.

To do that, Washington would need to violate a few of the less-important articles of the Geneva Convention, such as being required to inform their government of the prisoners' status and granting them the right to communicate with their families.

The overriding priority at all times was to keep the captured crewmen isolated. In Bermuda, this presented no difficulty: The island was hardly on the beaten track, and its Naval Operating Base was guarded by a contingent of no-nonsense Marines.

Despite the ferocious fighting reputation of the U-boat corps, the prisoners remained remarkably passive. Most were in some kind of cognitive shock that for them the war was over, but on the plus side they were free from the incessant dread of a horrible death, fed three square meals a day, allowed outside to feel the antiseptic sunshine on their skin, led through the same exercise routines that American sailors undertook every day, and had their teeth seen to by good dentists while their medical issues were taken care of by excellent doctors.

After disembarking from *Guadalcanal*, they had been physically examined and treated for any complaints. The only serious case was that of *U-505*'s wounded captain, Harald Lange, who had to have one of his shrapnel-studded legs taken off mid-thigh. The rest of the crew's afflictions were minor ailments caused by living in filthy quarters in close proximity for months at a time, and exacerbated by having to endure the sweat-inducing jail on *Guadalcanal*.

The most common issues were "furuncles" (reddish boils), rashes, and other bacterial skin infections. These were simple to cure with boric-acid soaks, and sufferers were removed from the sick list after a few days.

Then it was time for questioning.

II

The three OP-16-Z interrogators who had flown to Bermuda with Knowles—Lieutenant Commander Gherardi and Lieutenants Erek and Hart—called the crew in one by one. *Interrogation* was too strong a word for what followed: They essentially had a conversation, some briefer than others, with each man. In the case of *U-505*, there was little information they needed.

Names, ranks, service dates, and addresses were the bread-and-butter substance of these chats. There were also a few questions about what had happened to Captain Zschech, and about *U-505*'s troubled history. The interrogators used a blunt shorthand to distinguish who was useful, who was recalcitrant, and who really didn't know anything.

The first category included men such as the machinists Werner Hönemann and Josef Juriza, who both had "Good Man" written at the top of the buff-colored, lined A4 pages the interrogators used to scribble their notes. Others, such as Karl Schmidt, needed some coaxing but were otherwise "Meek and O.K., Will Talk." To persuade these shy ones that it was permissible to speak freely, the interrogators looked for men who came across as leaders, such as the radioman Erich Laun, who "will answer anything." If they sang, the others would, too.

Laun was important in another respect as well: With Gottfried Fischer dead, only by cross-referencing the testimonies of Laun and his surviving fellow radio operator, Erich Kalbitz ("Completely O.K."), could the interrogators confirm that "no signal [was] made about final attack." That proved U-Boat Command was still in the dark—and Gallery in the clear.

The chattiest of all proved to be twenty-two-year-old Willi Kneisel, who may have been the same "Willi" who'd once approached Hans Goebeler to suggest going AWOL to Switzerland. His answers filled no fewer than seven pages—evidence that Kneisel was severely disaffected from the regime. In reward, his interrogator wrote: "A very, very good boy. One of the best."

By contrast, some of the crewmen dug in their heels, though the degree of their hostility varied widely. Goebeler, for instance, was noted as being "Security Conscious!," which meant that he could not be drawn out on *U-505*'s weapons or operations but was otherwise fine to deal with. Similarly, Hans Decker proved "a little sticky" but was otherwise "O.K."

Reserved for the most hardcore hold-outs was the term "Bastard," which referred to extreme Nazi sympathies and signaled that the flagged individual bore watching. One of these was Hans Senft, aged only twenty, who "refuses all answers and is to be treated as a bastard."

And then there were the harmless ones. Twenty-year-old Hans

Rasch, who had joined *U-505* only recently, was a "very nice lad. But knows nothing because he is quite without experience." Seaman Walter Baumert, however—who may have entered the service as far back as April 1940 and should therefore have been a font of information—turned out to be "O.K. but dumb!!"

Quite often, the interrogators, a couple of whom were exiled German Jews, would linger to reminisce about the old country and happy days gone by. When Wolfgang Schiller was questioned by (probably) Lieutenant Erek, who already knew everything the submariner could possibly tell him, Erek informed Schiller that "he came from the same town I came from. From Breslau. And then we spoke only about my home town. And it was a really nice conversation."

Absent from the interrogation list were the helpful Ewald Felix, who was being comfortably provided for elsewhere, and Josef Hauser, the chief engineer nicknamed the Raccoon. He was kept separately, with the officers, who included Dr. Friedrich Rosenmeyer (a drunk greatly disliked by the crew), *Leutnant* Kurt Brey, and the popular Paul Meyer, who had assumed temporary command after Zschech's death.

Hauser was fortunate to be shielded by his rank. Without it, he would have been housed with the crewmen. As Zschech's incompetent appointee and suspected sneak, Hauser had long been hated, but now he had a new crime to answer for: Everyone blamed him for failing to sink *U-505*, an ignominy that in turn had heaped dishonor upon *them*.

Surrendering was one thing; surrendering with ship (mostly) intact was traitorous. When Lange had regained consciousness for the first time after being rescued and discovered that *U-505* was not at the bottom of the sea, he moaned, "I will be punished for this."

He wouldn't be, but Hauser would. As chief engineer, it had been his responsibility to stay behind and set the demolition charges that would sink the submarine. Yet numerous crewmen recalled that instead of scuttling the ship Hauser had scuttled up the ladder and was one of the first out.

As the Raccoon would soon discover, inactions had consequences.

III

The crew would stay in Bermuda for six weeks—long enough for U-Boat Command to assume the worst, but also sufficient to allow special arrangements to be made for them in Louisiana, their new home.

The prisoners would miss Bermuda. Werner Reh deemed it paradise—"the freedom, the fresh air, the climate, food and drink"—and considered his time there a vacation paid for by the United States government.

But all good things come to an end, and on August 1 two large coastal-patrol boats, *Rockville* and *Brattleboro,* departed Bermuda bound not for Norfolk, home to a huge naval base, but for Newport News, Virginia, where Marine escorts would surreptitiously disembark their human supercargo. A sole survivor stayed behind: In no condition to travel, the one-legged Captain Lange recuperated in sunny Bermuda for the next nine months.

The men were destined for Camp Ruston, a POW camp that had been built two years prior on a 750-acre swath of piney woods outside the eponymous Louisiana town. Sent south by special train scheduled to arrive on the night of August 5–6, the prisoners were preceded by a request from Admiral King that they be permanently sequestered from all other POWs. A naval intelligence officer accompanying them reiterated to the camp commandant that this particular batch of Germans was not to be permitted to mingle with anyone, ever.

Moreover, any letter they wrote must be separated from the rest of the camp mail and forwarded to the Chief Postal Censor in New York so it could be held back. It was just as important to intercept any *other*

POW's mail that might mention the arrival of these mysterious internees. (There would be a scare several months later when a German prisoner in another sector of the camp joyfully wrote home saying that he'd just seen so-and-so, a *U-505* crewman who happened to be his wife's cousin.)

Camp Ruston was well-chosen for secrecy. Until shortly before the submariners' arrival, it had been home to around 4,000 of Rommel's *Afrika Korps* soldiers. Most had since been moved to other camps, and in their place were non-Germans—many volunteers, but some conscripted—who had joined the Wehrmacht. These included Russians (a few died by suicide but the rest were later returned to the USSR to face Stalin's wrath), Hungarians, Poles, Czechs, Romanians, Lithuanians, Vichy French, and even some Muslim Chechens (erroneously believed to be "Mongolians"), all of whom divided themselves into groups along national lines to defend their turf.

Few of the resident POWs, then, spoke German, and fewer still knew anything about U-boats. From the outset they shunned Germans like the *U-505*ers, and the *U-505*ers were forbidden to associate with them, so it was a mismatch made in heaven.

Key as well to maintaining security was to conceal the *U-505* prisoners from the prying eyes of the International Red Cross and the Swiss Legation, which served as intermediaries for the Reich government. Whenever delegates of either organization were due to visit, the *U-505* men were taken on a camping trip to the nearby forest or driven a couple of hours south to another holding center.

For the rest of the time, they were relegated to a far corner of Compound III. The first few months were hard on the crew: They were desperate to show that while they had surrendered, they were not beaten.

Enterprisingly, they captured tortoises—perhaps as many as one hundred—painted swastikas on their shells, and let them trundle under the wire. They also acquired enough cellophane to piece together several small balloons, upon which they wrote U-505 LIVES!, and tried to float them out, not very successfully. Next came a *Great Escape*-style attempt to tunnel outside from their barracks, which was busted when they were a mere five feet from freedom. The camp commandant urbanely directed those responsible to fill the tunnel back in, applying the same characteristic diligence with which they had dug it.

IV

More seriously, the *U-505* prisoners held an illicit midnight tribunal. The American authorities had recently cracked down on these mock military trials, often called "courts of honor," owing to a series of murders, forced suicides by noose or slashed wrists, and severe punishment beatings carried out by rabid Nazi loyalists who had established *Terrorgruppen* within camps to exact retribution on "anti-Nazis."

Membership in these private Gestapos was often signified by a pinpricked tattoo of a homemade swastika-and-sword logo, and their definition of *anti-Nazi* was a loose one: Alleged cowards, informers, defeatists, or anyone suspected of criticizing the regime were liable to be disciplined. The worst offenders were members of the Afrika Korps—so often still conceived as the honorable good *Soldaten* of the Reich—who'd been captured in 1942, when Hitler was still on top of the world. Cut off from much communication, and still thoroughly indoctrinated in Nazi ideology, as late as 1944 they continued to believe that Germany was winning; when America inevitably surrendered, they promised the targets of their intimidation, they would be shot upon returning home.

The power of these Terrorgruppen had recently been sapped when the authorities had begun filtering out the hardest Nazis from incoming batches of POWs. The former were sent to a special camp for irredeemables in Oklahoma, where they kept themselves busy persecuting each other for moral laxity for the rest of the war.

At Camp Ruston, nevertheless, the survivors from *U-505* managed to set up their own kangaroo court. The interrogators on Bermuda had noted that several of the crewmen were "bastards," and it's probable that some of these were the instigators. Owing to the need for secrecy, none of the bastards could be sent to Oklahoma and so they all had to stay at Camp Ruston. Their thrall over the others, however, was limited because they formed a small minority compared with the bulk of the less-political crew. Still, the fact that they had succeeded in convening a court of honor implies that it was a popular move.

And understandably so. *U-505* had been ingloriously stolen from them—and someone needed to pay. One of the accused was Hans Goebeler, who was ordered to explain why he had not ensured the sinking of *U-505* by throwing the sea-strainer lid into the bilge (where it could not have been found) instead of across the control room (where it was). After his testimony, Goebeler was judged innocent and commended for his initiative and bravery.

The man who was truly on trial, Josef "Raccoon" Hauser, defended himself from the charge of dereliction of duty (for failing to set the demolition charges) by claiming that the boat was already sinking fast and he assumed her end was near. That cut no ice with his judges, who found him guilty and told him that a court-martial would be his due when they were released. In the meantime, his comrades would treat him as a traitor. The threat was serious enough to convince Hauser that he wasn't safe and he prevailed upon the camp authorities to transfer him elsewhere.

It was a wise decision on the Raccoon's part. Only a few months earlier, Werner Drechsler of *U-118* (a U-tanker that Knowles had helped sink), accused of being a rat like Ewald Felix, had been tried, beaten, strangled, and lynched by his former comrades within six hours of arriving at a POW camp.

Whether Hauser was in similar jeopardy cannot be known, but surely it's revealing that more than five decades later his former comrades, most notably Goebeler, still cursed his very name. Asked to talk about Hauser, the normally amiable Werner Reh clammed up and replied, "I have no comment to make about that," while Machinist's Mate Karl Springer gave a curt "No" to the same question. The subject was "taboo," he added.

Josef Hauser may have escaped fatal retribution at Camp Ruston, but the men there had nevertheless succeeded in executing his memory.

V

Over time, the prisoners grew more accustomed to, even fond of, camp life. For one thing, this was America, and food portions were large—larger than anything they'd ever get in Germany, even in peacetime. Despite a few complaints about too much white bread, many put on weight and had to be issued larger uniforms. Hence the introduction of a daily exercise regimen consisting of calisthenics, running, and drills.

Thinking about what would happen the day after the inevitable defeat of the Nazis, the Americans had smartly instituted a comprehensive education program. Karl Springer recalled that the *U-505* prisoners "took Spanish lessons, we learned Greek history, we had math lessons." They even set up a glee club for jolly sing-alongs.

Considered more important, though, was to inoculate the prisoners against Communist propaganda by giving lectures and showing films touching on the virtues of democracy and liberty. There was a Cold War coming, and just as the Soviets had established front groups of Wehrmacht prisoners like the Federation of German Officers, the Americans wanted their own cadre of friendly Germans on the ground.

For the prisoners' free time, there was the impressive camp library, hobby clubs, and art classes—many a German earned cash and favors from his American guards with an ability to whittle and paint and sculpt. Sports were encouraged, though pole-vaulting was forbidden. Even if they didn't take to baseball, much to their guards' disappointment, the Germans leveled an area to fit a regulation soccer pitch and taught the Americans how to play a proper European game. For the less sporty, prisoners could subscribe to virtually any newspaper or magazine—*Life*, *Reader's Digest*, and the *Saturday Evening Post* were popular choices—and they were allowed to purchase cigarettes, Coca-Cola, beer, toiletries, and treats from the camp store.

They earned their scrip via contracted labor. The Geneva Convention guaranteed enlisted men a wage of eighty cents per day if they worked. Inside the camp there were always vacancies for electricians, mechanics, and carpenters, but Louisiana was cotton country; once the Germans had built enough trust to be let out of the camp, they were assigned to picking cotton in the nearby fields—under an armed escort, of course.

The cotton fields, like the nearby rice farms and lumber mills, were a topsy-turvy world for the POWs. Taught since childhood that they were the master race, the Germans now found themselves on par with an allegedly inferior one, although the white planters treated them far better than they did their black laborers. For their part, the latter were aggrieved that the newcomers not only undercut their wages but also, being immune from Jim Crow laws, enjoyed higher social status than actual American citizens. Some of the planters even encouraged the Germans to date their daughters once the current unpleasantness was over.

The South's peculiarity in these matters was as strange to the Germans as the Nuremberg Race Laws were to Americans. One German prisoner, escorted by a black MP through Atlanta on his way to Camp Ruston, was shocked to discover that his guard was relegated to standing outside the WHITES ONLY lavatory, with his foot wedged inside the door, as the prisoner relieved himself. Another POW took the sentiment a step further, declaring that he would never travel willingly in a WHITES ONLY train carriage.

All very worthy, but no German POW seemed to think it odd, much less abhorrent, that Jews back home had lost their jobs and businesses, been banned from public transport, had their belongings and residences seized, and ultimately been "sent East," never to return.

VI

By the opening months of 1945, the U-boat war was as good as over, even as Grand Admiral Karl Dönitz, chipper as ever, continued to reassure the Führer that he was commissioning no fewer than 450 submarines, of which 84 would be the next-generation Type XXIs the admiral had long been touting as "wonder weapons."

With so much bad news streaming in from every other front, Hitler was delighted to hear Dönitz's boast at the end of February that the imminent arrival of the first Type XXIs would mean "the U-boat once more can operate successfully even in areas of the strongest escorts." Indeed, the grand admiral sunnily promised, the "rebirth of the U-boat war" would be "significant for the overall war situation."

Just the ticket for raising everyone's spirits—except that in truth, while the Type XXI's performance in trials exceeded even the most elevated expectations, rocketing it far past anything the Allies had, its construction program had been a disaster. As a result, when he spoke to Hitler, Dönitz's Type XXI armada remained a phantom fleet: The first operational one, *U-2501*, would be ready to sail at the end of April, but it was scuttled on May 3, a few weeks before the German surrender.

Given its incredible underwater speed, streamlined design, ability to stay submerged for seventy-four hours, maximum depth of 919 feet, special "silent running" electric motor, and rapid-fire torpedo salvos, the outcome of the war at sea might have been very different had the Type XXI appeared en masse in 1943 or early 1944.

But it hadn't, and the stark reality was that the Type VII and Type IX U-boats were being slaughtered left, right, and center. In January 1945, fourteen were lost; in February, twenty-one; and in March, thirty-three, including thirteen destroyed in a single day when the U.S. Army Air Forces bombed their dockyards. In those months alone, Peter Cremer of *U-333*—the longest-serving commander and a man blessed with lottery-winning luck—lost three of his four former watch officers who'd gone on to command their own boats. They and all their men had died for no good reason at all.

By April 18, when Dönitz conferenced with a palsied Hitler in Berlin—aside from an audience to wish the Führer happy birthday two days later in the Bunker, it would be the last time he saw him—even the grand admiral felt bound to acknowledge that the Type XXI would not save them. In fact, whatever was left of the U-boat fleet was a spent force, at sea at least. Still, as he informed his Führer, he had reassigned their remaining crews to rapidly organized land-based naval units directed to defend the Reich to the very end.

One engineering petty officer accordingly wrote that "a single day's training has made an infantryman out of a U-boat man." He was handed a single-shot *Panzerfaust* anti-tank weapon, then—along with Captain Cremer and a motley collection of sixteen-year-old Hitler Youths and disabled Great War veterans—he was sent out to confront the British armor spearheading toward Hamburg.

Hitler was impressed by Dönitz's unstinting, unyielding loyalty. The Wehrmacht, the Luftwaffe, the SS—all had betrayed their death-drunk Führer but the Kriegsmarine had remained steadfast. The generals and the field marshals—the old Prussian elites with their monocles and *Grafs* and *Vons*—had tried to kill him during the Bomb Plot in 1944;

Reichsmarschall Göring, fat and rouged, had moved to seize power and was now under house arrest; and even the supremely murderous crank *Reichsführer* Himmler was trying to strike a deal with the Americans by offering his remaining SS as Washington's Praetorian Guard against the Soviets.

But not dear Dönitz. As a reward, before he committed suicide on April 30, Hitler appointed Dönitz to the post of Supreme Commander and Head of State of the Thousand-Year Reich, currently aged twelve.

On May 3, as anointed heir to the golden throne and bloody altar of the Nazi empire, Dönitz began using the sports gym at the Naval Academy in Flensburg in northern Germany as the government's new headquarters. If Dönitz considered a gym a step down from the Chancellery in Berlin, he gamely made no mention of it. Instead he issued Cremer and his men, still in their blue Navy uniforms, field-gray ones and instructed them to form a "Guard Battalion" for the final defense of the Reich around the academy from which they had once graduated with such high hopes.

Dönitz's very last order of that day, as if he had been postponing it for as long as he could, was to direct the few U-boats still at sea to cease operations and return home. He signed off by addressing the remnants of his once-feared force in his distinctively familiar tone: "Comrades! Preserve your brave U-boat spirit, with which you have fought through the long years bravely, toughly, and unflinchingly; preserve it for the future, to the benefit of the Fatherland. Long live Germany! Your Grand Admiral."

Over the next couple of days, some 218 captains—loyal to the end to Navy and state—would scuttle or destroy their own penned U-boats, the great majority of which were barely functioning or only half-built. Just 156 mostly useless submarines would formally surrender to the Allies.

And then it was all over, as Germany unconditionally capitulated on May 8, 1945. At the Naval Academy, however, a life of mummery and pomp continued, as in some Roman palace whose decadent courtiers were studiously deaf to the clattering of barbarian swords outside its walls. In the grim eclipse of an exhausted regime, elaborate ceremonial duties carried on and portentous titles for defunct jobs like "Minister for the Occupied Territories in the East" retained so as to extend, for a delicious little while longer, the delusions of vanished supremacy.

It all came to a head in the Third Reich's last state funeral on May 15.

Two days earlier, *Kapitän zur See* Wolfgang Lüth, the head of the Naval Academy and the most decorated U-boat commander of all (and also the humorless Nazi prig who had banned girlie pinups), had been shot by a sentry after he fumbled his own password of the day.

Dönitz and the remaining cohort of U-boat veterans attended the somber affair, with six Knight's Cross recipients bearing Lüth's coffin. The ceremony marked the benighted conclusion to the longest military campaign of World War II: the Battle of the Atlantic, which had begun on the very first day of the war, when *U-30* had torpedoed SS *Athenia*, a British liner, killing 117 civilian passengers and crew, including twenty-eight Americans.

On May 16, a day after Lüth's burial, the U.S. Navy Department revealed to an astounded nation that, according to its press release, "on June 4, 1944, a U.S. Navy escort carrier task group reverted to the tactics of the early Continental Navy and hunted down, attacked, boarded, and captured the Nazi submarine *U-505.*"

Featuring prominently was, of course, Gallery, who in his inimitable style was quoted as saying, "I consider this capture to be proof for posterity of the versatility and courage of the present day American sailor. All ships in this task group were less than a year old and 80 percent of the officers and men were serving in their first seagoing ship. All hands did their stuff like veteran sea dogs, and airplane mechanics became submarine experts in a hurry, when the chips were down. I'm sure John Paul Jones and his men were proud of these lads and of the day's work when the U.S. colors went up on the *U-505.*"

Perhaps Lüth's death is a fitting way to mark The End—or perhaps a better one is the U.S. Navy's proud announcement of its immortal achievement. Whatever the case, a week later, on May 23, British troops entered Dönitz's headquarters and arrested him like a common criminal. The spell was at last broken.

At Nuremberg, Dönitz would be sentenced to ten years at Spandau Prison, time that he would serve alongside his fellow fallen princes of the Reich Albert Speer, Erich Raeder, and Rudolf Hess. During their imprisonment, they seemed to spend most of their time bickering over who got an extra pair of socks or a larger serving of peas.

VII

The Navy's announcement of *U-505*'s capture obviated the need for any further secrecy. At Camp Ruston, the crew was finally permitted to write to their families, and the German government was informed of their internment. The shock their families must have felt after nearly a year of assuming that their husbands, fathers, and sons had died would have been both horrible and wonderful.

Those living in eastern Germany or central Europe, however, often did not hear the news until perhaps a year (or even two) later, and sometimes more. Once refugees from the advancing Soviets, they had usually ended up in displaced-persons camps or were otherwise untraceable in the chaotic aftermath of the war. Wolfgang Schiller, for instance, was unable to contact his Silesian parents until 1948—three years after the German surrender.

The *U-505* men were treated no differently than any of the thousands of other POWs in Allied hands. Given the millions of Allied soldiers who needed to be demobilized—and the many millions more refugees in Europe who had to be taken care of—the process of repatriation was necessarily a slow and circuitous one for all.

The crew had left Camp Ruston by the end of 1945, with most being transported to Camp McCain, Mississippi, an Army training base. By April 1946 they were at Camp Shanks in New York, once an embarkation point for soldiers heading to Europe for D-Day. There was a brief hunger strike when they discovered that they were being sent to France, Belgium, or Britain—anywhere but Germany—though Europe, at least, was closer to home.

At that point, they were broken up into twos and threes. Karl Springer went to Liverpool; Werner Reh ended up in Yorkshire; Wolfgang Schiller was housed outside London; and Hans Goebeler was sent to a farm in Scotland. Owing to severe labor shortages, POWs were widely used as cheap laborers and workers. By the end of 1947, though, the crunch had eased and virtually all of the prisoners had returned to Germany. Awaiting them was a new world very alien to the one they had left behind in headier days.

Despite the delays, none of the crew had anything substantive to complain about. They had, depending on one's inclinations, either cheated fate or drawn a royal flush: They were *alive*. They had not perished, as so many others did, in the hideous dark amid crumpling iron and cold surging seawater, anguishedly praying to God and pleading for their mothers.

Relatively few men survived Dönitz's U-boats. Of the 48,000 to 50,000 sailors who entered the submarine service from 1939 to 1945, more than 30,000 died—a fatality rate of roughly 60 percent, and one never exceeded by any other modern military branch. Of 863 U-boats that embarked on war patrols, 739 never came back.

U-505 may once have been disparaged as the Unluckiest Boat in the Fleet. But she turned out to be the Luckiest Boat of All.

"THEIR DESIRED HAVEN"

(Psalm 107:29)

I

Some achievements deserve admiration simply because they are admirable achievements. In and of themselves, they inspire, they astonish, they fascinate, they thrill—they make history *interesting*. The first ascent of Mt. Everest is one such, and so too is Charles Lindbergh's solo flight across the Atlantic and the discovery of *Titanic's* final resting-place on the chilly seabed.

The hunt for and heist of *U-505* is another case in point. Its importance lies not in whether it "changed the course of the war"—it didn't, not to any major degree—but in the fact that, well, it was one *hell of a thing*. Pulling it off against towering odds took guts, instinct, mettle, smarts, planning, luck, and, if you're of that mind, a divine thumb on the scale of human affairs. To use a perhaps now-unfashionable term, the capture of *U-505* was a *Glorious Adventure* on the high seas.

U-505 sails serenely, if perhaps disconcertingly, beneath New York's Brooklyn Bridge.

Gallery knew it, and so did Knowles, and so did King and Low and everyone else at Tenth Fleet and aboard Task Group 22.3—and that is exactly how it should be remembered, and celebrated.

II

The official announcement on May 16 of *U-505*'s capture made Gallery and his boys famous—so much so that the Navy urgently recruited what was now the U.S. submarine *Nemo* into a war-bond drive that saw her tour the East Coast to raise money for the ongoing fight against Japan.

Helping to spark interest and excitement was a documentary movie,

Now It Can Be Told, spliced together from the footage Gallery had shot during the battle and some staged action scenes filmed off the coast of Florida. The photograph that Clifford Werlla had snapped of Gallery posing on the captured *U-505*'s bridge also helped sell the story. Republished widely, for a time it became almost as iconic a shot as Joe Rosenthal's of the Marines raising the flag at Iwo Jima.

Until her reemergence into the spotlight, however, *U-505* had been ignominiously mistreated by the Navy. To maintain secrecy, she had stayed in Bermuda after her crew was taken to Camp Ruston and was used as an experimental vessel to test new Allied anti-submarine technology. After the war-bond tour, in common with the titanic haul of Axis matériel and surplus Allied ships that now cluttered American ports, *U-505* was to be scrapped or used for target practice until fate, or fortune, intervened.

Casting his eye down page after page of ship listings, the Navy official in charge of the decommissioning program happened to notice a "U-505" lodged inconspicuously amidst all the hundreds of once-valuable destroyer escorts that no one needed anymore. He contacted Gallery, who swung into action to save "his" U-boat—in such pitiable condition by now that it would be charitable to call her a rust bucket.

Transforming himself into a one-man marketing operation, Gallery mounted a years-long crusade to bring *U-505* to Chicago, his hometown. He raised funds, organized exhibitions, conducted a ceaseless publicity drive, exercised his considerable charm on admirals and industrialists alike, and persuaded war-weary Americans that here they had, wasting away, one of the great trophies of the war. In the end, he battered down all resistance and won his battle.

In the early 1950s, the names of those who had been involved in *U-505*'s capture began to emerge. Gallery's boys had been as good as gold about keeping their mouths shut to respect his warning of dire retribution if they blabbed, but it didn't matter anymore. Numerous wives of the men in the boarding parties only now discovered their husbands' roles when they read about them in a magazine story or attended a Gallery-sponsored fundraiser and watched him raise his glass to their heroism.

The final voyage of *U-505* under her last captain—fittingly, Gallery's *Guadalcanal* engineer, Earl Trosino—came in mid-1954: She was towed from her Navy berth in Portsmouth, New Hampshire, to Montreal, and thence to a succession of crowd-cheering (and fundraising) whistle-stops by river, canal, and lake past Buffalo, Cleveland, Detroit, and Milwaukee before reaching Chicago.

For *U-505*, it had been a long odyssey—one that originated in Hamburg's *Deutsche Werft* shipyard in 1941 and ended on the southern shore of Lake Michigan in September 1954. Today the brutal, magnificent creature reposes in state (and restored in splendid fashion) in a specially built wing of the Griffin Museum of Science and Industry.

Her first commander, Loewe, remarked during a postwar visit that "it is an odd feeling to consider that every month thousands of people enter the boat and stroll through the places where we so often stood while sweating out depth charges and bombs falling upon us." Indeed, when you tour the exhibit today, it is undeniably eerie to walk past where Zschech shot himself or to imagine Goebeler desperately flinging the sea strainer lid into a corner to try to scuttle the very vessel you're on. It's like walking across a perfectly preserved Civil War battlefield with only the ghosts for company.

During this time, Gallery became fast friends with Herman Wouk, a naval veteran himself and the bestselling author of *The Caine Mutiny*. For Wouk, then being attacked for undermining the Navy's reputation by his portrayal of Captain Queeg, having a famous fan like Gallery (by then a rear admiral) tell him it was "the best book about the modern Navy that I've ever read" came as a tremendous morale-booster.

To repay him, the writer suggested that his literary agent take Gallery on as a client. In gratitude for all the well-paid *Saturday Evening Post* pieces that resulted, Gallery invited Wouk to come along for a training cruise with his carrier group. The flagship's captain was obligingly displaced from his comfortable quarters to make room for the former lieutenant. Later on, Gallery would serve as Wouk's naval consultant for *The Winds of War* and *War and Remembrance*.

It was an incongruous relationship, recalled Wouk: the observant, abstemious Jew and the faithful, hard-drinking Catholic. But after Gallery retired to the Virginia suburbs, they talked often of God's role in the world—and perhaps also of His role in the hunt for and heist of *U-505*.

For some years, Gallery kept up an illuminating correspondence with his prize's two living captains, Loewe and Lange, both of whom became managers of businesses—construction in Loewe's case, fruit in Lange's—that played a modest part in West Germany's postwar economic miracle.

In 1956, armed with insights provided by Loewe and Lange, Gallery published an entertaining memoir, *Twenty Million Tons Under the Sea*, narrating his fun adventure. He even cheekily sent a copy to Dönitz a couple of months after the last Führer was released from his ten-year stretch in Spandau Prison. The grand admiral, still reveling in the title, thanked him in a politely noncommittal manner, choosing to focus on the spirit of "comradeship" that unites sailors and studiously not mentioning the con that Gallery had orchestrated by making him believe *U-505* had been lost in action.

Dönitz would outlive Gallery by three years. The Can-Do King died of emphysema on January 16, 1977. According to his nephew, Gallery had been pensive for several months before the inevitable, but he at least was succored by his faith that in doing his duty he had earned a place at the Lord's right hand.

III

In 1974, RAF Group Captain Frederick Winterbotham was permitted to publish *The Ultra Secret*, which revealed to an astonished world the British decryption of Enigma and its strategic deployment, not least during the Battle of the Atlantic.

There had been hints about Enigma before, and those in the know understood that euphemisms such as *radio intelligence* in World War II books up to that time generally meant *Ultra*, but Winterbotham's was the first to make it part of the popular discourse. To this day, there remains, as a result of his being prime mover, a heavy skew toward the extraordinary British achievement of penetrating Enigma, whereas the American side in this cryptographic war-within-a-war, especially after 1943, is barely known.

Whether an aged Gallery read *The Ultra Secret* is unknown—Dönitz frankly refused to believe any of its revelations—but if he had he might just have been able to guess, after wondering for thirty long years, how Knowles, that soothsayer of Tenth Fleet, had been able to predict the movements and positions of U-boats so unerringly. In truth, Knowles had generally relied more on other sources for his Working Fictions, tending to use *Ultra* to confirm or zoom in on the stories he'd already seen in his mind's eye.

Though not a cryptanalyst, Knowles was nevertheless familiar with the state and progress of U.S. Navy Enigma work. In the Secret Room, he saw more highly classified material than probably anyone else in the country. At the end of the war, all of it, including the confidential Tenth Fleet material, was packed into boxes and transferred to a secure naval facility in Indiana. Those documents, for the most part opened only in 2001, now reside in the National Archives.

Knowles was similarly disinclined to reveal his role in Tenth Fleet and the anti-submarine campaign. He was a man of secrets, and never one to brag. In 1946, in an unremarkable ceremony at Main Navy, Rear Admiral Richard Edwards—first buttonholed by Rodger Winn to set up an American Room 41—awarded Knowles the Legion of Merit. Fittingly, Knowles then joined the CIA, rising to Assistant Director. Later he would work once more with Gallery, when he was briefly detached to a committee discussing the future of submarine warfare. Together, as their friend Admiral Low circumspectly put it, they "stopped some silly things."

Whether Knowles stayed in touch with Winn, however, is a matter for conjecture. Probably not at any level much beyond exchanging Christmas cards. Though Knowles's admiration for his counterpart's talents remained unalloyed, the betrayal over *Ultra*, the campaign against the U-tankers, and the Wolf Pack *Trutz* trap may have been unforgivable, at least from Winn's side.

For his part, Winn returned to the law and eventually became a judge. In 1970 he suffered a severe stroke that rendered him unable to speak or write, and he died in 1972—two years before the Enigma revelation that changed everything. His loyal deputy, Patrick Beesly, would publish *Very Special Intelligence* in 1977, finally telling the world about the role of Winn and Room 41 in helping to win the struggle against the U-boat.

In it, Beesly magnanimously laid old grievances to rest and granted that while "our concern was not unreasonable" about the Americans' relatively wanton use of *Ultra* to hunt and kill submarines, "Knowles was proved right and no harm, except to the unfortunate U-boats, resulted." In return, Knowles reluctantly shuffled into the (dim) light and wrote an appreciative review of the book for the then-classified CIA journal, *Studies in Intelligence,* in which he paid due honor to Winn, "the brilliant London barrister" with whom "this reviewer...worked closely."

The only time, however, that Knowles ever said anything even remotely publicly about his wartime work was in the fall of that year, 1977, at a symposium at the U.S. Naval Academy. He was one of three expert speakers on the subject of "Ultra and the Battle of the Atlantic"— Beesly was another—and he mounted a polite but frank retort to what he regarded as Britain's hogging the limelight when it came to Enigma.

The United States, Knowles countered, was very far from being "spoon-fed" Ultra: "[O]nce we got into the act, the American contribution to Ultra was at least equal to the British effort." In fact, Admiral King's "calculated risk" strategy of leveraging U.S.-produced Ultra was not only "sound" but "paid off in rich dividends, culminating in the capture by Dan Gallery's task group of U-505."

Having died nine months earlier, Gallery, sadly, was not present to hear those laudatory words, but for the rest of his own life Knowles always remembered him.

On August 19, 1986, the National Security Agency sent T. R. Johnson down to Stuart, Florida, to interview the long-retired Knowles as part of an oral-history series for its records. At the end of a long and tiring conversation, the 82-year-old, trailing an oxygen tank, offered to show Johnson "a little photograph" he had of Gallery he kept on display in another room. It was the famous shot of the wiry Chicagoan standing triumphantly atop U-505's conning tower—but this one was an original, personally given to Knowles, his brother-in-arms and partner-in-crime, all those decades ago.

His work done, his life recorded, his friend consecrated, three months later Knowles himself departed in peace.

ACKNOWLEDGMENTS

I talk a lot about luck and fate in this book, and I *think* the idea for *Phantom Fleet* came about by happy accident—or perhaps it was by some kind of providence. I was pitching a series of assuredly brilliant ideas to my agent, Eric Lupfer of UTA, who was not quite as enthused about their broad commercial appeal as I'd anticipated, until, reaching the end of my list, I mentioned that I'd heard about a Japanese submarine that had been tracked by the U.S. Navy during World War II. It might make for an exciting story. To which Eric responded, "Oh, you know there's a U-boat in Chicago? They tracked that one, too."

I did not, in fact, know that there was a U-boat in Chicago—which, to be fair, is a rather unlikely place for a U-boat to be—but we both understood there and then that we'd hit upon the Next Book. So yet again my thanks go to him for that vital assist, his fine judgment, and his expert guidance on the subsequent proposal.

Authors write their books alone, but they benefit from a crack team to publish them. In this instance, I must thank my terrific editor, Alexander Littlefield of Little, Brown, for again taking on one of my proposals and seeing it through with his usual style, aplomb, and judicious comments on the manuscript. Shepherding the book through a notably smooth process was Pat Jalbert-Levine, Senior Production Editor, while Allan Fallow performed sterling service in copyediting my clumsy prose into readable form and proofreader Barbara Jatkola ruthlessly laser-targeted my dangling modifiers. I thank them all profusely, and I must also express my gratitude to Kirin Diemont, Associate Art Director, for the striking cover, as well as Morgan Wu, Alex's assistant, for arranging the always-tricky photo rights.

As I've followed the tortuous trail of *U-505*, I've accumulated numerous other debts that I shall now strive to pay.

I'd like to thank Dr. Kenneth A. Knowles, Jr., the son of one of the stars of this book. He sent me the only copy of a family history, written by his uncle, and trusted me to return it to him safe and sound. Dr. David Kohnen of the U.S. Naval War College, the reigning expert on "King's Navy," has been of inestimable assistance and provided a number of key documents, as well as sage advice.

Books like this, I've said before (and I'll say again), cannot be written without archives and libraries. Any experienced historian knows that 99 percent of the world's documents are not digitized—and most never shall be. For supplying copies of important items, I need to mention: Robert Simpson, National Cryptologic Museum (National Security Agency); Adam Minakowski, Nimitz Library (U.S. Naval Academy); Blair Williams, Cumberland County Historical Society of Carlisle, Pennsylvania; Brynn White, Century Association Archives Foundation (New York); and Emily Hegranes, U.S. Naval Institute.

I'm particularly grateful to Douglas Zimmer, Special Project Volunteer at the Griffin Museum of Science and Industry, who was gracious enough to allow me free rein of its voluminous *U-505* archive while turning a conveniently blind eye to my son clambering atop a (defused) German torpedo that was lying around the storeroom.

And I must also praise two remarkable websites, both extraordinarily useful and both clearly labors of love, which proved invaluable to my research: Uboat.net and Uboatarchive.net.

Family is the most important source of encouragement and sustenance during the lengthy process of writing a book, and I'm blessed to have the best around. I'd like to thank Ari and Michelle, Zoë and Craig (and Dean and Drew), and my extended family (Liz and Chad, Ben and Jaime, Erna, and David and Carolyn) for their support.

As always, I count myself a fortunate man to be providentially married to my beloved of beloveds, Rebecca, she who walks in beauty, and a proud one to have a son like Edmund. Without them this book would never have emerged from its chrysalis, nor been launched fluttering into the world, and so to them it is dedicated.

NOTES

PROLOGUE—"WONDERS IN THE DEEP"

Gallery's views of fate: *Twenty Million Tons*, 4–5, 257.

CHAPTER 1—THE EMERALD CITY

I

Gannon, *Operation Drumbeat*, 224–25, 231; U-123 War Diary, Jan. 14, 15, https://www.uboatarchive.net/U-123/KTB123-7.htm; *Movie-Radio Guide*, Jan. 10–16, 1942, 27–29; Mulligan, *Neither Sharks Nor Wolves*, 17; Bergmeier and Lotz, *Hitler's Airwaves*; Weather Archive (http://wxarchive.uppermw.com/) for Jan. 1942. The Internet Archive contains a large collection of surviving *Goldbergs* episodes, including that of Jan. 14, "Mr. Way to Receive a Pardon."

II

Gannon, *Operation Drumbeat*, 231–32; War Diary, Jan. 15, https://www.uboat archive.net/U-123/KTB123-7.htm; "Strange Life of a Big Ship That Never Goes Anywhere," *Popular Science Monthly*, Feb. 1931, 68.

III

War Diary, Jan. 15, https://www.uboatarchive.net/U-123/KTB123-7.htm; Gannon, *Operation Drumbeat*, 233–34; "Coimbra," https://www.uboat.net/allies/merchants/1251.htm. In 2019 the wreck of the *Coimbra*, now an artificial reef, began leaking oil to the surface; up to a million gallons was thought to remain in her tanks.

IV

Brooklyn Eagle, Jan. 16, 17; *New York Times,* Jan. 17.

V

Gannon, *Operation Drumbeat,* 173. More precisely, it was the North Atlantic Naval Coastal Frontier until Feb. 6.

VI

Padfield, *War Beneath the Sea,* 201–04; Love, "U.S. Navy and Operation *Roll of Drums,*" 103; ESF War Diary, Jan. 1942, Ch. 2, 1–2; Gannon, *Operation Drumbeat,* 158–59; Blair, *Hunters,* 454; Dimbleby, *Battle of the Atlantic,* 245; Andrews, quoted in Farago, *Tenth Fleet,* 56. All references to ESF War Diary are to the transcribed version of the Eastern Sea Frontier's war diary at Uboat archive.net.

VII

ESF War Diary, Dec. 1941, App. 2; Ch. 2, 10–14; App. 1 (JCIC floor plan); Jan. 1942, Ch. 4, 6–8; Table, "Availability of Forces—January 1942," App. 2. Andrews's character: Farago, *Tenth Fleet,* 53; Morison, *Battle of the Atlantic,* vol. 1, 208, 229–34; "fusspocket," quoted in Morison, *Turmoil and Tradition,* 569; Gannon, *Operation Drumbeat,* 168, 176–77. Army Air Forces: Blair, *Hunters,* 465–66; Craven and Cate, *Army Air Forces,* vol. 1, 532.

CHAPTER 2—THE GOLDEN TIME

I

German Submarine Activities on the Atlantic Coast, 18–23, 139–41; *New York Times,* Jan. 21, 24, Mar. 22, Apr. 28, May 19, 24, 31; Farago, *Tenth Fleet,* 68–70; Table 12.1, in Mawdsley, *War for the Seas,* 253; Morison, *Battle of the Atlantic,* vol. 1, 155; Karig, Burton, and Freeland, *Battle Report,* 92.

III

ESF War Diary, Jan., App. 2; Feb., App. 2; Mar. 1942, App. 3; Milner, *Battle of the Atlantic,* 81; Dimbleby, *Battle of the Atlantic,* 251–52; Report by Oshima, Mar. 24, 1942, quoted in Lewin, *American Magic,* 234; Holland, *War in the West: Allies Fight Back,* 110. Hitler's views of America: Simms and Laderman, *Hitler's American Gamble,* 5–6, 15–16, 33; Schmider, *Hitler's Fatal Miscalculation,* 16–18, 20–23, 26, 33–36. Size of U.S. Army and American preparedness: Royle, *Patton,* 75; Roberts, *Storm of War,* 214.

IV

Simms and Laderman, *Hitler's American Gamble*, 33; lack of war plan: Warlimont, *Inside Hitler's Headquarters*, 208; Dimbleby, *Battle of the Atlantic*, 249–50; Kennedy, *Victory at Sea*, 209; Morison, *Battle of the Atlantic*, vol. 1, 126; Minutes, Dec. 12, 1941, Thursfield, *Führer Conferences*, 244–45; Dönitz, *Memoirs*, 206. Hitler's fear of a British invasion of Norway: Cremer, *U-Boat Commander*, 53, and Hessler, *U-Boat War*, para. 177. German divisions: Roberts, *Storm of War*, 214.

V

Letters, Churchill-Roosevelt, Mar. 12, 20, 29, 1942, in Churchill, *Hinge of Fate*, 119–21; Milner, *Battle of the Atlantic*, 84; Morison, *Battle of the Atlantic*, vol. 1, 131, 133. The decline was probably due to having earlier sunk so many tankers. Hessler, *U-Boat War*, paras. 191, 195; Minutes, May 13 and 14, 1942, Thursfield, *Führer Conferences*, 281. Oil-supply figures: Blair, *Hunters*, 467–68, 521 note. New York: Meany, Jr., "Port in a Storm," 282–94; Binford, "New York Harbor," 55; Morison, *Battle of the Atlantic*, vol. 1, 128; Farago, *Tenth Fleet*, 61.

CHAPTER 3—SHEEPDOGS AND WOLVES

I

Character and biography: In general, Buell, *Master of Sea Power*, and King and Whitehill, *Fleet Admiral King*; and see also Love, Jr., "Ernest Joseph King," 137–79; Thorndike, Jr., "King of the Atlantic," 92–108. Naval reorganization: Exec. Order 8984, Dec. 18, 1941; Exec. Order 9096, Mar. 12, 1942.

II

Hilarious Dönitz joke: Van Der Wat, *Atlantic Campaign*, 461. Character: Padfield, *Dönitz* and "Grand Admiral Karl Dönitz."

III

Morison, *Battle of the Atlantic*, vol. 1, 257; App. 1, Table 4, "Atlantic Areas of Most Severe Losses by Submarine Attack," 413; ESF War Diary, Apr. and May; Hessler, *U-Boat War*, para. 118; Dönitz, *Memoirs*, 216, 220; tanker shipments: Blair, *Hunters*, 591; Minutes, May 13 and 14, 1942, 282–83; Aug. 26, 290, in Thursfield, *Führer Conferences*.

IV

Cremer, *U-Boat Commander*, 79; British and American convoy views and research: Waters, "Mathematics of Convoy," 22–26, 78; Milner, *Battle of the Atlantic*, 86; Milner,

"The Atlantic War," 45–60; Ellis, *Brute Force,* 133; "tighten their belts": P. M. S. Blackett, quoted in Roskill, *War at Sea,* vol. 2, 370; supplies: P. M. Morse, "The Antisubmarine Problem," in NDRC, *Survey of Subsurface Warfare,* 3; Anzio, Reynolds, *Mirrors of Greatness,* 187. King on boxing: Quoted in Buell, *Master of Sea Power,* 193.

V

Life expectancy: Sternhell and Thorndike, *Antisubmarine Warfare in World War II,* Fig. 1, 84. The table gives life expectancy in this period of twelve months, but page 31 cites thirteen months. A similar minor discrepancy exists for the figure for number of ships sunk per U-boat loss.

CHAPTER 4—THE SEASON ON THE LINE

I

"List or Manifest of Alien Passengers for the United States," Aug. 4, 1942, for American Export Airlines NC-41881, in *Arriving Passenger and Crew Lists, 1820–1957,* Ancestry.com. This particular aircraft today resides at the New England Air Museum.

II

Winn's build and habits: Beesly, *Very Special Intelligence,* 58. Winn's visit: "Report on a Trip to Washington," June 3, 1942, No. 28, in Syrett, *Battle of the Atlantic and Signals Intelligence,* 100–04; Kohnen, "F-21 and F-211," 310–11; Memorandum, "The Americans, the Navy Department, and U-Boat Tracking," in *Operational Intelligence Centres: Formation and History,* 1945, ADM 223/286, National Archives, London; Reynolds, *Need to Know,* 237–39; Beesly, *Very Special Intelligence,* 114–15. King's "anti-Britishness" and reluctance to cooperate: Bath, *Tracking the Axis Enemy,* 88–89; Slessor, *Central Blue,* 491, 529–30; Low, "Personal Narrative," 42–47.

III–IV

"Under the weather": Quoted in Buell, *Master of Sea Power,* 65. Knowles background: NSA interview, National Cryptologic Museum, 1–4; Kohnen, "F-21 and F-211," 311–12; Heavilin, *Lucky Bag of 1927,* 252, 512–13; *Navy Directory (1943),* 506; *Annual Register of the United States Naval Academy, 1927–28,* Merit Roll, 31; Personnel jacket for Knowles, courtesy of the Nimitz Library, USNA; "Notes on His Father," personal reminiscences by Dr. K. A. Knowles, Jr., Jan. 13, 2023. I am greatly obliged to Dr. Knowles for providing a copy of his uncle's memoirs: F. Knowles, *Autobiography* (privately printed, 1976). Attitudes toward marksmanship: Rose, *American Rifle,* 214–17; Naval Academy rifle team: Stillwell, "Willis Lee."

V

The most important sources for life in Room 41 are Barrett's memorandum, "U-Boat Tracking and Anti-U-Boat Warfare: NID 8(S)," 1946–47, No. 173, in Syrett, *Battle of the Atlantic and Signals Intelligence,* 389–404; Beesly, *Very Special Intelligence,* 172–79; Hamilton, "Character and Organization of the Admiralty Operational Intelligence Centre," 295–324; Hastings, *Secret War,* 215–18. Beesly, *Very Special Intelligence,* photo insert between pages 68 and 69, notes the "Lenin's Tomb" nickname. On Winn and Beesly, see the latter's contribution on his old boss in *Oxford Dictionary of National Biography;* Beesly's Wikipedia entry; and https://archivesearch.lib .cam.ac.uk/repositories/9/archival_objects/461524; McLachlan, *Room 39,* 118–19; Barrett, "U-Boat Tracking and Anti-U-Boat Warfare," 400–01. Knowles's comments on the "brilliance" of Winn were made in a March 1985 interview with Parrish, *The Ultra Americans,* 152. Regarding Latin: Beesly later sniped of an unpopular superior, Commander Colpoys, whose claim to fame was designating the highest-grade signal intelligence ULTRA, that *ultra* was "about the only Latin he could remember." Beesly, *Very Special Intelligence,* 105. King as "megalomaniac": Personal note inserted by Winn into "The Americans, the Navy Department, and U-Boat Tracking," *Operational Intelligence Centre—Formation and History,* ADM 223/286.

CHAPTER 5—THE LAVATORY MAN

I

Building the Navy's Bases in World War II, 2, 54–59.

II–V

Gallery's background, career, and his amazing idea: Gilliland and Shenk, *Admiral Dan Gallery;* Gallery, *Clear the Decks!,* 2–14, 21–41; Gallery, *Twenty Million Tons,* 91–93; Gallery, U.S. Naval Institute (USNI) interview, 1–70. Hopgood's co-pilot, Lieutenant Bradford "Tex" Dyer, also related a version of the *U-464* story in Karig, Burton, and Freeland, *Battle Report,* 128–29; see also *U-464: Report on Interrogation of Survivors from U-464,* at https://www.uboatarchive.net/Int/U-464INT.htm. The state of American aviation is covered in chapter 25, "The Visionary," in my *Empires of the Sky. U-570:* Kohnen, "Tombstone of Victory," 7, which notes Gallery's inspection.

CHAPTER 6—THE HERBIVORE

I

Early history: Paterson, "From the Lion's Roar," 57–62. Need to know every inch of the boat: According to *Matrosenobergefreiter* (Leading Seaman Machinist) Hans

Eckert on *U-616*, quoted in Paterson, *U-Boat Combat Missions*, 34–35. Loewe's age: Table 18, "Ages of U-Boat Commanders at Time of First Command," in Mulligan, *Neither Sharks Nor Wolves*, 154. Life in Weimar Navy: Mulligan, *Neither Sharks Nor Wolves*, 223. Loewe background is based on a letter he sent to Gallery after the war dated Sept. 29, 1955, in Gallery Papers, Box 9, Folder 4. See also Mulligan, "Community Bound by Fate," 26–27. Cadet entry and training: Mulligan, *Neither Sharks Nor Wolves*, 90; selectiveness: Mulligan, "German U-Boat Crews in World War II," 264.

II

Freetown: Whinney, *U-Boat Peril*, 71–74. Stifling heat: Decker, "404 Days!," 36. Number of veterans: letter, Loewe to Gallery, Sept. 29, 1955, Gallery Papers. Roll with the boat: Werner, *Iron Coffins*, 15, 19–20. Strain of long patrol: Decker, "404 Days!," 37. Cramped conditions: Paterson, *U-Boat Combat Missions*, 38–39; price of torpedoes: Cremer, *U-Boat Commander*, 25. Toilets: Paterson, *U-Boat Combat Missions*, 25, 63–64, 72, 76–77; Werner, *Iron Coffins*, 22, 90; Mulligan, *Lone Wolf*, 66–67; Mulligan, *Neither Sharks Nor Wolves*, 12–13; on the eggs: letter, Loewe to Gallery, Oct. 18, 1955, Box 9, Folder 4, Gallery Papers. Prunes: Interview, Heinrich Klippisch, Griffin Museum of Science and Industry (MSI). Library and record collection: Mulligan, "Community Bound by Fate," 53; letter, Loewe to Gallery, Oct. 18, 1955; interview, Klippisch. Politics: Mulligan, *Lone Wolf*, 85; Schiller's recollections, quoted in Paterson, *U-Boat Combat Missions*, 39. Lüth: see his lecture, "Problems of Leadership in a Submarine," Dec. 17, 1943, 8, at https://www.uboatarchive.net/Misc/LuethLecture.htm; Padfield, *War Beneath the Sea*, 302–03; Hughes and Costello, *Battle of the Atlantic*, 290–91. Fischer diary: Paterson, *U-Boat Combat Missions*, 70. Dönitz's decree: Herwig, "Germany and the Battle of the Atlantic," 84. *Blechkoller*: Goebeler, *Steel Boat*, 221–22. *West Irmo*: Paterson, "From the Lion's Roar," 63–67.

III

Dönitz comment: U-505 War Diary, Feb. 11–May 7, 1942, at https://www.uboat archive.net/U-505/KTB505-2.htm. Loewe's view: letter, Loewe to Gallery, Sept. 29, 1955, Gallery Papers. *U-505's* patrol: Paterson, "From the Lion's Roar," 68–70; App. B, "U-505 Combat Chronology," in Savas, *Hunt and Kill*, 224–27; U-505 War Diary, June 7–Aug. 25, 1942, esp. 9–10, at https://www.uboatarchive.net/U-505/KTB505-3.htm. Gallery, *Twenty Million Tons*, 125–46, reprints lengthy statements from several *McKean* crew; see also Albert Rust interview, MSI.

IV

Car: Goebeler, *Steel Boat*, 53. Strong patrol: Entry, July 21, p. 43, in "War Diary and War Standing Orders of Commander in Chief, Submarines," at https://www

.uboatarchive.net/BDU/BDUKTB30309B.htm. Crash-dives: Werner, *Iron Coffins*, 16. People on *Roamar*: Interview, Aloysius Hasselberg, MSI.

V

Loewe's assistance: This is attested to in several places, not least the U-505 War Diary and also letter, Loewe to Gallery, Sept. 29, 1955, Gallery Papers. Machine-gunnings: Dunn, "Treatment of Merchant Ship Survivors by U-Boat Crews 1939–1945," https://uboat.net/articles/index.html?article=55 (2003); Mulligan, *Neither Sharks Nor Wolves*, 195–214. It was common practice at this time to stop to assist lifeboats and survivors (see Cremer's memoir, *U-Boat Commander*, 41–42). Some of these claims were, of course, self-serving, but Gallery, in his memoirs, *Twenty Million Tons*, 61–62, states that "they did not machine gun life boats as our propaganda claimed they did." It worked both ways, too: "When we sank one of their subs and paused to fish them out of the water they were grateful—and surprised. Their propaganda had told them to expect machine-gun bullets instead of rescue!" Killing merchant seaman: See, for example, Minutes, May 14, 1942, in Thursfield, *Führer Conferences*, 283. As Padfield notes on p. 297 of *War Beneath the Sea*, Dönitz had been telling Hitler about a new type of torpedo that would sink ships faster and thus "the crew will no longer be able to be rescued. This greater loss of ships' crews will doubtless aggravate the manning difficulties for the great American shipbuild-ing programme." It was an eccentricity of German thinking that the Americans were permanently short of sailors, despite their colossal population. Hitler's view: "Memorandum on the Conversation between the Führer and Ambassador Oshima," in "Presence of the Reich Foreign Minister in the *Wolfsschanze* on 3 January 1942," in Office of United States Chief of Council for Prosecution of Axis Criminality, *Nazi Conspiracy and Aggression*, 7, Document D-423, 53–54. Dönitz ignores: In his affidavit at Nuremberg after the war, Admiral Raeder said that at a conference of May 14, 1942, Hitler had again broached the idea of killing sailors but both he and Dönitz had rejected it. See Anon., "Trial of Admiral Doenitz," 32. Colombia: Laud-erbaugh, "Bolivarian Nations: Securing the Northern Frontier," 115–19.

A special note on the *Roamar* Affair: The circumstances surrounding the sinking of the *Roamar* were obscured in two memoirs by *U-505* crewmen, almost certainly owing to their loyalty to Loewe (and desire to avoid awkward questions), as well as in the War Diary and Loewe's postwar remarks. Thus Goebeler (*Steel Boat*, 53–54) alleges that *Roamar* was acting suspiciously by not stopping, and that Loewe ordered Gunnery Officer Stolzenberg to send a warning shot. This was done and tore away the mainmast, but the ship "refused to stop." Then Loewe said, "Sink her, Stolzenberg, but make it quick." Goebeler claims that the first shot persuaded the crew to abandon the *Roamar*. After waiting for them to get "well clear," the deck gunners destroyed the schooner, and that is the last we hear of the Colombians. In his book, Goebeler elsewhere devotes significant space to describing Loewe's considerate treatment of survivors, which makes his circumspection here as to the fate of the *Roamar* crew more than a trifle odd. Decker, "404 Days!," 39, hews more or less to Goebeler's version, but omits any mention of the crew whatsoever and asserts of the *Roamar* that just three shots "finished her off." Moreover, he claims that only "much later did we discover she belonged to neutral Colombia," an assertion belied by Loewe's own contemporary note that she was flying the Colombian flag. Further, in the official War Diary entry (July 22, p. 19), Loewe states the deck gun used no fewer than *twenty-two* 105mm rounds. Suspiciously, he also makes no mention of the fate of *Roamar*'s crew. Then, ten years after the war, Loewe wrote Gallery a letter that detailed his consideration for survivors, but when he gets to the *Roamar* (which he misremembers as *Roma* or *Romar*) he mysteriously omits any mention of her crew. As he says, "I met this ship in the Caribbean Sea and while surfaced I shot several cannon shots in front of her bow to stop her. Rather suspiciously it did not react and I sunk it with the 10.5cm cannon, since it might have been a submarine trap." (Letter, Loewe to Gallery, Sept. 29, 1955, Gallery Papers.) The only person who seems to have noticed the evasion was Gallery, who in a follow-up letter of November 8 pointed out that *U-505*'s log "makes no mention of any survivors…Surely some of the crew must have escaped." In his reply of November 27, Loewe came the closest he ever would, or could, to admitting the truth: "While sinking the *Romar* a whole row of shots missed after the first warning shot. The first hit must have killed the small crew for after sinking the sail ship, I saw outside of some wreckage, no trace of survivors." (Letters, Gallery to Loewe, Nov. 8; Loewe to Gallery, Nov. 27, in Box 61, Folder 25, MSI.) According to the authoritative Uboat.net website, there were at least thirteen crew, and an unknown number of passengers. Gallery returned to the subject at greater length in his memoirs (*Twenty Million Tons*, 154–59). He empathized with Loewe, saying that he genuinely might have been sick in the days preceding the affair, that he might have thought it was a trap, and that *Roamar*'s captain panicked and refused to heave to. But ultimately Gallery judged that "there is little use speculating and philosophizing about things like this thirteen years after the event. It's just one of the messy little incidents of a global war which are important only to the men concerned in them." In other words, Gallery knew that Loewe had committed a crime.

VI

U-505's return: Goebeler, *Steel Boat*, 57. Decades later, Goebeler loyally alleged that Loewe's "worrying himself sick" was prompted by his fear that sinking *Roamar* would provide "the political grounds for Colombia to declare war against Germany." Goebeler, however, elided dates, thus making it seem that the *Roamar* and Colombia's eventual declaration of war were related. Colombia did not declare war until November 27, *1943*—more than a year later. See Goebeler, *Steel Boat*, 54, 60. Messages and comments: U-Boat Command War Diary, July 28, p. 56, https://www.uboatarchive.net/BDU/BDUKTB30309B.htm; U-505 War Diary, 24, at https://www.uboatarchive.net/U-505/KTB505-3.htm. U-Boat Command duly logged the message, but dated it July 31 because of the time difference. Submarines kept to German summer time, no matter their location (https://www.uboat archive.net/BDU/BDUKTB30309B.htm). U-505 War Diary, https://www.uboat archive.net/U-505/KTB505-3.htm. London Naval Treaty: Anon., "Trial of Admiral Doenitz," 30. Guilt: Goebeler, *Steel Boat,* 60.

VII

Terraine, *U-Boat Wars*, App. D, "Shipping and U-Boat Losses, 1939–1945, Yearly and Monthly," 767–68.

CHAPTER 7—THE HUMAN FACTOR

I

Estimates: McLachlan, *Room 39*, 115; Barrett, "U-Boat Tracking and Anti-U-Boat Warfare," No. 173, in Syrett, *Battle of the Atlantic and Signals Intelligence,* 396. As Knowles put it, successful tracking entailed employing all "available intelligence to reproduce as nearly as possible the operations rooms of the enemy" (F-21 War Report, 13).

II

German headquarters: Dönitz, *Memoirs,* 317; see also the recollection by his communications officer, Captain Hans Meckel, in Hughes and Costello, *Battle of the Atlantic,* 247. A list of Dönitz's staff officers may be found at https://www.uboat.net/men/bdu.htm. Kretschmer, quoted in McLachlan, *Room 39,* 166. Winn's visit: "Report on a Trip to Washington," June 3, 1942, No. 28, in Syrett, *Battle of the Atlantic and Signals Intelligence,* 100–04; "The Americans, the Navy Department, and U-Boat Tracking," in *Operational Intelligence Centres,* ADM 223/286. "Flair" and "osmosis": Barrett, "U-Boat Tracking and Anti-U-Boat Warfare," No. 173, in Syrett, *Battle of the Atlantic and Signals Intelligence,* 390, 392; Knowles, NSA interview, p. 4.

III

Intelligence: Beesly, *Very Special Intelligence,* 28; Cremer, *U-Boat Commander,* 176-77. Interrogations: Interview with Angus MacLean Thuermer, Fort Hunt Oral History

Project, Oct. 25, 2006, 23 (see also 28–29), https://www.nps.gov/museum/exhibits/fohu_oral_history/transcripts/nps_pobox1142_athuermer.pdf; Thuermer's recollection: printed in Paterson, *U-Boat Combat Missions*, 142–43; McLachlan, *Room 39*, 166; *U-643*, Interrogation of Survivors, Dec. 1943, https://www.uboatarchive.net/U-643A/U-643INT.htm. Emblems: Mulligan, *Neither Sharks Nor Wolves*, 180; Paterson, *U-Boat Combat Missions*, 110–11; Cremer, *U-Boat Commander*, 31. Cremer's file: *U-Boat Commander*, 126. Strategy change: Dönitz, *Memoirs*, 240–41.

IV

Enigma versions: App. 4, "Enigma Keys Attacked by GC & CS up to Mid-1943," Part 1, "GAF Enigma Keys Before the End of June 1942," in Hinsley et al., *British Intelligence*, vol. 2, 659–61. Starting combinations: DeBrosse and Burke, *Secret in Building 26*, 19. Radio intelligence: Erskine, "Shore High-Frequency Direction-Finding in the Battle of the Atlantic," 1–32; Syrett, "Infrastructure of Communications Intelligence," 163–72; Kahn, *Seizing the Enigma*, 4, 145, 215–16; Syrett, *Battle of the Atlantic and Signals Intelligence*, 4–6, and memoranda by Kemp, "The D/F Plotting Section of the OIC," No. 171, 380–85, and "HF/DF Organisation, 1939–1945," No. 172, 386–89; Rohwer, "Allied and Axis Radio-Intelligence in the Battle of the Atlantic," 77–100; Rohwer, "Ultra and the Battle of the Atlantic: The German View," 9–13. Radio traffic: Kahn, *Seizing the Enigma*, 119, 121; Knowles, NSA interview (19–20), discusses it as Dönitz's weak spot; Anon., "Origination and Evolution of Radio Traffic Analysis," 23–38. Extrapolation: Montagu, *Beyond Top Secret Ultra*, 86; McLachlan, *Room 39*, 103; Knowles, NSA interview (15), notes the importance of message length.

VI

Main Navy: Whitehill's recollection in King and Whitehill, *Fleet Admiral King*, 647–49. F-21 layout: Knowles, "F-21 War Report," drawing. Meetings: Farago, *Tenth Fleet*, 216–17; Knowles, NSA interview, 30–31; Knowles, "F-21 War Report," 15. Relationship with Winn: Knowles, interview with Parrish, *The Ultra Americans*, 152; Telephone: Knowles, "American View," 14; NSA interview, 5. Winn's memory: Beesly, *Very Special Intelligence*, 175; Knowles, "F-21 War Report," 19. Archive: Kohnen, *Winn and Knowles*, 103; Parsons, "Functions of Secret Room," 3–4. Staff and organization: Knowles, "F-21 War Report," 7–12, 14. Parsons's background: two letters proposing him for membership of the Century Association, dated June 14 and Oct. 3, 1961, as well as a memorial printed in the *1976 Yearbook*, 232–36; *Thirty Year Record of the Class of 1925, Yale College*, 286–87, reprinted in "Finding Aid for the John E. Parsons Papers," MS 792, at Yale University Library. WAVES: Godson, *Serving Proudly*, 106–30. "In awe": Personal communication from K. A. Knowles, Jr., Jan. 13, 2023.

CHAPTER 8—THE CARNIVORE

I

Loewe's career and popularity: Paterson, "From the Lion's Roar," 72; letter, Loewe to Gallery, Sept. 29, 1955, Box 9, Folder 4, Gallery Papers; Goebeler, *Steel Boat*, 60; letter, Loewe to Gallery, Oct. 18, 1955, Box 9, Folder 4, Gallery Papers. Zschech: Goebeler, *Steel Boat*, 60–77; Mulligan, "Community Bound by Fate," 31–35. Knight's Cross: Mulligan, *Neither Sharks Nor Wolves*, 183.

II

Informality and uniforms: Goebeler, *Steel Boat*, 60; Cremer, *U-Boat Commander*, 85; Mulligan, *Neither Sharks Nor Wolves*, 22. Motivations, background, discipline: Gannon, *Operation Drumbeat*, 109, 112–13; Mulligan, "Community Bound by Fate," 45, 48, 52; Mulligan, *Lone Wolf*, 81–82. Hitler's view: Cameron and Stevens, *Hitler's Table Talk*, No. 293, Aug. 20, 1942, 639.

III

Tradition: Goebeler, *Steel Boat*, 66; letter, Loewe to Gallery, Oct. 18, 1955, Box 9, Folder 4, Gallery Papers; interview, Karl Springer (who remembered hearing Zschech say, "The flowers will not be thrown overboard. We'll keep them"). Zschech and Bode: Springer interview; Wolfgang Schiller interview; Goebeler, *Steel Boat*, 62–63, 83, 96–97. See his intriguing comment, 94, noting that Bode "comforted his friend [Zschech] with his usual degree of tenderness and intimacy." Class of 1936: https://uboat.net/men/commanders/crews.html?crew=36. Hauser: Mulligan, "Community Bound by Fate," 38, notes Party membership (No. 6,956,390, joined Sept. 1938 as an eighteen-year-old engineering student). Förster's transfer: War Diary, Oct. 20, 1942, 10–11, https://www.uboatarchive.net/U-505/KTB505-4.htm.

IV–V

Verdigris: Werner, *Iron Coffins*, 13. *U-505* operations and Sillcock attack: War Diary, Nov. 7, 10–12, 22–23, 27–41; https://www.uboatarchive.net/U-505/KTB505-4 .htm; Goebeler, *Steel Boat*, 76, 82–112; Kelshall, *U-Boat War in the Caribbean*, 228–29; Decker, "404 Days!," 40–42. Torpedoes: Mulligan, *Lone Wolf*, App. I, "The Place of Henke in the U-Boat War," 227. Comments on Zschech: Dönitz, War Diary commendation, https://www.uboatarchive.net/U-505/KTB505-4.htm; letter, Loewe to Gallery, Sept. 29, 1955, Gallery Papers, Box 9, Folder 4.

VI–VII

"Z Plan": Mallmann Showell, *German Navy*, 23–24. Grand names: Rose, *Empires of the Sky*, 387. Hitler and Raeder: Rhys-Jones, "German System: A Staff Perspective," in Howarth and Law, *Battle of the Atlantic,* 145. Dönitz and Navy at the time: Pad-field, "Grand Admiral Karl Dönitz," 196–98; Padfield, *War Beneath the Sea,* 306–08; Dimbleby, *Battle of the Atlantic,* 344–49. Hitler on Navy: "useless ships," quoted in Mawdsley, *War for the Seas,* 309; minutes of January 6, in Thursfield, *Führer Conferences,* 306–08. Comparisons of U-boats: Mulligan, *Lone Wolf,* 60; Mulligan, *Neither Sharks Nor Wolves,* 66. Building schedule and production bottlenecks: Rössler, "U-Boat Development and Building," 129–30; Tooze, *Wages of Destruction,* 567–72. Dönitz and Goebbels: Herwig, "Germany and the Battle of the Atlantic," 80–81.

CHAPTER 9—THE FUNHOUSE

I

Rate of construction and destruction: Hinsley et al., *British Intelligence,* vol. 2, 565. Dönitz and flotillas: Ellis, *Brute Force,* 134 and note. Size of groups and strategy: Werner, *Iron Coffins,* 90; "Survey of German Submarine Strategy and Tactics: Northern Convoy Lanes," Apr. 13, 1943, in Syrett, *Battle of the Atlantic and Signals Intelligence,* No. 45, p. 141. TM-1 and HX-224: "Attacks on Convoy TM 1," Jan. 1943, in Syrett, *Battle of the Atlantic and Signals Intelligence,* No. 32, 110–16; Hinsley et al., *British Intelligence,* vol. 2, 558–60; Knowles, "American View," 15–16, vividly recalled the disaster more than forty years later. Routing issues: Highlighted by the First Sea Lord, March 30, cited in Hinsley et al., *British Intelligence,* vol. 2, 563.

II

U-boat shadowing: Report, "Compromise of Allied Communications, March 1943, Convoy TO 2," in Syrett, *Battle of the Atlantic and Signals Intelligence,* No. 43, 137; memorandum, "Compromise of Allied Communications, March 1943: Convoy HX 229," No. 44, 138–40, reaches the same conclusion; see also App. 12, "Confirmed Cases of Allied Cipher Compromise," 179–80, and App. 13, "Cases of Presumed and Confirmed Compromise," 181–200, in OP-20-G Report, *Battle of the Atlantic—Appendices,* at https://www.ibiblio.org/hyperwar/ETO/Ultra/SRH-BA-Appendix/index.html. Tranow: Kahn, *Seizing the Enigma,* 211; Jörgensen, *Hitler's Espionage Machine,* 194–95. Cypher No. 3: Bray, *Ultra in the Atlantic,* vol. 1: *Allied Communication Intelligence and the Battle of the Atlantic,* 68–69; Barnett, "German Successes Against British Codes and Ciphers," No. 175, in Syrett, *Battle of the Atlantic and Signals Intelligence,* esp. 411–12, which concludes that "the patient and careful work of the submarine trackers [i.e., Winn and Knowles] was in fact being used against our own ships"; Hinsley et al., *British Intelligence,* vol. 2, App. 1, Part (i), "British Cypher Security During the War," 635–38, covers the same ground; the most detailed examination is a report by OP-20-G, in Bray, *Ultra in the Atlantic,* vol. 3: *German Naval Intelligence Communications,* 35–55; see also

Erskine, "Tunny Reveals B-Dienst Successes Against the 'Convoy Code,'" 868–89. No. 5: Budiansky, *Battle of Wits*, 293; Kahn, *Seizing the Enigma*, 213.

III

Tucker, *Naval Service of Canada*, vol. 2, 410–17; Morison, *Atlantic Battle Won*, vol. 10, 19–20; Slessor, *Central Blue*, 497–99; Tidman, *Operations Evaluation Group*, 55. Iwo Jima: Rose, *Men of War*, 224. Unconditional surrender: Churchill and Gilbert, *Winston S. Churchill*, vol. 7, 300–13; Balfour, "Another Look at 'Unconditional Surrender,'" 719–36; Campbell, "Franklin Roosevelt and Unconditional Surrender," 219–41. Two questions: Gorodetsky, *Maisky Diaries*, entry of Feb. 9, 1943, 482. Stalin: Reynolds, *Mirrors of Greatness*, 197, 205–06. Number of divisions: Ellis, *Brute Force*, xx. FDR's bragging (to Hopkins): Quoted in Persico, *Roosevelt's Secret War*, 236. *Dorchester*: "Narrative of U-Boat Attack on Convoy SC 118," No. 36, in Syrett, *Battle of the Atlantic and Signals Intelligence*, 118–26; Dimbleby, *Battle of the Atlantic*, 378; young officer: quoted in Hughes and Costello, *Battle of the Atlantic*, 255.

IV

Dönitz: Quoted in Hughes and Costello, *Battle of the Atlantic*, 272; Meigs, *Slide Rules and Submarines*, 103. Convoy failure: Roskill, *War at Sea*, vol. 2, 367; Ellis, *Brute Force*, 152; Hughes and Costello, *Battle of the Atlantic*, 261; Kennedy, *Engineers of Victory*, 23; Milner, *Battle of the Atlantic*, 155–57; Rohwer, *Critical Convoy Battles*, 187; Pound, quoted in Barnett, *Engage the Enemy*, 600. Mineral oil: Hughes and Costello, *Battle of the Atlantic*, 257. King speech: Quoted in Meigs, *Slide Rules and Submarines*, 91; Morison, *Atlantic Battle Won*, vol. 10, 19.

CHAPTER 10—BLACK MAY

I

Dönitz: Minutes, Apr. 21, 1943, in Thursfield, *Führer Conferences*, 318. Construction estimates: Hessler, *U-Boat War*, para. 194 and Table. Actual construction: The official number was 14.585 million tons in 1943, in King, *U.S. Navy at War, 1941–1945*, vol. 3, Table, 206. There are inconsequential discrepancies in the data. Hessler, *U-Boat War*, para. 194 and Table, for example, gives 14.39 million tons, while Ellis, *Brute Force*, Table 6, 157, gives the figure of 15.45 million tons. The most detailed breakdown is Fischer, *Statistical Summary of Shipbuilding*, Tables B-1 and B-4, 39, 43. The differences can be accounted for by excluding or including certain categories of civilian and military vessels. "Integral Tonnage" and older ships: Morison, *Atlantic Battle Won*, vol. 10, 58; Morison, *Battle of the Atlantic*, vol. 1, 404. Dönitz's complaints about Göring: Minutes, Feb. 26, 1943, in Thursfield, *Führer Conferences*,

311. The feud dated from 1941, when Göring had starved Dönitz of long-range Focke-Wulf 200 *Kondor* planes that he wanted to use to reconnoiter for convoys ahead of the U-boats (see Ellis, *Brute Force*, 142–43 and note).

II

Production: Heinrich, "Fighting Ships That Require Knowledge and Experience," 288–91; Morison, *Atlantic Battle Won*, vol. 10, 34–36. (Of the 1,005, 442 would be canceled owing to the decline of the U-boat threat, and ultimately 373 would see service.) Destroyer escorts: Andrews, *Tempest, Fire, and Foe*, 1–4; Cross, *Shepherds of the Sea*, 19–20; Williamson, *U-Boats vs. Destroyer Escorts*, 19, 23–24, 33–34. Technology: Barnett, *Engage the Enemy*, 580–82; Kennedy, *Engineers of Victory*, 55, 58–59; Radar Research and Development Sub-Committee, "U.S. Radar: Operational Characteristics of Radar Classified by Tactical Application," FTP-217, Aug. 1, 1943; Report, "History of the Anti-Submarine Measures of the Tenth Fleet," 32A–33; Dring, "Steep Learning Curve," esp. 48–50; Cremer, *U-Boat Commander*, 117; Dönitz, *Memoirs*, 325. Fido: Williams, "See Fido Run," 115–25. Rotterdam and German development: Sternhell and Thorndike, *Antisubmarine Warfare*, 156–57.

III

Catalinas: Morison, *Atlantic Battle Won*, vol. 10, 43. CVEs: Sternhell and Thorndike, *Antisubmarine Warfare*, 39; Hobbs, "Ship-Borne Anti-Submarine Warfare," 395; Y'Blood, *Hunter-Killer*, 29–40; Knowles, *Battle of the Atlantic: U-Boat Operations*, 40. (Erskine, "Ultra and Some U.S. Navy Carrier Operations," p. 84, note 13, states Knowles's authoring of this volume. The others in the series were primarily produced by OP-20-G.) "Crow can fight a mole": Quoted in Slessor, *Central Blue*, 522.

IV

Strength: Kennedy, *Victory at Sea*, 269, and Chart 3, "Daily U-Boat Availability for Combat, 1939–45." ONS-5: Syrett, *Defeat of the German U-Boats*, 63–95; Kennedy, *Victory at Sea*, App. A, "Sinking U-Boats in the Dark, May 6, 1943," 439–42. There are minor discrepancies, none important.

V

Padfield, "Grand Admiral Karl Dönitz," 199, and *Dönitz*, 299, notes the admiral's coldness. In his *Memoirs*, 340, Dönitz restricts himself to saying that "it was only bit by bit that I received definite details of the losses we had suffered." Gretton and Forsythe: Gretton's entertaining *Convoy Escort Commander*, 150–51.

VI

Conference and losses: Minutes, May 31, 1943, in Thursfield, *Führer Conferences,* 331–36; Plan 59, "Analysis of U-Boat Numbers and Losses in the North Atlantic," in Hessler, *U-Boat War,* opp. para. 333; Milner, *Battle of the Atlantic,* 179. Life expectancy: Herwig, "Germany and the Battle of the Atlantic," 83. Tonnage loss ratio: Hessler, *U-Boat War,* para. 333, note; Ellis, *Brute Force,* 156, notes, equally strikingly, that "the average quarterly tonnage sunk per U-boat at sea [fell] from 70,000 in late 1940 to 2,000 by the end of 1943." Fountain pens: Padfield, "Grand Admiral Karl Dönitz," 201. Herwig, "Germany and the Battle of the Atlantic," 85, notes that Dönitz attended the meeting at Posen on October 4, 1943, in which Himmler spoke of "the extermination of the Jewish race." Undefeated: Only in his *Memoirs,* 341, would Dönitz finally admit that "we had lost the Battle of the Atlantic." Dönitz tells his captains: Mawdsley, *War for the Seas,* 305; Knowles, *Battle of the Atlantic: U-Boat Operations,* 67; full talk of June 3 printed in Rössler, "U-Boat Development and Building," 131–32. Conference: Minutes, May 31, 1943, in Thursfield, *Führer Conferences,* 334–35. Guderian: Quoted in Hughes and Costello, *Battle of the Atlantic,* 286; see also Speer, *Inside the Third Reich,* 272–73. Lack of torpedoes: Herwig, "Germany and the Battle of the Atlantic," 83. Winn and more U-boats sunk: Report, May 24, cited in Hinsley et al., *British Intelligence,* vol. 2, 566. Dönitz and victory: "sharper weapons" quoted in Padfield, *War Beneath the Sea,* 336; future years will be better: quoted in Herwig, "Germany and the Battle of the Atlantic," 83. Schäffer: *U-Boat 977,* 179–80; War Diary, quoted in Barnett, *Engage the Enemy,* 612.

CHAPTER 11—THE PHANTOM FLEET

I

Farago, *Tenth Fleet,* 163–81; "History of the Anti-Submarine Measures of the Tenth Fleet," 29–30A; Meigs, *Slide Rules and Submarines,* 95–103, 113–16; Tidman, *Operations Evaluation Group,* 56–58; Morison, *Atlantic Battle Won,* vol. 10, 21–26.

II

Low's character, background, relationship with King: Low, "Personal Narrative," 27–31; "knew precisely," letter, Low to Sir Arthur Bryant, Jan. 22, 1960, in "Personal Narrative," 42–47 (see also page 16 on leadership methods); Buell, *Master of Sea Power,* 293. Farago, *Tenth Fleet,* 177–80, 358 note. Tenth Fleet: Memorandum, May 19, 1943, quoted in Morison, *Atlantic Battle Won,* vol. 10, 23; see also King, *U.S. Navy at War,* vol. 3, 206. Knowles: Personal communication, K. A. Knowles, Jr.; Farago, *Tenth Fleet,* 18.

III

British views: "Office," quoted in Budiansky, "Bletchley Park and the Birth of the Very Special Relationship," 213; Budiansky, *Battle of Wits*, 254. Enigma: Hinsley et al., *British Intelligence*, vol. 2, 55, 233. Secret Room: Report by Parsons, "Functions of 'Secret Room' of COMINCH Combat Intelligence." King and *Ultra*: On April 27, 1943, King signaled the Admiralty that "while I am equally concerned with you as to security of Z [*Ultra*] information it is my belief that we are not deriving from it fullest value." Quoted in DeBrosse and Burke, *Secret in Building 26*, 118. *Neptun* and *TGD*: App. 4, "Enigma Keys Attacked by GC & CS Up to Mid-1943," in Hinsley et al., *British Intelligence*, vol. 2, 664, 668.

IV

Knowles memorandum, Dec. 24, 1943, printed in Y'Blood, *Hunter-Killer*, App. 3, "The Anglo-American CVE Controversy," 286; Knowles, "American View," 15; Knowles, NSA Interview, 6.

V

"Square 87": Erskine, "Ultra and Some U.S. Navy Carrier Operations," 82; Knowles, *Battle of the Atlantic: U-Boat Operations*, 74. For the full text, *Battle of the Atlantic—Appendices*, App. 13, "Cases of Presumed and Confirmed Compromise, 1943–1945," 191. Naval Grid: Erskine, "German Naval Grid in World War II," 39–51; Mallmann Showell, *German Navy in World War Two*, App., "German Naval Charts," 217–18; Beesly, *Very Special Intelligence*, 170.

VI

Sable Island: Erskine, "Ultra and Some U.S. Navy Carrier Operations," 83; U-Boat Command War Diary, June 5, 465, remarks that "the enemy definitely suspects a considerable number of U-boats in the sea area," https://www.uboatarchive.net/BDU/BDUKTB30325.htm. Uphoff and ruse: "Memorandum from OP-20-GI-2," Apr. 16, 1943, No. 47, in Syrett, *Battle of the Atlantic and Signals Intelligence*, 144. U-Boat Command War Diary, June 5, 465; Knowles, *Battle of the Atlantic: U-Boat Operations*, 77.

VII

Knowles, *Battle of the Atlantic: U-Boat Operations*, 74 (formation of Wolf Pack *Trutz*); Dönitz, quoted in Syrett, *Defeat of the German U-Boats*, 149; Dönitz's trap, Signal 1832/29 to Wolf Pack *Trutz*, May 27, in *Battle of the Atlantic—Appendices*, App. 13, "Cases of Presumed and Confirmed Compromise," 191; day's delay: Knowles, *Battle of the Atlantic: U-Boat Operations*, 101; Dönitz orders not wasting torpedoes: Memorandum, "Compromise of Allied Communications, May 1943: Flight 10,"

June 26, 1943, No. 70, in Syrett, *Battle of the Atlantic and Signals Intelligence,* 191–92; "carrier-borne airpower": Knowles, *Battle of the Atlantic: U-Boat Operations,* 75, 79, 90.

VIII

Ship losses and June 11: Erskine, "Ultra and Some U.S. Navy Carrier Operations," 87. Czygan: Knowles, *Battle of the Atlantic: U-Boat Operations,* 100. Type VII fuel: OP-20-GI memorandum, "U-Boat Cruising Speeds, Fuel Consumption, and Torpedo Capacity," May 10, 1943, No. 56, in Syrett, *Battle of the Atlantic and Signals Intelligence,* 165–66. "Week or ten days": Memorandum, late Jan. 1943, quoted in Rielage, "Indirectly by Operational Signals." Rielage states (note 4) that the memorandum is anonymous, but in fact it was almost certainly written by Knowles. King and Low back Knowles: Low had written a memorandum for King on April 14, 1943, discussing U-tanker strategy and proposing to station American submarines near rendezvous points. That was an impractical scheme, as it turned out, but Low was a keen supporter of Knowles's idea to deploy carrier groups instead. See No. 46, in Syrett, *Battle of the Atlantic and Signals Intelligence,* 143–44. Looks: quoted in Erskine, "Ultra and Some U.S. Navy Carrier Operations," 89. U-boats with empty tanks: Knowles, *Battle of the Atlantic: U-Boat Operations,* 115.

IX

King promise: letter to Pound, Apr. 27, 1943, in Snow, *Measureless Peril,* 274; Barlow, "Navy's Escort Carrier Offensive." Knowles admitted to "skat[ing] on some pretty thin ice" in Knowles, "American View," 14. Dönitz's comment: U-Boat Command War Diary, July 11, 1943, 24, at https://www.uboatarchive.net/BDU /BDUKTB30327.htm. "Too true": Knowles, NSA interview, 8. Beesly, *Very Special Intelligence,* 176, also mentions it.

X

Americans visit Bletchley Park: Gladwin, "Cautious Collaborators," 123–25; Budiansky, *Battle of Wits,* 175–79; Alvarez, "Most Helpful and Co-Operative," 164–66, and Fig. 9.1, "Diplomatic Cryptosystems Read at GC&CS and SIS, 1940," 162. Bombes: Hastings, *Secret War,* 75–86, 102. American bombe development: DeBrosse and Burke, *Secret in Building 26,* esp. xxvii–xxviii, 9, 69, 77–78, 103–04, 108–10, 124–30, 138–39, 166–72; Burke, *It Wasn't All Magic,* 111–12. Number of British bombes: Erskine, "Naval Enigma: A Missing Link," 494; Hinsley et al., *British Intelligence,* vol. 2, 748, 750; Hastings, *Secret War,* 102; Kahn, *Seizing the Enigma,* 227. Sub cards: Kohnen, *Winn and Knowles,* 103; Parsons report: "Functions of Secret Room," 3–4. Knowles receiving OP-20-G intelligence: Benson, *History of U.S. Communications Intelligence During World War II,* 78. Knowles's own view was that "our capabilities actually exceeded that [sic] of the British" and that "we were able

to do a lot of breaking, once we got into the business, more so than the British did"
(Knowles, NSA interview, pp. 20–21).

XI

Size of Royal Navy: Hanson, *Second World Wars*, 149. U.S. ships commissioned: Jones,
WW2, 105. There were also 200 submarines, which I have omitted as they were not
part of the surface fleet. U.S. Navy in 1945: Based on Chart 5, "Overall Warship Ton-
nages of the Powers, 1939–1945," in Kennedy, *Victory at Sea*, 299. "Boots and spurs":
Cited in Hathaway, *Ambiguous Partnership*, 316. "All the gold": letter, Churchill to
Roosevelt, Nov. 28, 1944, quoted in Reynolds, *Mirrors of Greatness*, 189.

CHAPTER 12—THE SUICIDE STRETCH

I

One particular list of *U-505 Ultra* signals—those after Zschech received permission
to enter Lorient on December 11, 1942, up until his announcement on July 2, 1943,
that he would arrive soon at a rendezvous point—is blank. See https://www.uboat
archive.net/U-505A/U-505Messages.htm. Willi: Goebeler, *Steel Boat*, 129–33. Morale
and reprimand: Hinsley et al., *British Intelligence*, vol. 2, 567–68; Beesly, *Very Special
Intelligence*, 187–88; Milner, *Battle of the Atlantic*, 158. Torpedo range: Memorandum, "U-Boat Offensive Tactics," June 16, 1943, No. 66, in Syrett, *Battle of the
Atlantic and Signals Intelligence*, 188.

II

Wells, "Persuading the U-Boats"; Daugherty, "Commander Norden and the German Admirals," 494–97; Farago, *Burn After Reading*, 276–82; Farago, *Tenth Fleet*, 194,
203; Memorandum, "OP-16-W Broadcasts to German U-Boats," Sept. 24, 1943,
https://www.uboatarchive.net/U-662A/U-662NordenInterview.htm. Mulligan,
Lone Wolf, 130–35, has an excellent analysis of OP-16-W and Farago's propaganda
work. Farago gained something of a reputation among Tenth Fleet veterans and
old intelligence hands after the war as an indiscreet fabulist who exaggerated truths
to make better stories. The *Tenth Fleet* book itself, however, contains much that is
interesting and was the first to bring its existence and work to light, even if there
are numerous errors and exaggerations. The final say should surely go to Knowles
himself, who reviewed the book for the CIA journal, *Studies in Intelligence*. His
judgment was thus: "This is the best comprehensive account of U.S. antisubmarine
operations in World War II that has come to this reviewer's attention...The main
criticism that can be directed at the book arises from the author's dramatic com-
pulsions." Knowles, "*The Tenth Fleet* (Review)," A19–23. On the losses amongst

the Crew of 1936, my analysis is based on the list at https://uboat.net/men/commanders/crews.html?crew=36.

III–IV

These sections are primarily based on Goebeler, *Steel Boat,* 125–49, 164; Decker, "404 Days!," 42–43; Paterson, "From the Lion's Roar," 80–86. Knowles's knowledge of *U-505*'s movements and damage is clear from intercepted *Ultra* signals, provided at https://www.uboatarchive.net/U-505A/U-505Messages.htm. Dönitz's suspicion: Memorandum, including POW interrogation statements, "History of U-505," June 5, 1944, Box 61, Folder 56, MSI.

CHAPTER 13—THE LEMON

I

Leaflet: Cremer, *U-Boat Commander,* 50. Zschech gossip: Memorandum, including POW interrogation statements, "History of U-505," June 5, 1944, Box 61, Folder 56, MSI. Loewe: letter, Loewe to Gallery, Nov. 27, 1955, Box 61, Folder 25, MSI. Wrench: Werner, *Iron Coffins,* 19. The itching-powder story is mentioned in Foot, *SOE in France,* 271, who confirms that not even Special Operations Executive teams ever infiltrated the Biscay U-boat bases. Foreigners: Cremer, *U-Boat Commander,* 96. Dislike of Todt workers: Goebeler, *Steel Boat,* 150–53, 161. Sabotage stories: Compare Decker, "404 Days!," 43, with Goebeler, *Steel Boat,* 144–45.

II

Changes to production methods: Tooze, *Wages of Destruction,* 616–17. Problems with departures: "U-Boats Sailing from Biscay: False Starts Due to Defects or Nostalgia," Oct. 9, 1943, No. 91, in Syrett, *Battle of the Atlantic and Signals Intelligence,* 213; letter, Lange to Gallery, June 27, 1955, Box 42, Folder 14, MSI; interview, Aloysius Hasselberg, MSI.

III

Mile figures: "U-505 Combat Chronology," App. B, in Savas, *Hunt and Kill,* 225–29. *U-505* false starts: "U-Boats Sailing from Biscay," Syrett, *Battle of the Atlantic and Signals Intelligence,* 213. Winn does not specify the hull number, but it is clear to which U-boat he is referring.

IV–V

Date of *U-505* departure: Paterson, "From the Lion's Roar," 84. Sound of sonar: Schäffer, *U-Boat 977,* 103. Musing on others: Goebeler, *Steel Boat,* 163. Deaths: Based on my analysis of Crew of 36, at https://uboat.net/men/commanders/crews.html?crew=36. Only suicide: Mulligan, *Neither Sharks Nor Wolves,* 159, 190. Zschech's final voyage: Goebeler, *Steel Boat,* 164–80; Paterson, "From the Lion's Roar," 84–86; Meyer's log entries, U-505 War Diary 10, https://www.uboatarchive.net/U-505/KTB505-10.htm.

VI–VII

Lange: Goebeler, *Steel Boat,* 186–90; Mulligan, "Community Bound by Fate," 36–39, esp. note 40 concerning Lange's NSDAP (Nazi Party) membership. Relationship between the Party and the Navy: Mulligan, *Neither Sharks Nor Wolves,* 215–36; Gallery, *Twenty Million Tons,* 233–36, also has some remarks. For *U-505* at this time, Goebeler, 193–204; Paterson, "From the Lion's Roar," 87–90.

VIII

"Raising havoc": Decker, "404 Days!," 44.

CHAPTER 14—THE CAN-DO KING

I

Gallery's movements and thoughts at this time: USNI interview, 63–70. New role for CVEs: memorandum, Knowles to Low, Nov. 23, 1943, No. 105, in Syrett, *Battle of the Atlantic and Signals Intelligence,* 235–36; captain (probably *Bogue*), quoted in Grosvenor, "Cruise on an Escort Carrier," 520.

II

Gallery, *Twenty Million Tons,* 248–50.

III

Gallery, *Twenty Million Tons,* 251. Gallery gets *U-129* confused with *U-516*: It was the latter that was refueling, not *U-129*. See https://uboat.net/allies/ships/uss_guadalcanal.htm. On Knowles, NSA interview, 74–76.

IV

Gallery, USNI interview, 78–82; Gallery, *Twenty Million Tons,* 260–61; Mulligan, *Lone Wolf,* 193–201, has an excellent account of the *U-515* fight. Cremer and Henke: Cremer, *U-Boat Commander,* 165–66.

V–VI

Interrogation setup and procedure: Gallery, *Twenty Million Tons,* 263; Mulligan, *Lone Wolf,* 206–09. Knowles and intelligence: He "received all the interrogation reports in my room, I went over all of them as they came in." A Fort Hunt interrogator would often visit F-21 "to amplify what we would consider the significant aspect" (NSA interview with Knowles, 22–23). Captured U-boats: The captain of

U-110 was Fritz-Julius Lemp, mentioned in section 1 of chapter 6, who happened to be Loewe's cousin; he died during the battle. There was one more U-boat taken by the Allies during the war, *U-1024*, but that would not occur until April 12, 1945, when she was captured by two British frigates. Like the others, she would sink soon afterward. *YYY*: "Alphabetical List of *Feste Funknamen* of U-Boats Extracted from the *Geheime Marinefunknamenliste*," June 18, 1943, No. 67, in Syrett, *Battle of the Atlantic and Signals Intelligence*, 189. Gallery's interests and scuttling methods: *Twenty Million Tons*, 273; Vause, "Desperate Decisions," 147–48, 151–55.

VII

Gallery, *Twenty Million Tons*, 273–74; Gallery, "Reminiscences," 94. On *Chatelain*: Mulligan, *Lone Wolf*, 200. There are discrepancies in the chronology, but this timing seems consistent with the facts.

VIII

Smith-Hutton, USNI interview, 402–03; Gallery, *Clear the Decks!*, 93.

IX

Gallery, *Clear the Decks!*, 150.

XI

OP-16-W collected letters written by Axis captives for a radio program called *Prisoner of War Mail*, in which the prisoners' letters home would be read out (with their knowledge) as a propaganda tool to show that those who surrendered were alive, well, and being treated leniently. Had there been a mistake that allowed one of Gallery's POWs to have his letter broadcast, the ruse would have been over. Daugherty mentions the show in "Commander Norden and the German Admirals," 495.

XII

Zschech missing from boat: OP-16-Z Report, "U-Boat Officers List," Box 31, Folder 19, MSI. Voyage: "Ultra Intercepts from U-505," Apr. 10, 13, May 14, 15, at https://www.uboatarchive.net/U-505A/U-505Messages.htm, and for copies of the originals, Box 31, Folder 10, MSI; Paterson, "Collision Course," 125; Kohnen, "Tombstone of Victory," 27, note 12; Decker, "404 Days!," 44; Goebeler, *Steel Boat*, 222–27.

CHAPTER 15—NINETEEN MINUTES

I

Schedule: "Plan of the Day," June 4, 1944, Encl. H, in TG 22.3 Report, https://www.uboatarchive.net/U-505A/U-505PlanOfTheDay.htm; and Grosvenor,

"Cruise on an Escort Carrier," 514. Watts: Interview, MSI. Radio communications: The complete transcript of the day's radio transmissions, which were recorded onto phonographic discs, "Log of Communications During Action Resulting in Capture of U-505," June 4, 1944, is available at https://www.uboatarchive .net/U-505A/U-505CommunicationsLog.htm. See also Y'Blood, *Hunter-Killer*, 183–90. Unless otherwise noted, all quotes are from these sources. Whales: Gallery, *Twenty Million Tons*, 292; Grosvenor, "Cruise on an Escort Carrier," 535. "Hot on trail": Quoted in Kohnen, "Tombstone of Victory," 13. Half-power: Report by Gallery, "Capture of German Submarine U-505," 2, https://www.uboatarchive .net/U-505A/U-505TG22.3Report.htm. *Ultra* message to Lange, May 26, 1944, https://www.uboatarchive.net/U-505A/U-505Messages.htm. Knowles and *U-505* position: Paterson, "Collision Course," 131. Transport planes: Gallery, *Twenty Million Tons*, 240–41. Crash-dives: U-505 War Diary, May 29, 30, 1944, 57–58, https:// www.uboatarchive.net/U-505/KTB505-11.htm. Movements: Plots in Encl. C, "Track Chart" (TG 22.3 Report), and the "COMINCH Estimate" (i.e., Knowles), "Capture of German Submarine U-505," https://www.uboatarchive.net/U-505A/U-505Track Chart.htm. Lange's comments about heading eastward are in his War Diary, May 30, 05:48 a.m. See also Gallery's narrative of the pursuit, *Twenty Million Tons*, 240–44.

II

Gallery on chance, flipping nickel, goose, and Casablanca: *Twenty Million Tons*, 4–5, 285–90. Lange outwits Gallery: Goebeler, *Steel Boat*, 227. Gallery himself professed admiration at the exploit. "I had based all my operations on the assumption that U-boats were submerged all day long [and so] I had been flying only token patrols in daylight" (*Twenty Million Tons*, 242–43). "Bastard": Interview, Earl Trosino, MSI.

III–VII

U-505 before attack: Goebeler, *Steel Boat*, 229; "The Secret Around Felix," *Kristall* (1956), translated copy in Box 60, Folder 2, MSI, p. 4. "No big stuff": Gallery, *Twenty Million Tons*, 292. Audio/video: Kohnen, "Tombstone of Victory," 12; footage can be seen at https://archive.org/details/NPC-9050. "Barroom brawl": Gallery, *Twenty Million Tons*, 292; interview, Don Carter, MSI Archives. Marking the spot: Cadle's (and Wolffe's) "Report of Antisubmarine Action by Aircraft," June 4, 1944, Encl. A7, TG 22.3 Report, https://www.uboatarchive.net/U-505A/U-505VC-8ASW -6Report.htm. Sounds and lights out inside *U-505*: Decker, "404 Days!," 45; Goebeler, *Steel Boat*, 230. "Battle stations": Goebeler, *Steel Boat*, 232–33. Lange recalled these moments in "The Secret Around Felix," 5. "Disgusted tone": Gallery, TG 22.3 Report, "Capture of German Submarine U-505," 4, https://www.uboatarchive .net/U-505A/U-505TG22.3Report.htm.

CHAPTER 16—THE BOARDING PARTY

I

Boarding party: Encl. F, "Boarding Party," TG 22.3 Report, esp. Boat No. 1; interview, Philip Trusheim, MSI; "Boarding and Salvage Bill for Enemy Submarines," report in Kohnen, "Tombstone of Victory," 32. Backgrounds: In the Gallery Papers, Box 29, Folder 1, there is a collection of postwar cards on some of the first boat's crewmen. Volunteers and training: Interviews, Wayne Pickels, Zenon Lukosius, Don Carter, MSI. "Attaboy": "Log of Communications," 12:05 p.m., https://www .uboatarchive.net/U-505A/U-505CommunicationsLog.htm. Diesel oil: Interviews, D. E. Hampton, Carter, MSI. Four to six inches: interview, Earl Trosino, MSI. Secret documents location: "Boarding and Salvage Bill," in Kohnen, "Tombstone of Victory," 32. Gallery, memorandum, "Stowage Space for Classified Documents in Board U/Bs," May 7, 1946, Box 61, Folder 56, MSI. Enigma: Interviews, Pickels and Lukosius. Jack Dumford, in his MSI interview, was certain "there were two machines. One of them looked to be inoperable." A Naval Intelligence message dated June 19 confirms that "machines actually aboard U-505 were numbered 3467 and 4473." This was in reply to a message sent the previous day, which had erroneously stated that there was one machine, numbered 2802 (Item 2802 was in fact an instruction manual). See the two messages in Box 61, Folder 62, MSI. I have confirmed the two numbers with NSA. Unless otherwise noted, times in this chapter are based on the relevant dated entries in *Guadalcanal's* "Report of A/S Cruise of Task Group 22.3," https://www.uboatarchive.net/U-505A/U-505ASCruise.htm.

II

"Machinery": Gallery, *Clear the Decks!,* 225. Trosino comes aboard: Interview, Earl Trosino, MSI. Jacobson: Interviews, Pickels and Lukosius. According to Lieutenant Hampton, who joined Trosino in the control room, "It's a terrible feeling not really knowing where you're going, and what you're doing and everything in German" (interview, D. E. Hampton, MSI).

III

Actions aboard *U-505*: Interviews, Trosino, Hampton, Carter, MSI. Decoded messages: Interview, Jack Dumford, MSI. Patrol perimeters: June 5, 5:02 a.m., "Report of A/S Cruise of Task Group 22.3," https://www.uboatarchive.net/U -505A/U-505ASCruise.htm. Radio communication: See note on p. 33, "Report of A/S Cruise of Task Group 22.3." Souvenirs: Interviews, Trusheim, Pickels, Carter, and Lukosius; "mountain of stuff": Gallery, *Clear the Decks!,* 228–29. One especial prize would always elude Gallery: Lange's personal Mauser HSc 7.65mm pistol. He knew someone had stolen it, but the mystery would be solved only after Gallery's death. The Chief Photographer's Mate, Clifford Werlla, had been one of the first aboard. He had tagged along in Trosino's boat and had helped himself to Lange's gun as well as his Zeiss Ikon camera. Later on, when Gallery was demanding every souvenir to be handed in, Werlla had hidden the Mauser and the Zeiss in the one place that couldn't be searched: the carrier's darkroom, where he was developing the very photos Gallery was so eager to see. Years later, somewhat embarrassed by the episode, Werlla had told his wife not to sell the gun or camera until after the Old Man was dead. Werlla himself died in the 1960s and Lorraine, his wife, loyally held on to the trophies until January 23, 1977, four days after Gallery's death, when they passed to a military-memorabilia dealer. See Bill Shea's post, "The Saga of the Never Been Told Story of the U-505 Commander's Pistol," at https://www .therupteddduck.com/blogs/bill-sheas-wwii-memorabilia-blog/so-here-is-the-rest -of-the-story.

IV

Officers' reactions: Gallery, *Clear the Decks!*, 226. The two messages are printed in Waller, "U-505 in the US Navy," 181. Low's description: see "Personal Narrative," 38A.

CHAPTER 17—NEMO

I

"Report of A/S Cruise of Task Group 22.3," June 4; interview, Jack Dumford, MSI.

II

Ewald Felix: Encl. E, "Prisoners Taken from U/B U-505," TG 22.3 Report; Gilliland and Shenk, *Admiral Dan Gallery*, 124–31; Trosino and Hampton interviews, MSI. Dislike: Schiessl, "*Volksdeutsche* of Eastern Europe." After Christmas 1945, Felix was repatriated to Germany and ended up in the Russian Zone. Trosino and Gallery tried to get him permission to return to the U.S., but by then Felix had left for his parents' farm in Poland and was beyond reach. He wrote to Trosino in 1948, a terrible time, to ask for secondhand clothing. Trosino's wife's church group sent a number of packages. Some years later, Felix succeeded in getting to Germany, where he lived with his son, and corresponded intermittently with Trosino until the early 1990s.

III

Waller, "U-505 in the US Navy," 182; TG 22.3 Report, 6; Gallery, *Clear the Decks!*, 223; Wise and Mallmann Showell, "Deciphering the U-Boat War," 118; Dispatch,

CINCLANT to FOCWAF, forwarded to Gallery, June 5, 1944, Box 61, Box 64, MSI; interview, Dumford, MSI.

IV

Gallery arrives: Encl. F, "Boarding Parties," Boat No. 7, June 5, 1944, TG 22.3 Report. Can-Do Junior: Gallery, *Clear the Decks!*, 223. War flag: Speer, *Inside the Third Reich*, 102. Don Carter tells the flag story in his interview, MSI. There is some debate about the veracity of Carter's version, which may have been misremembered. No one else, including Gallery or Low, either mentioned or noticed the switcheroo and believed the ensign to be the real deal. See, for instance, Kohnen, "Tombstone of Victory," 28, note 18. I tend to believe Carter. It's very possible that one of the German sailors grabbed the ensign before departure, to avoid the dishonor of it falling into American hands, and threw it overboard before the Americans arrived.

V

Escorts: "Report of A/S Cruise of Task Group 22.3," June 7, 1944; Gallery, *Clear the Decks!*, 226; TG 22.3 Report, 7. Safe room: Encl. F, "Boarding Parties," Boat No. 9, June 7, 1944, TG 22.3 Report; relevant dates in "Report of A/S Cruise of Task Group 22.3," June 7–9, 1944; Encl. A6, *Jenks* Report, of TG 22.3 Report, Part V, notes refueling amounts.

VI

Jenks: dispatch, Jenks to Naval Operating Base, Bermuda, June 11, noting planned arrival at 2:30 a.m. on June 13, Box 61, Folder 39, MSI. Documents: App. 3, "Captured Documents," in Bray, *Battle of the Atlantic—Appendices*, 85–87; Wenger, OP-20 memorandum, "Benefits Gained from U-505 Documents," July 13, 1944, in Clay Blair Papers, Box 128, Folder 8. The importance of the Address Book is given in Hinsley et al., *British Intelligence*, vol. 2, App. 9, 682. Exchange of messages: dispatches, Admiralty to King, June 4, 1944; and King to Admiralty, June 5, in Box 61, Folder 39, MSI; Knowles's reply, Wise and Mallmann Showell, "Deciphering the U-Boat War," 123. On August 28, 1944, King, with undisguised pleasure, lectured the British on using U-505 instead of the cover name *Nemo*, saying that it "endangers security." The British, with good grace, apologized for the lapse and assured him that circulation had been heavily restricted. See dispatches, King to U.S. Commander of Naval Forces, Europe, Aug. 28; and Admiralty to King, Aug. 31, in Box 61, Folder 54, MSI.

VII

Interview, Dumford, MSI. Name: Kohnen, "Tombstone of Victory," 14–15; Farago, *Tenth Fleet*, 270. On June 6, Low suggested a short list to King, *Ark* and *Nemo*, with the latter circled in pen, making it the clear favorite. In Box 61, Folder 56, MSI. On the *Yehudi* reference, see the Wikipedia entries "Crazy Cruise" and "Who's Yehoodi?" Probably unbeknownst to Gallery and Knowles, the U.S. Navy had initiated Project *Yehudi* in 1943. It was a research program directed toward developing special lights for aircraft that would camouflage their dark shapes against a bright sky so as to allow them to sneak up on U-boats. Since Tenth Fleet's Low was likely aware of the project, avoiding confusion between a serious Navy project and Gallery's jokey name would have been sufficient reason to reject it as *U-505*'s cover name.

VIII

Flight: Low, "Memorandum for the Admiral [King]," June 18, 1944, Clay Blair Papers, Box 105, Folder 3; "Memorandum for Vice Chief of Naval Operations," June 15, 1944, Clay Blair Papers, Box 128, Folder 8; for flight details: memorandum by Low, June 10, in Box 61, Folder 54, MSI; names of travelers: "Distribution List," June 18, Box 61, Folder 54, MSI. Knowles quietly mentioned that he and Low were in Bermuda, where they inspected *U-505*, in his article, "American View," 14. Sea-lane clearance: Interview, Raymond Watts, MSI. Flare gun and ensign: Interview, Carter, MSI. He later donated the flare gun to the museum. Gallery enjoins secrecy: Gallery, memorandum to all hands of TG 22.3, June 14, 1944, in Box 61, Folder 39, MSI; interview, Carter; Roger Cozens, chief sonarman of the *Flaherty*, kept his signed copy of Gallery's printed oath, dated June 8, photocopy in Box 58, Folder 10, MSI. Prize money: Gallery, *Clear the Decks!*, 231. Lange's interesting choice of reading: letter, Roosevelt to Gallery, Aug. 19, 1944, printed in Gallery, *Clear the Decks!*, 237. The letter would enrage Francis Low, who accused Gallery of compromising national security by sending a book lifted from *U-505* to White House staffers. Gallery told him that in fact King had given it to FDR. Nothing more was said about it. Buell, *Master of Sea Power*, 296–97. The book itself is kept at the Roosevelt Library.

IX

See relevant *Ultra*/Enigma intercepts, https://www.uboatarchive.net/U-505A/U-505Messages.htm. D-Day: Cremer, *U-Boat Commander*, 180–82. For U-Boat Command judgment, entry of July 16, 1944, in War Log, https://www.uboatarchive.net/BDU/BDUKTB30351.htm (and Box 61, Folder 56, MSI). Shortly after the war, there was a rumor that in fact the Germans had known about *U-505* almost all along. This was based on an editor's mistaken note in Hessler's official *U-Boat War*, para. 457. After stating that U-Boat Command initially did not "know of the capture of U.505, owing to the excellence of Allied security and to the strict isolation of her crew by the Americans," Hessler went on to say that either at the end of 1944 or the beginning of 1945 "a U-boat officer held in a Canadian prisoner-of-war camp managed to pass us a message warning of the probable capture of a U-boat, intact and complete with signal publications." Of his own volition, the British editor of Hessler's once-secret report added that this referred to *U-505*. But it didn't: It referred to *U-110*, captured May 9, 1941, along with its secret documents. The submarine sank while being towed. Her surviving crew members, as mentioned by Hessler, were lodged at Camp 23 / Monteith in Canada. Worthwhile noting was that it *took three and a half years* for word to reach German ears, which makes it even less likely that news of *U-505* could have leaked so soon. Part of the reason for the error was due to Anglo-American rivalry. The British were immensely (and justly) proud of their capture and the official historian, Capt. Stephen Roskill, always thought Gallery was showboating even as he himself was hamstrung by more onerous security regulations. The "clarification" was a discreet way of putting Gallery back in his place. Accordingly, in his *War at Sea,* vol. 3, Part 2, p. 174, Roskill devoted just one sentence to *U-505*'s capture. He would later write an excellent if incomplete account (because he could not mention Enigma) of *U-110, The Secret Capture*; see esp. 14–15, where Roskill discusses his irritation with Gallery. Hessler, it's worth mentioning, was Dönitz's son-in-law and a U-boat staff officer; if the grand admiral really had known that *U-505* had fallen into American hands, Hessler was in a good position to have stated so definitively.

CHAPTER 18—TOPSY-TURVY

I

The medical records of the *U-505* crew are in Box 31, Folder 145, MSI. Some men were already afflicted with furuncles before they left *U-505*. But others, among them Werner Reh, said, "Good health, that's what I jumped into the water with. But, what happened then on the aircraft carrier, until Bermuda, probably ninety percent of us were all sick there! We broke out in boils in particular." See interviews, Reh, Wolfgang Schiller, and Heinrich Klippisch (who'd since left *U-505*, but who recalled that a lot of men suffered from skin conditions), MSI.

II

Interrogator names and notes: "Distribution List," June 18, Box 61, Folder 54, MSI; OP-16-Z, "Interrogation Notes—Crew Members of U-505," Gallery Papers, Box 29, Folder 2, USNI; full list of prisoners: Encl. E, "Prisoners Taken from U/B U-505," TG 22.3 Report. Breslau: Interview, Wolfgang Schiller, MSI. Lange's moan: Gallery, *Clear the Decks!,* 227. Hauser: Goebeler, *Steel Boats,* 234.

III

Bermuda and voyage: Interview, Werner Reh, MSI; Dispatches, July 24 and 29, Box 61, Folder 54, MSI; Lange in Bermuda: J. Bell, "German Sailor Helped US Navy

Seize U-505," *Royal Gazette,* June 19, 2019; S. Jones, "Historian Uncovers New Twist in U-Boat Story," *Royal Gazette,* Jan. 12, 2015; S. Jones, "My Wife and the U-Boat Secret," *Royal Gazette,* Dec. 30, 2014. Mail: memorandum, War Department, "Transfer of Naval Prisoners of War," July 31, 1944, MG-146-001-032, Pine Grove Furnace, POW Interrogation Camps, and Camp Michaux Research Collection, Cumberland County Historical Society, Carlisle, Pennsylvania; "Special Handling of Prisoners of War," Jan. 25, 1945; "Special Naval Prisoners of War," Jan. 25, Box 61, Folder 65, MSI; Waller, "U-505 in the U.S. Navy," 187. Camp Ruston: Scalia, "History, Archaeology, and the German Prisoner of War Experience," 312–13, 325, and Map 3, "Schematic Layout of Camp Ruston," 318; Shea and Pritchett, "*Wehrmacht* in Louisiana," 7, 9; "U-505: The Secret Around Felix," *Kristall,* 11–12; Waller, "U-505 in the U.S. Navy," 187–89; Karl Springer, interview, notes the dates they were taken to Camp Livingston, MSI; tortoises and getting rid of dirt from the tunnel: Reh, interview, MSI. Goebeler, *Steel Boat,* 247, exaggerates the success of the balloon wheeze. It is questionable, in fact, whether it happened. Several times the interviewers at MSI asked former POWs about the incident, but none could attest to it. Goebeler seems convinced, however, so it's possible that it was a small-scale effort.

IV

Nazis: Shea and Pritchett, "*Wehrmacht* in Louisiana," 13, but the fullest discussion is in Krammer, *Nazi Prisoners of War,* 147–88. An inspection of the POW quarters at Pine Grove Furnace, Pennsylvania, uncovered a piece of paper containing a tattoo outline, smeared in blood, that was tucked into a crack in a wall. See memorandum, War Department, "Tattooing," Nov. 1, 1944, MG-146-001-005, in MG-146, Pine Grove Furnace Collection. See also memoranda, War Department, "Segregation of Prisoners of War," Feb. 18, 1943, and May 10, 1944, MG-146-001-020, Pine Grove Furnace Collection. Hauser's time as POW: Kohnen, "Tombstone of Victory," p. 28, note 16; Goebeler, *Steel Boat,* 246–47, circumspectly outlines the trial. Interviews, Reh and Springer, MSI. For Lange's view that Hauser had been derelict, see his letter to Gallery, June 27, 1955, in Box 42, Folder 14, MSI. Less directly, Lange (the author's source) would use the alias "L. I." to disguise Hauser's identity in the 1956 *Kristall* article, "U-505: The Secret Around Felix," 5–6, where Lange put on the record that he ordered, "All men abandon the ship! Scuttle the boat!" (Box 50, Folder 2, MSI). Goebeler recounts that "after the war, Hauser's son told me his father claimed to have single-handedly saved U-505 on three separate occasions, and that he deserved a great medal for his bravery. In my opinion, he deserved a medal from the Allies, because that guy did a lot more harm to us than good."

V

Life in camp: Shea and Pritchett, *"Wehrmacht* in Louisiana," 9, 12; Scalia, "History, Archaeology, and the German Prisoner of War Experience," 316–17, 321–25; interview, Springer, MSI; Gelpi, "Piney Hills Stalag," 347–48; Heisler, "Returning to America," 537–56, discusses German eagerness to emigrate to the U.S. after the war. Jim Crow: Schott, "Prisoners Like Us," 279–80; Scalia, "History, Archaeology, and the German Prisoner of War Experience," 319, 324.

VI

Dönitz's promises and new U-boats: Minutes, Feb. 15 and 17, Apr. 18, 1945, in Thursfield, *Führer Conferences,* 445–48, 485 (and also July 8, 1943, 338–39); "strongest escorts" and "rebirth of the U-boat war": Conference of February 28, quoted in Herwig, "Germany and the Battle of the Atlantic," 84; Cremer, *U-Boat Commander,* 198–207; Hughes and Costello, *Battle of the Atlantic,* 301–02. Technical specifications and operations of the Type XXI: Relevant pages at Uboat.net, and Williamson, *Kriegsmarine U-Boats,* 33–37. Hessler, *U-Boat War,* para. 464, discusses the disparity between calculated and actual performance. He concludes that the Type XXI, notwithstanding some real-world issues, possessed "outstanding fighting qualities." Cremer, who put *U-2519* through her paces in the winter of 1944, describes his amazement, *U-Boat Commander,* 194–96. Scuttled U-boats: Mulligan, *Neither Sharks Nor Wolves,* 239; the number of surrendered vessels varies a little, but the most authoritative list is D. Waller and A. Niestlé, "U-Boats That Surrendered," https://uboat.net/articles/83.html and https://uboat.net/fates/surrendered.htm. Press release, "Capture of Nazi Submarine in 1944 Revealed," May 16, 1945, https://www.uboatarchive.net/U-505A/U-505Press.htm.

VII

Interviews, Schiller, Springer, Reh, MSI; Goebeler, *Steel Boat,* 250. U-boat losses and fatalities are impossible to nail down precisely, and figures are revised continually. The most detailed analysis is in Mulligan, *Neither Sharks Nor Wolves,* App. 2, "Numbers and Losses of the U-Boat Service," 251–56. Mulligan's book was published in 1999, and he cites 28,748 names being catalogued at the Möltenort U-Boat Memorial in Germany. Today the memorial lists 30,002.

EPILOGUE—"THEIR DESIRED HAVEN"

II–III

U-505's postwar career is covered in Gill, "Project 356: U-505 and the Journey to Chicago," 161–220; and Kohnen, "Tombstone of Victory," 17–23. Loewe: Quoted in Mulligan, "Community Bound by Fate," 54. Gallery and Wouk: Wouk, *Language God Talks*, 125–27; Wouk, "Admiral Dan: A Reminiscence," in Gilliland and Shenk, *Admiral Dan Gallery*, ix–xi. Gallery sends out his book: letters, Dönitz, Nov. 30, 1956; see also Nimitz (Oct. 20); Low (Nov. 27, "silly things"), Gallery Papers, Box 9, Folder 5. Death: Gilliland and Shenk, 303. Beesly and Winn: Beesly's contribution on Winn, *Oxford Dictionary of National Biography*; Beesly, *Very Special Intelligence*, 197. Knowles career and writing: Notices and announcements, in Clay Blair Papers, Box 170, Folder 14; NSA interview, 32; Knowles, "Very Special Intelligence (Review)," 35; Knowles, "American View," 14, 16.

BIBLIOGRAPHY

Interviews

GRIFFIN MUSEUM OF SCIENCE AND INDUSTRY, COLLECTIONS & ARCHIVES DEPARTMENT, CHICAGO

GERMAN:

Aloysius Hasselberg

Heinrich Klippisch

Werner Reh

Albert Rust

Wolfgang Schiller

Karl Springer

AMERICAN:

Don Carter

Jack Dumford

D. E. Hampton

Zenon Lukosius

Wayne Pickels

Earl Trosino

Philip Trusheim

Raymond Watts

NATIONAL CRYPTOLOGIC MUSEUM, ANNAPOLIS JUNCTION, MARYLAND

Kenneth Knowles, NSA OH-22-86, August 19, 1986

NATIONAL PARK SERVICE

Angus MacLean Thuermer, NPS Fort Hunt Oral History Project, October 25, 2006

U.S. NAVAL INSTITUTE, ANNAPOLIS, MARYLAND

Rear Admiral Daniel V. Gallery, June 1976

Captain Henri Smith-Hutton, August 1976

Archives

Century Association Archives Foundation, New York

Clay Blair Papers, American Heritage Center, University of Wyoming

Daniel Gallery Papers, Special Collections & Archives Department, Nimitz Library, U.S. Naval Academy

Griffin Museum of Science and Industry, Collections & Archives Department, Chicago

National Archives, London, United Kingdom

National Cryptologic Museum, National Security Agency, Annapolis Junction, Maryland

Pine Grove Furnace Collection, POW Interrogation Camps, and Camp Michaux Research Collection, Cumberland County Historical Society, Carlisle, Pennsylvania

Official Publications, Histories, and Documents

Admiralty-COMINCH Serial Messages. www.uboatarchive.net.

Annual Register of the United States Naval Academy, 1927–28. Washington, D.C.: GPO, 1927.

Bray, J. K., ed. *Ultra in the Atlantic.* 6 vols. Laguna Hills, CA: Aegean Park Press, 1994.

Building the Navy's Bases in World War II: History of the Bureau of Yards and Docks and the Civil Engineer Corps, 1940–1946. 2 vols. Washington, D.C.: GPO, 1947.

Burke, C. B. *It Wasn't All Magic: The Early Struggle to Automate Cryptanalysis, 1930s–1960s.* Annapolis Junction, MD: Center for Cryptologic History/National Security Agency, 2002.

Craven W. F. and Cate, J. L., eds. *The Army Air Forces in World War II.* 7 vols. Chicago, IL: University of Chicago Press, 1948.

Fischer, G. J. *A Statistical Summary of Shipbuilding Under the U.S. Maritime Commission During World War II.* Washington, D.C.: GPO, 1949.

Foot, M. R. D. *SOE in France: An Account of the Work of the British Special Operations Executive in France, 1940–1944.* London: HMSO, 1966.

Furer, J. A. *Administration of the Navy Department in World War II.* Washington, D.C.: GPO, 1959.

German Submarine Activities on the Atlantic Coast of the United States. Washington, D.C.: Office of Naval Records and Library, 1920.

Heavilin, J. S., ed. *The Lucky Bag of 1927.* Annapolis, MD: United States Naval Academy, 1927.

Hessler, G. *The U-Boat War in the Atlantic, 1939–1945.* 3 vols. London: HMSO, 1989 edn.

Hinsley, F. H., Thomas, E. E., Ransom, C. F. G., Knight, R. C., Simkins, C. A. G., and Howard, M. *British Intelligence in the Second World War.* 5 vols. New York: Cambridge University Press, 1979–1990.

History of the Anti-Submarine Measures Division of the Tenth Fleet. 1946.

King, E. J. *U.S. Navy at War, 1941–1945: Official Reports to the Secretary of the Navy.* Washington, D.C.: Navy Department, 1946.

Knowles, K. A. *Battle of the Atlantic: U-Boat Operations, December 1942 to May 1945.* Report SRH-008, 1945.

———. *F-21 War Report.* Atlantic Section, COMINCH, May 15, 1945.

Morison, S. E. *The Atlantic Battle Won, May 1943–May 1945.* 15 vols. History of United States Naval Operations in World War II. Boston, MA.: Little, Brown and Company, 1968.

———. *The Battle of the Atlantic, September 1939–May 1943.* 15 vols. History of United States Naval Operations in World War II. Boston, MA.: Little, Brown and Company, 1946.

National Defense Research Committee. *A Survey of Subsurface Warfare in World War Two: Summary Technical Report of Division 6.* Washington, D.C.: GPO, 1946.

Navy Directory: Officers of the United States Navy and Marine Corps. Washington, D.C.: GPO, 1943.

Office of United States Chief of Council for Prosecution of Axis Criminality. *Nazi Conspiracy and Aggression.* 8 vols. Washington, D.C.: GPO, 1946.

Parsons, J. E. *Functions of Secret Room of COMINCH Combat Intelligence, Atlantic Section.*

Radar Research and Development Sub-Committee. *U.S. Radar: Operational Characteristics of Radar Classified by Tactical Application.* 1943.

Roskill, S. W. *The War at Sea, 1939–1945.* 4 vols. London: HMSO, 1954–1961.

Sternhell, C. M. and Thorndike, A. M. *Antisubmarine Warfare in World War II.* OEG Report No. 51. Washington, D.C.: Navy Department, 1946.

Syrett, D. *The Battle of the Atlantic and Signals Intelligence: U-Boat Tracking Papers, 1941–1947.* New York/Abingdon, England: Routledge (orig. Ashgate/Navy Records Society), 2018.

Thursfield, R. G., ed. *Führer Conferences on Naval Affairs.* New York: Macmillan Co., 1948.

Tucker, G. N. *The Naval Service of Canada: Its Official History.* Ottawa, Canada: King's Printer, 1952.

Secondary Sources

Alvarez, D. "Most Helpful and Co-Operative: GC&CS and the Development of American Diplomatic Cryptanalysis, 1941–42." In *Action This Day,* edited by R. Erskine and M. Smith, 152–73. New York: Bantam Press, 2001.

Andrews, Jr., L. M. *Tempest, Fire, and Foe: Destroyer Escorts in World War Two and the Men Who Manned Them.* Charleston, SC/Miami, FL: Narwhal Press, 1999.

Anon. "The Origination and Evolution of Radio Traffic Analysis: World War II." *Cryptologic Quarterly* 6, no. 1 (1987): 23–38.

Anon. "The Trial of Admiral Doenitz." *The ONI Review* 1, no. 12 (1946): 26–35.

Balano, R. C. and Symonds, C. L., eds. *New Interpretations in Naval History: Selected Papers from the Fourteenth Naval History Symposium.* Annapolis, MD: Naval Institute Press, 2001.

Balfour, M. "Another Look at 'Unconditional Surrender.'" *International Affairs* 46, no. 4 (1970): 719–36.

Barlow, J. G. "The Navy's Escort Carrier Offensive." *Naval History* 27, no. 6 (2013).

Barnett, C. *Engage the Enemy More Closely: The Royal Navy in the Second World War.* New York: W. W. Norton & Co., 1991.

Bath, A. H. *Tracking the Axis Enemy: The Triumph of Anglo-American Naval Intelligence.* Lawrence, KS: University Press of Kansas, 1998.

Beesly, P. *Very Special Intelligence: The Story of the Admiralty's Operational Intelligence Center, 1939–1945.* New York: Doubleday & Co., 1978.

Bergmeier, H. J. P. and Lotz, R. E. *Hitler's Airwaves: The Inside Story of Nazi Radio Broadcasting and Propaganda Swing.* London/New Haven, CT: Yale University Press, 1997.

Binford, J. "New York Harbor." *Life,* November 20, 1944: 55–60.

Blair, C. *Hitler's U-Boat War: The Hunted, 1942–1945.* London: Weidenfeld & Nicolson, 1999.

———. *Hitler's U-Boat War: The Hunters, 1939–1942.* New York: Random House, 1996.

Budiansky, S. *Battle of Wits: The Complete Story of Codebreaking in World War II.* New York: Touchstone, 2002.

Buell, T. B. *Master of Sea Power: A Biography of Fleet Admiral Ernest J. King.* Boston, MA: Little, Brown and Company, 1980.

Cameron, N. and Stevens, R. H., trans. *Hitler's Table Talk, 1941–1944.* Oxford, England: Oxford University Press, 1988.

Campbell, A. E. "Franklin Roosevelt and Unconditional Surrender." In *Diplomacy and Intelligence During the Second World War,* edited by R. Langhorne, 219–41. Cambridge, England: Cambridge University Press, 1985.

Churchill, R. S. and Gilbert, M. *Winston S. Churchill.* 8 vols. London: Heinemann, 1966–1988.

Churchill, W. S. *The Hinge of Fate.* Boston, MA: Houghton Mifflin Company, 1950.

Cremer, P. *U-Boat Commander: A Periscope View of the Battle of the Atlantic.* Translated by L. Wilson. Annapolis, MD: Naval Institute Press, 1984.

Cross, R. F. *Shepherds of the Sea: Destroyer Escorts in World War Two.* Annapolis, MD: Naval Institute Press, 2010.

Daugherty, W. E. "Commander Norden and the German Admirals." In *A Psychological Warfare Casebook,* edited by W. E. Daugherty and M. Janowitz, 494–97. Baltimore, MD: The Johns Hopkins Press, 1958.

DeBrosse, J. and Burke, C. *The Secret in Building 26: The Untold Story of America's Ultra War Against the U-Boat Enigma Codes.* New York: Random House, 2004.

Decker, H. J. "404 Days! The War Patrol Life of the German U-505." *Proceedings of the United States Naval Institute* 86, no. 3 (1960): 33–45.

Dimbleby, J. *The Battle of the Atlantic: How the Allies Won the War*. London: Penguin, 2016.

Dönitz, K. *Memoirs: Ten Years and Twenty Days*. Translated by R. H. Stevens. 2012 edn. London/Annapolis, MD: Frontline Books/Naval Institute Press, 2012.

Dorwart, J. M. *Conflict of Duty: The U.S. Navy's Intelligence Dilemma, 1919–1945*. Annapolis, MD: Naval Institute Press, 1983.

Dring, T. R. "A Steep Learning Curve: The Impact of Sonar Technology, Training, and Tactics on the Initial Years of U.S. Navy Antisubmarine Warfare in World War II." *Warship International* 55, no. 1 (2018): 37–57.

Ellis, J. *Brute Force: Allied Strategy and Tactics in the Second World War*. New York: Viking, 1990.

Erskine, R. "Captured *Kriegsmarine* Enigma Documents at Bletchley Park." *Cryptologia* 32, no. 3 (2008): 199–219.

———. "Naval Enigma: A Missing Link." *International Journal of Intelligence and Counterintelligence* 3, no. 4 (1989): 493–508.

———. "Naval Enigma: An Astonishing Blunder." *Intelligence and National Security* 11, no. 3 (1996): 468–73.

———. "Naval Enigma: The Breaking of *Heimisch* and *Triton*." *Intelligence and National Security* 3, no. 1 (1988): 162–83.

———. "Shore High-Frequency Direction-Finding in the Battle of the Atlantic: An Undervalued Intelligence Asset." *Journal of Intelligence History* 4, no. 2 (2004): 1–32.

———. "Tunny Reveals B-Dienst Successes Against the 'Convoy Code.'" *Intelligence and National Security* 28, no. 6 (2013): 868–89.

———. "Ultra and Some U.S. Navy Carrier Operations." *Cryptologia* 19, no. 1 (1995): 81–96.

Erskine, R. and Smith, M., eds. *Action This Day: Bletchley Park from the Breaking of the Enigma Code to the Birth of the Modern Computer*. New York: Bantam Press, 2001.

Farago, L. *Burn After Reading*. Los Angeles, CA: Pinnacle Books, 1961.

———. *The Tenth Fleet*. New York: Ivan Obolensky, 1962.

Gallery, D. V. *Clear the Decks!* New York: William Morrow & Co., 1951.

———. *Twenty Million Tons Under the Sea*. Chicago, IL: Henry Regnery Company, 1956.

Gannon, M. *Operation Drumbeat: The Dramatic True Story of Germany's First U-Boat Attacks Along the American Coast in World War Two*. New York: Harper & Row, 1990.

Gardner, W. J. R. *Decoding History: The Battle of the Atlantic and Ultra*. Annapolis, MD: Naval Institute Press, 1999.

Gelpi, Jr., P. D. "Piney Hills Stalag: The Internment of Axis Prisoners of War in Camp Ruston, Louisiana." *Louisiana History* 50, no. 3 (2009): 341–50.

Gill, K. R. "Project 356: U-505 and the Journey to Chicago." In *Hunt and Kill: U-505 and the U-Boat War in the Atlantic,* edited by T. P. Savas, 161–220. El Dorado Hills, CA: Savas Beatie, 2004.

Gilliland, C. H. and Shenk, R. *Admiral Dan Gallery: The Life and Wit of a Navy Original.* Annapolis, MD: Naval Institute Press, 1999.

Gladwin, L. A. "Cautious Collaborators: The Struggle for Anglo-American Cryptanalytic Co-Operation, 1940–43." *Intelligence and National Security* 14, no. 1 (1999): 119–45.

Godson, S. H. *Serving Proudly: A History of Women in the U.S. Navy.* Annapolis, MD: Naval Institute Press, 2001.

Goebeler, H. and Vanzo, J. *Steel Boat, Iron Hearts: A U-Boat Crewman's Life Aboard U-505.* El Dorado Hills, CA: Savas Beatie, 2008.

Gorodetsky, G., ed. *The Maisky Diaries: The Wartime Revelations of Stalin's Ambassador in London.* London/New Haven, CT: Yale University Press, 2015.

Gretton, P. *Convoy Escort Commander.* London: Cassell and Company, 1964.

Grosvenor, M. B. "Cruise on an Escort Carrier." *National Geographic* 84, no. 5 (1943): 513–46.

Hanson, V. D. *The Second World Wars: How the First Global Conflict Was Fought and Won.* New York: Basic Books, 2017.

Hastings, M. *The Secret War: Spies, Ciphers, and Guerrillas, 1939–1945.* New York: HarperCollins, 2016.

Hathaway, R. M. *Ambiguous Partnership: Britain and America, 1944–1947.* New York: Columbia University Press, 1981.

Heinrich, T. "Fighting Ships That Require Knowledge and Experience: Industrial Mobilization in American Naval Shipbuilding, 1940–1945." *Business History Review* 88, no. 2 (2014): 273–301.

Heisler, B. S. "Returning to America: German Prisoners of War and the American Experience." *German Studies Review* 31, no. 3 (2008): 537–56.

Herwig, H. "Germany and the Battle of the Atlantic." In *A World at Total War: Global Conflict and the Politics of Destruction, 1937–1945,* edited by R. Chickering, S. Förster, and B. Greiner, 71–88. Cambridge, England: Cambridge University Press; 2004.

Hinsley, F. H. and Stripp, A., eds. *Codebreakers: The Inside Story of Bletchley Park.* Oxford, England: Oxford University Press, 1993.

Hobbs, D. "Ship-Borne Air Anti-Submarine Warfare." In *The Battle of the Atlantic, 1939–1945: The 50th Anniversary International Naval Conference,* edited by S. Howarth and D. Law, 388–407. Annapolis, MD: Naval Institute Press, 1994.

Holland, J. *The War in the West: The Allies Fight Back, 1941–1943.* London: Bantam Press, 2017.

Howarth, S., ed. *Men of War: Great Naval Leaders of World War II.* New York: St. Martin's Press, 1992.

Howarth, S. and Law, D., eds. *The Battle of the Atlantic, 1939–1945: The 50th Anniversary International Naval Conference.* London/Annapolis, MD: Greenhill Books/Naval Institute Press, 1994.

Hughes, T. and Costello, J. *The Battle of the Atlantic.* New York: Dial Press/James Wade, 1977.

Jones, J. *WW2.* New York: Ballantine Books, 1975.

Kahn, D. *Seizing the Enigma: The Race to Break the German U-Boat Codes, 1939–1943.* London: Arrow Books, 1996.

Karig, W., Burton, E., and Freeland, S. *Battle Report: The Atlantic War.* New York: Farrar & Rinehart, 1946.

Kelshall, G. T. M. *The U-Boat War in the Caribbean.* Annapolis, MD: Naval Institute Press, 1994.

Kennedy, P. *Engineers of Victory: The Problem Solvers Who Turned the Tide in the Second World War.* New York: Random House, 2013.

———. *Victory at Sea: Naval Power and the Transformation of the Global Order in World War Two.* London/New Haven, CT: Yale University Press, 2022.

King, E. J. and Whitehill, W. M. *Fleet Admiral King: A Naval Record.* New York: W. W. Norton & Co., 1952.

Knight, R. *Convoys: The British Struggle Against Napoleonic Europe and America.* London/New Haven, CT: Yale University Press, 2022.

Knowles, F. *Autobiography.* Privately printed, 1976.

Knowles, K. A. "The Tenth Fleet (Review)." *Studies in Intelligence* 7, no. 2 (1963): A19–23.

———. "Ultra and the Battle of the Atlantic: The American View." In *Changing Interpretations and New Sources in Naval History: Papers from the Third United States Naval Academy History Symposium,* edited by R.W. Love, Jr., 13–16. New York: Garland Publishing, 1980.

———. "Very Special Intelligence (Review)." *Studies in Intelligence* 21, no. 4 (1977), 34–36.

Kohnen, D. *Commanders Winn and Knowles: Winning the U-Boat War with Intelligence, 1939–1943.* Kraków, Poland: Enigma Press, 1999.

———. "F-21 and F-211: A Fresh Look into the 'Secret Room.'" In *New Interpretations in Naval History: Selected Papers from the Fourteenth Naval History Symposium,* edited by R. C. Balano and C. L. Symonds, 298–339. Annapolis, MD: Naval Institute Press, 2001.

———. "Tombstone of Victory: Tracking the U-505 from German Commerce Raider to American War Memorial, 1944–54." *Journal of America's Military Past 33,* no. 105 (2007): 5–33.

Krammer, A. *Nazi Prisoners of War in America.* New York: Stein and Day, 1979.

Kurzak, K. H. "German U-Boat Construction." *Proceedings of the United States Naval Institute* 81, no. 4 (1955).

Lauderbaugh, G. M. "Bolivarian Nations: Securing the Northern Frontier." In *Latin America During World War II,* edited by T. M. Leonard and J. F. Bratzel, 109–25. Lanham, MD: Rowman & Littlefield, 2007.

Levie, H. "Submarine Warfare: With Emphasis on the 1936 London Protocol." In *Levie on the Law of War,* edited by M. N. Schmitt and L. C. Green, 70, 293–337. Newport, RI: Naval War College, 1998.

Lewin, R. *The American Magic: Codes, Ciphers and the Defeat of Japan.* New York: Farrar, Straus and Giroux, 1982.

Love, Jr., R. W., ed. *Changing Interpretations and New Sources in Naval History: Papers from the Third United States Naval Academy History Symposium.* New York: Garland Publishing, 1980.

———. "Ernest Joseph King, 26 March 1942–15 December 1945." In *The Chiefs of Naval Operations,* edited by R. W. Love, Jr., 137–79. Annapolis, MD: Naval Institute Press, 1980.

———. "The U.S. Navy and Operation *Roll of Drums,* 1942." In *To Die Gallantly: The Battle of the Atlantic,* edited by T. J. Runyan and J. M. Copes, 95–120. Boulder, CO: Westview Press, 1994.

Mallmann Showell, J. P. *The German Navy in World War Two: A Reference Guide to the Kriegsmarine, 1935–1945.* Annapolis, MD: Naval Institute Press, 1979.

Mason, J. T., ed. *The Atlantic War Remembered: An Oral History Collection.* Annapolis, MD: Naval Institute Press, 1990.

Mawdsley, E. *The War for the Seas: A Maritime History of World War II.* New Haven, CT: Yale University Press, 2020.

McLachlan, D. *Room 39: Naval Intelligence in Action, 1939–45.* London: Weidenfeld & Nicolson, 1968.

Meany, Jr., J. F. "Port in a Storm: The Port of New York in World War II." In *To Die Gallantly: The Battle of the Atlantic,* edited by T. J. Runyan and J. M. Copes, 282–94. Boulder, CO: Westview Press, 1994.

Meigs, M. C. *Slide Rules and Submarines: American Scientists and Subsurface Warfare in World War Two.* Honolulu, HI: University Press of the Pacific, 2002.

Milner, M. "The Atlantic War, 1939–1945: The Case for a New Paradigm." *Global War Studies* 14, no. 1 (2017): 45–60.

———. "The Battle of the Atlantic." *Journal of Strategic Studies* 13, no. 1 (1990): 45–66.

———. *Battle of the Atlantic.* Stroud, England: History Press, 2011.

Montagu, E. *Beyond Top Secret Ultra.* New York: Coward, McCann & Geoghegan, 1978.

Morison, E. E. *Turmoil and Tradition: A Study of the Life and Times of Henry L. Stimson.* Boston, MA: Houghton Mifflin Company, 1960.

Mulligan, T. P. "A Community Bound by Fate: The Crew of U-505." In *Hunt and Kill: U-505 and the U-Boat War in the Atlantic,* edited by T. P. Savas, 25–55. El Dorado Hills, CA: Savas Beatie, 2004.

———. "German U-Boat Crews in World War II: Sociology of an Elite." *Journal of Military History* 56, no. 2 (1992): 261–82.

———. "The German Navy Evaluates Its Cryptographic Security, October 1941." *Military Affairs* 49, no. 2 (1985): 75–79.

———. *Lone Wolf: The Life and Death of U-Boat Ace Werner Henke.* Westport, CT: Praeger, 1993.

———. *Neither Sharks Nor Wolves: The Men of Nazi Germany's U-Boat Arm, 1939–1945.* London: Chatham Publishing, 1999.

Offley, E. *The Burning Shore: How Hitler's U-Boats Brought World War II to America.* New York: Basic Books, 2014.

Padfield, P. *Dönitz: The Last Führer: Portrait of a Nazi War Leader.* New York: Harper & Row, 1984.

———. "Grand Admiral Karl Dönitz." In *Men of War: Great Naval Leaders of World War II,* edited by S. Howarth, 177–206. New York: St. Martin's Press, 1992.

———. *War Beneath the Sea: Submarine Conflict During World War II.* New York: John Wiley & Sons, 1998.

Parrish, T. *The Ultra Americans: The U.S. Role in Breaking the Nazi Codes.* Briarcliff Manor, NY: Stein and Day, 1986.

Paterson, L. "Collision Course: Task Group 22.3 and the Hunt for U-505." In *Hunt and Kill: U-505 and the U-Boat War in the Atlantic,* edited by T. P. Savas, 125–36. El Dorado Hills, CA: Savas Beatie, 2004.

———. "From the Lion's Roar to Blunted Axe: The War Patrols of U-505." In *Hunt and Kill: U-505 and the U-Boat War in the Atlantic,* edited by T. P Savas, 57–90. El Dorado Hills, CA: Savas Beatie, 2004.

———. *U-Boat Combat Missions: The Pursuers and the Pursued: First-Hand Accounts of U-Boat Life and Operations.* New York: Barnes & Noble, 2007.

Persico, J. E. *Roosevelt's Secret War: FDR and World War II Espionage.* New York: Random House, 2001.

Redford, D. "Inter- and Intra-Service Rivalries in the Battle of the Atlantic." *Journal of Strategic Studies* 32, no. 6 (2009): 899–928.

Reynolds, D. *Mirrors of Greatness: Churchill and the Leaders Who Shaped Him.* New York: Basic Books, 2024.

Reynolds, N. *Need to Know: World War II and the Rise of American Intelligence.* New York: HarperCollins, 2022.

Rielage, D. C. "Indirectly in Operational Signals." *Naval History* 16, no. 6 (2002).

Roberts, A. *The Storm of War: A New History of the Second World War.* New York: Harper, 2011.

Rohwer, J. "Allied and Axis Radio-Intelligence in the Battle of the Atlantic: A Comparative Analysis." In *The Intelligence Revolution: A Historical Perspective; Proceedings of the Thirteenth Military History Symposium,* edited by H. T. Hitchcock, 77–100. Washington, D.C.: Office of Air Force History, U.S. Air Force Academy, 1991.

———. *The Critical Convoy Battles of March 1943: The Battle for HX229/SC122.* Annapolis, MD: Naval Institute Press, 1977.

———. "Ultra and the Battle of the Atlantic: The German View." In *Changing Interpretations and New Sources in Naval History: Papers from the Third United States Naval Academy History Symposium,* edited by R. W. Love, Jr., 9–13. New York: Garland Publishing, 1980.

Rose, A. *American Rifle: A Biography.* New York: Delacorte, 2008.

———. *Empires of the Sky: Zeppelins, Airplanes, and Two Men's Epic Duel to Rule the World.* New York: Random House, 2020.

Roskill, S. W. *The Secret Capture.* Annapolis, MD: Naval Institute Press, 2011.

Rössler, E. "U-Boat Development and Building." In *The Battle of the Atlantic, 1939–1945: The 50th Anniversary International Naval Conference,* edited by S. Howarth and D. Law, 118–37. Annapolis, MD: Naval Institute Press, 1994.

Royle, T. *Patton: Old Blood and Guts*. London: Weidenfeld & Nicolson, 2005.

Runyan, T. J. and Copes, J. M., eds. *To Die Gallantly: The Battle of the Atlantic*. Boulder, CO: Westview Press, 1994.

Rust, E. C. "No Target Too Far: The Genesis, Concept, and Operations of Type IX U-Boats in World War II." In *Hunt and Kill: U-505 and the U-Boat War in the Atlantic*, edited by T. P. Savas, 1–24. El Dorado Hills, CA: Savas Beatie, 2004.

Sanders, H. "King of the Oceans." *United States Naval Institute Proceedings* 100, no. 8 (1974).

Savas, T.P., ed. *Hunt and Kill: U-505 and the U-Boat War in the Atlantic*. El Dorado Hills, CA: Savas Beatie, 2004.

Scalia, J. M. "History, Archaeology, and the German Prisoner of War Experience in Rural Louisiana: The Ruston Alien Internment Facility, 1943–45." *Louisiana History* 38, no. 3 (1997): 309–27.

Schäffer, H. *U-Boat 977*. New York: W. W. Norton & Co., 1952.

Schiessl, C. "The *Volksdeutsche* of Eastern Europe as Nazi Collaborators During World War II." In *German-Occupied Europe in the Second World War*, edited by R. Scheck, F. Théofilakis, and J. Torrie. New York: Routledge, 2004.

Schmider, K. H. *Hitler's Fatal Miscalculation: Why Germany Declared War on the United States*. Cambridge, England: Cambridge University Press, 2021.

Schott, M. J. "Prisoners Like Us: German POWs Encounter Louisiana's African-Americans." *Louisiana History* 36, no. 3 (1995): 277–90.

Shea, W. L. and Pritchett, M. R. "The *Wehrmacht* in Louisiana." *Louisiana History* 23, no. 1 (1982): 5–19.

Simms, B. "Against a 'World of Enemies': The Impact of the First World War on the Development of Hitler's Ideology." *International Affairs* 90, no. 2 (2014): 317–36.

Simms, B. and Laderman, C. *Hitler's American Gamble: Pearl Harbor and Germany's March to Global War*. New York: Basic Books, 2021.

Slessor, J. *The Central Blue: Recollections and Reflections*. London: Cassell and Company, 1956.

Smith, B. F. *The Ultra-Magic Deals and the Most Secret Special Relationship, 1940–1946*. Novato, CA: Presidio, 1993.

Smith, M. *Station X: The Codebreakers of Bletchley Park*. London: Pan Books, 2004.

Snow, R. *A Measureless Peril: America in the Fight for the Atlantic, the Longest Battle of World War II*. New York: Scribner, 2010.

Soybel, P. L. *A Necessary Relationship: The Development of Anglo-American Cooperation in Naval Intelligence*. Westport, CT: Praeger, 2005.

Speer, Albert. *Inside the Third Reich*. New York: Simon & Schuster, 1970.

Stille, M. *U.S. Navy Escort Carriers, 1942–1945*. Oxford, England: Osprey Publishing, 2017.

Stillwell, P. "Willis Lee: The Naval Academy Years." *Naval History* 36, no. 2 (2022).

Syrett, D. *The Defeat of the German U-Boats: The Battle of the Atlantic*. Columbia, SC: University of South Carolina Press, 1994.

———. "The Infrastructure of Communications Intelligence: The Allied D/F Network and the Battle of the Atlantic." *Intelligence and National Security* 17, no. 3 (2002): 163–72.

Terraine, J. *The U-Boat Wars, 1916–1945*. New York: G. P. Putnam's Sons, 1989.

Thorndike, Jr., J. J. "King of the Atlantic." *Life*, November 24, 1941: 92–108.

Tidman, K. R. *The Operations Evaluation Group: A History of Naval Operations Analysis*. Annapolis, MD: Naval Institute Press, 1984.

Tooze, A. *The Wages of Destruction: The Making and Breaking of the Nazi Economy*. New York: Penguin, 2008.

Van Der Vat, D. *The Atlantic Campaign: The Great Struggle at Sea, 1939–1945*. London: Grafton Books, 1990.

Vause, J. "Desperate Decisions: The German Loss of U-505." In *Hunt and Kill: U-505 and the U-Boat War in the Atlantic*, edited by T. P. Savas, 137–59. El Dorado Hills, CA: Savas Beatie, 2004.

Waller, D. "U-505 in the US Navy, 1944–45: From Capture to Disposal to Display." *Bermuda Journal of Archaeology and Maritime History* 21 (2018): 177–212.

Warlimont, W. *Inside Hitler's Headquarters, 1939–45*. Translated by R. H. Barry. London: Weidenfeld & Nicolson, 1964.

Waters, D. W. "The Mathematics of Convoy." *Navy International* (1978): 22–26, 78.

Wells, R. D. "Persuading the U-Boats." *Proceedings of the United States Naval Institute* 90, no. 12 (1964).

Werner, H. A. *Iron Coffins: A Personal Account of the German U-Boat Battles of World War II*. New York: Da Capo Press (orig. Henry Holt and Co.), 2002.

Whinney, B. *The U-Boat Peril: A Fight for Survival*. London: Cassell and Company, 1986.

Williams, K. B. "See Fido Run: A Tale of the First Anti-U-Boat Acoustic Torpedo." In *New Interpretations in Naval History: Selected Papers from the Sixteenth Naval History Symposium Held at the United States Naval Academy, 10–11 September 2009*, edited by C. C. Felker and M. O. Jones, 115–25. Washington, D.C.: GPO, 2012.

Williamson, G. *Kriegsmarine U-Boats, 1939–45 (2)*. Oxford, England: Osprey Publishing, 2002.

———. *U-Boats vs. Destroyer Escorts: The Battle of the Atlantic*. Oxford, England: Osprey Publishing, 2007.

Wise, M. E. and Mallmann Showell, J. P. "Deciphering the U-Boat War: The Role of Intelligence in the Capture of U-505." In *Hunt and Kill: U-505 and the U-Boat War in the Atlantic,* edited by T. P. Savas, 91–124. El Dorado Hills, CA: Savas Beatie, 2004.

Wouk, H. *The Language God Talks: On Science and Religion*. New York: Little, Brown and Company, 2010.

Y'Blood, W. T. *Hunter-Killer: U.S. Escort Carriers in the Battle of the Atlantic*. Annapolis, MD: Naval Institute Press, 1983.

ILLUSTRATION CREDITS

161: USS *Bogue* attacks *U-118*. Note bullet splashes, depth-charge explosions, and the evasive trail behind the target. National Archives / Naval History and Heritage Command.

167: A WAVE works alongside an American bombe. Wikimedia Commons.

192: Harald Lange, third commander of *U-505*. German U-Boat Museum, Cuxhaven.

208: *Chatelain* attacks the ailing *U-515*. Flora B. McCabe Collection, Naval History and Heritage Command.

221: *Guadalcanal*'s Combat Information Center (CIC) on June 3, 1944. National Archives / Naval History and Heritage Command.

231: Away Boarding Party!: *Pillsbury*'s pirates. National Archives / Naval History and Heritage Command.

233: David's boat, bottom right, approaches *U-505*. National Archives / Naval History and Heritage Command.

238: *U-505* slips perilously low in the water. National Archives / Naval History and Heritage Command.

240: Beginning the tow. National Archives / Naval History and Heritage Command.

245: *U-505* prisoners file aboard *Guadalcanal*. National Archives / Naval History and Heritage Command.

249: Gallery and *Can-Do Junior*. National Archives / Naval History and Heritage Command.

253: Admiral King, as jocular as ever. National Archives / Naval History and Heritage Command.

276: *U-505* sails serenely, if perhaps disconcertingly, beneath New York's Brooklyn Bridge. Griffin Museum of Science and Industry, Chicago / Bridgeman Images.

INDEX

Note: *Italic* page numbers refer to photographs.